Fletcher W. Hewes

## History of the Formation, Movements, Camps, Scouts and Battles

of the Tenth Regiment Michigan Volunteer Infantry. Containing a short historical

sketch of every officer connected with the regiment

Fletcher W. Hewes

**History of the Formation, Movements, Camps, Scouts and Battles**
*of the Tenth Regiment Michigan Volunteer Infantry. Containing a short historical sketch of
every officer connected with the regiment*

ISBN/EAN: 9783337011048

Printed in Europe, USA, Canada, Australia, Japan

Cover: Foto ©ninafisch / pixelio.de

More available books at **www.hansebooks.com**

# HISTORY

OF THE

### FORMATION, MOVEMENTS, CAMPS, SCOUTS AND BATTLES.

OF THE

# TENTH REGIMENT

## MICHIGAN VOLUNTEER INFANTRY.

CONTAINING

## A Short Historical Sketch of Every Officer

CONNECTED WITH THE REGIMENT.

ALSO,

THE NAMES, DATES OF ENLISTMENTS, NATIVITY, OCCUPATION ETC.,
OF EVERY MEMBER OF THE ORGANIZATION, TOGETHER WITH
DATES AND PLACES OF DISCHARGE, DEATHS,
ECT., FROM THE FIRST ENLISTMENT
TO DATE OF RE-ENLISTMENT.

WRITTEN AND COMPILED BY F. W. H.,

A MEMBER OF THE REGIMENT.

[Fletcher Willis Howes]

### DETROIT:
JOHN SLATER'S BOOK AND JOB PRINTING ESTABLISHMENT

## 1864.

# PREFACE.

A history of the events of our lives, which are fraught with importance either to ourselves or to others, is always interesting as well as useful.

And, as our country is engaged in a struggle such as modern history nowhere records, a memoranda of the part we have played in the great drama cannot fail to be of interest to ourselves in years to come, when, in imagination, we can live over again

Th' exciting scenes, as we look back,
Of camp, or macrh, or bivouack,
Or fiercely 'gainst the rebels strive,
To keep our nation's strength alive;

And it will be of no little interest to our friends to see through what scenes we have passed, and trace out our long and tedious marches, and hear of the hardships we have endured for their sakes, and our country's honor and right.

On account of the data it contains, we hope this history may prove interesting to those who have taken part in the scenes it seeks to represent. As to its correctness, we would say that we have spared no pains to procure the most correct data which could be obtained, relying upon regimental and company records and daily journals kept during the whole time. We have endeavored to avoid all coloring of events, seeking a medium between the exaggeration of some and the eccentricities of others. Our aim has been to give a plain, truthful statement of facts as they occurred.

Hoping that the reader will excuse the absence of high or polished style which is so necessary in most works at the present age, of whatever kind, and accept it for the data it contains, the author would respectfully subscribe himself

YOUR OBEDIENT SERVANT.

# History of the Tenth Regiment.

## FORMATION.

The 10th Regiment Michigan Volunteer Infantry was organized under the first call for three years troops, and was rendezvoused at Flint, Genesee county. The camp was pleasantly situated, just east of the village, on the left bank of Flint River, on a piece of undulating ground, including a small piece of woods, separated from the drill grounds by a low marsh, which, in the spring time, was overflowed by the high water from the river. This piece of woods was designated "the island," and the boys will not forget "the island" of camp at Flint. This camp of instruction was named Camp Thomson, in honor of E. H. Thomson, who had charge of the formation of the regiment, as no Colonel was appointed for some time.

The company known at its organization as Saginaw Rangers (now Co. B.), commanded by Capt. Chas. H. Richman, was the first at the place of rendezvous, where it moved from Fort Wayne, Detroit, after the 9th Regiment Infantry (for which it was formed) had left for "Dixie," being full without the "Saginaw Rangers." This company served as a nucleus for the 10th—"Little Charley," as the boys called Capt. Richman, taking command until the appointment and arrival of Col. Lum.

E. H. Thomson directed the formation of the camp, and so fully and completely cared for the wants of the soldiers, that he found a place in the soldiers' hearts as the soldier's friend, and will not soon be forgotten. We learned to look upon him as a kind of father, and always called him Colonel, and, to this day he bears that title whenever his name is spoken among us.

The companies which first came to camp were quartered in tents, and, although it was late in the fall, and the weather severe, we were so well supplied with straw for beds, and, through the kindness of the citizens of Flint and vicinity, so well provided with blankets and quilts in addition to those drawn from the Government, that we were comfortable.

A large and commodious dining room, and a building for the Quartermaster's department, were constructed at an early date, and, through the energy and efficiency of Col. Thomson, comfortable barracks, with rooms attached for 1st Sergeants to transact company business in, were constructed soon afterwards. Cook rooms were also attached to the dining room, and we were " in out of the storm."

The wants of the men being thus supplied, attention was turnd to the wants of the officers, and quarters, pleasant and convenient, were constructed near by the barracks, consisting of fifteen rooms—the first being occupied by the Colonel, 2d by Lieutenant Colonel and Major, 3d by Adjutant, 4th by Quartermaster, 5th by Surgeons, and the remaining ten each by the commissioned officers of a company. There was a commodious cook room attached to the officers' quarters, and one Mr. Alport, living near camp, took the job of boarding the officers.

## AN ACCIDENT.

While the barracks were in course of construction, owing to a deficiency in bracing, the structure fell to the ground; but, fortunately, none were seriously hurt except a workman who was at the time on the roof. It was reconstructed in a better manner, and did good service in protecting us from the severity of the winter.

## DUTY AND PLEASURE.

Now that the barracks and other quarters were all done, the best part of our soldiering began, but we did not realize it, and often compared our situation with *home*. Our duties were drilling, guarding the camp, and eating our rations. Most of us took pride in drilling, despite " awkward squads," guard house, etc., and longed for the time to come when we could practice our evolutions in front of the enemy, where it would do some good. Camp guard was generally looked upon as a sort of " unnecessary evil," for we little knew the necessity of thoroughly understanding guard duty. We understand it pretty well now. As far as eating rations is concerned, most of us could and did eat our full share, although it was with more grumbling than at either of the other duties. It is but justice to say that our cooks did well. They performed the hardest part of the duty of that camp, as all cooks generally do everywhere.

## THANKSGIVING.

On thanksgiving day we received *extra* rations. The ladies of Flint gave us a dinner. Such a dinner! Better than Uncle Sam, with all his kindness, furnishes, as we well remember. And, could these tables have spoken, I dare say they would have said the *soldier's* day for giving thanks had surely come. Snowy cloths (strange articles to appear in camp) were spread upon the rude structures which we called tables, and then they were covered, *loaded*, with eatables of all sorts, and of the best quality, and dainties such as the epicure could well envy. Such as only our sisters know how to prepare. And a London dyspeptic might have been suited

> With any, all and *every* kind o' dish;
> Meats roasted, boiled and stewed, or fish;
> Cakes, jellies, custards, tarts and pies;
> Plum-puddings, salads, fricasees and "fries."

And had he even tried to taste the half,
You'd call him but the greater calf;
For 'twould have ta'en a stomach more fabulous in size
Than would have shamed "Old Nick" in all his lies.

We did good justice to this wondrous feast, and still there was enough and to spare. And for days afterwards we had tokens at almost every meal, to keep us in remembrance of the thanks we owed to the "good folk" of Flint for that expression of sympathy for the soldiers. And, in passing to and fro through the crowd, most of us found familiar faces, for the people came from far and near to our day of thanksgiving, and a kind of kindred feeling seemed to spring up in all our hearts, for it was as though we were all brothers and sisters, and we (soldiers) felt yet a firmer resolve to struggle to protect those kind ones whom we were soon to leave behind us.

## PRESENTATIONS.

The monotony of camp life during the long winter was often relieved by such scenes as the presentations of swords, belts and sashes. March 5th, 1862, a sword, belt and sash were presented to Adjt. Cowles, by the line officers, and at the same time a horse was presented to Maj. J. J. Scarritt, by his friends. At this time the battalion was called out and formed in a square. Capts. Bunnell, Co. C, and Deming, Co. G, also, Lieuts. Lyon, Co. B, and Hall, Co. F, were presented with swords and belts. Most, if not all, of these presentations were made by the companies. Appropriate speeches and replies accompanied the several scenes of presentation, and served to make all pleasant. On the occasion of the presentation to Adjt. Cowles, Lieut. Col. Dickerson made the presentation speech, and it was replied to by the noble recipient, whom all esteemed as worthy the gift. Besides these, several officers were presented at their homes with swords and belts by their friends. Col. Lum was in this way presented with a fine gray horse at Detroit. Such scenes served to keep our patriotism aglow, despite the severity of the weather and the disagreeableness of duty.

## RUMORS.

The exciting rumors of war and the excitement about going to " Dixie," gave us enough to think of in spare moments, so that weeks and months rolled quickly away. As the winter began to wane, and all the rumors of the paymaster's appearance with our "greenbacks" came one after another to be proved false, we began to be uneasy, for the homes we had left needed either us or them. But it was rumored at last that the paymaster was in the city, but out of funds, and, like a sensible officer, had gone to work sawing wood by the cord to get money to pay off the regiment. This placed the prospect of pay far in the future, but better then than never.

## MUSTER.

When the mustering officers came the "greenbacks" had not yet made their appearance, and most felt an inclination to "halt." Some were determined not to muster until they had their pay, but this was finally adjusted, and February 5th and 6th made us all Uncle Sam's boys.

## PAY DAY.

The paymaster at last came, although Christmas had come and gone long before ; and we received our first payment from Government April 17th, 1862. We were paid from date of enlistment to February 28th, 1862, and having got hold of the needful, we felt considerable better.

## FLAG PRESENTATION.

The ladies and citizens of Flint, who had all along shown their kindness and generosity by acts which will not soon be forgotten, gave us another token of interest in the cause in which we were engaged, by presenting Col. Lum, April 11th, 1862, with a splendid " stars and stripes," on which was inscribed the motto of our State and the number and name of our regiment. It would be interesting to relate in minutæ the details of the presentation, but we can only say that the appearance of the soldiers in their new clothes on parade and drill that day was better than ever before, and every soldier and citizen appeared intent upon doing what they could to make all agreeable. When the regiment was formed in hollow square, and the ladies, with a few gentlemen, admitted and the eager crowd surrounding the square gathered closer and yet closer, we could plainly read in their faces that they felt an interest for us, and again we were assured that we should be remembered. The presentation was made with appropriate speeches and ceremonies, heartily responded to by one and all in rounds of applause. Several songs were sung (national and patriotic) with good effect, and here it may not be improper to insert a song composed and sung by Mrs. Capt. Deming, assisted by one Mr. Bullock.

### THE FAREWELL SONG.

We are going far from home,
　As our fathers did before,
To fight upon the battlefield,
　Amid the cannon's roar.
To drive the traitors from our land,
　With the sword of liberty,
And guard with brave and dauntless love
　The banner of the free.
　　　CHORUS—So good bye! Good bye till then,
　　　　　　When we hope to meet again,
　　　　　　We never can forget you,
　　　　　　Oh no! we never can.

Shall we return again
　When the war is over?
With happy hearts we hope to meet
　With one and all once more;
But if we fall in battle,
　For this, our native land,
We ask our parting blessing,
　On this patriotic band.
　　　CHORUS—So farewell! farewell till then, etc.

Kind friends, we now must speak the word;
To one and all, farewell;
May heaven's blessing on you rest,
Say, will you sometimes think of us
When 'round your loved hearthstone,
And breathe a prayer to heaven,
For the soldiers far from home?
CHORUS—Home! Home! Sweet home!
There's no place like home,
There's no place like home.

After the ceremonies were ended, and the flag was really ours, so bright and beautiful (although stained and tarnished now, we felt glad, and a firm resolve to protect its sacred folds from insult, settled in our breasts, and is still rooted strongly there. After the speeches and songs, Col. Lum descended from the stand with the flag, and, placing it in the hands of the color Scargeant—William Lawrence, Co. H.—he charged the color company with its safe-keeping, giving it into their care in a kind and feeling manner.

Before the reducing of the square, Mrs. Morrison, Mrs. Fenton, and Mrs. Thayer, assisted by other ladies, presented each soldier with a testament, and their memories are blessed by us to this day for that Christian deed; and this but added another proof that they were the "soldier's friends."

After the dismissal of the battalion, and as the day wore away, greetings, true and heartfelt, were exchanged, which bound us closer to those we were preparing to protect. This was another day long to be remembered by the 10th.

## PREPARATIONS.

From the time we were paid to April 22d, 1862, the time set for our departure, there was considerable excitement and bustle. Getting ready: getting furloughs to go home for a few days to take leave of the loved ones, reducing the baggage, etc., etc. Guards were posted more thickly about camp, especially in the night, and pickets were thrown out on the principal roads leading from the city, to search all vehicles passing out, to prevent desertions and stealing of United States property. The camp became now, more than ever before, the resort of mothers, sisters, wives, fathers, brothers, relatives and friends of soldiers, and if, during the weary winter months we were blessed with the presence of fair ones to cheer us, we were now doubly blessed and more strongly reminded of the ties which bound us to our homes. Trying were the scenes enacted before and among us, and many a brave man's heart quailed and his lips quivered at the thought of parting from friends, who has never wavered or shrank back when the shells were flying all about, or *any danger* apparent.

The night before our departure was unpromising for the arrival of teams which had volunteered to carry us to Holly, the nearest railroad station; but a greater number of teams arrived than under the circumstances were expected. The tables were torn out of the dining hall in order to admit of sheltering the horses from the storm. Guards were doubled, and all admitted into camp, whether soldier or citizen, were subject to a search for liquor, and many were the canteens made to disgorge their contents of whisky upon the ground. Canteens, filled with liquors, were found upon citizens as well as soldiers. All was quiet in the night.

## OFF FOR DIXIE.

Preparations having been well completed the night before, we were astir the next morning at reveillee, which sounded at 2 o'clock. We packed our blankets—knapsacks having been packed the evening previous—and waited for the doors to open, for the guards were not removed from the barracks until just before we started—took breakfast as best we could, and fell in for roll call, loaded into the wagons while the snow, which had been falling for a number of hours, was still coming down, and bade farewell to Camp Thomson. We moved out of the city at 5½ o'clock A. M., and were *en route* for St. Louis. There were not wagons enough to hold all the regiment, and two companies had to walk until we struck the "plank" and met more teams coming, and those already loaded took on a few more.

The storm ceased soon after starting, the snow having fallen to a considerable amount, but had mellted so that it was only about one and a half inches deep. The ground, moistened by previous rain, was so softened by the melting of the snow that the plank road was entirely destroyed in some places, and in some instances had to be relaid before the train could pass. All along we were greeted with smiling faces, the waving of hands, hats and 'kerchiefs and by cheers, to give us courage and make us feel that we were doing well. On the road through which we passed in leaving the camp and going through Flint, the walks, yards, doors and winds were crowded with the friends of those "going to war." Many sad faces presented themselves, but most were hopeful. It was a passing good bye.

## DINNER.

At 2 o'clock P. M. the right wing had reached Holly, and were marched to tables loaded with luxuries provided by the people of Holly and vicinity. The roads were muddy, but we did not mind that. As soon as the right wing had eaten, the left were ready to take their places, and thus a "steady fire" was kept up, but we were unable to conquer those invincible tables. Our stomachs testified that their loss in slain must have been thousands, while our haversacks would have disclosed the fact that a large number of prisoners were "bagged." Hungry soldiers were never more thankful for a hearty meal, and we felt that our inner soldier was much reinforced. We shall long remember this generosity, and the spirit which prompted these kind people to prepare that meal on that stormy, muddy day.

## ON BOARD AND MOVING.

After as little delay as possible, we were on board the train and, amid the cheers, farewells, and tears of friends, the train moved us out and on. Stopped a few minutes at Pontiac, and found a goodly company of our acquaintances gathered there to greet us. Stopped at Royal Oak, and waited some time for a train due soon. The inhabitants "were sorry they did not know we were coming." "Would have prepared a 'bite' if they had known of it." As it was, the boys had quite a feast talking with the fair ones who came to the cars while we waited, and were very sociable. Nothing of note happened until we reached Detroit, at 9 o'clock P. M. Here we left the cars to march to the Central Depot, while the train backed to the Junction and came down to meet us there. Here a mistake occurred by which Company C. was left on board the train until the regiment had moved some distance. They were, however, soon missed, and, being notified, after some cursing, hurrying, etc., were brought up to the column. We had hoped to reach Detroit before dark, and it would have been more to the satisfaction of all. As it was, no demonstration on the part of the citizens could be made. A few rockets were fired, and we were met and escorted by the Detroit Light Guard, Capt. Mathews, and the Lyon Guard, G. S. Wormer, through the city and to the depot. We were obliged to wait at the depot until 11 o'clock P. M., when we again got under way, passing through in the night.

APRIL 23.—Daylight found us at Marshall, where we stopped half an hour, and drew rations of smoked hams and crackers. At 7 o'clock A. M., moved on, arrived at Kalamazoo at twenty minutes past 8 o'clock A. M., waited one hour for a train which was coming, and then moved on again. We were greeted everywhere by expressions of interest for our welfare and success. Wherever a house was in sight of the railroad, as soon as the inmates saw the "blue coats," the handkerchiefs, hats and bonnets, and, in no few cases, flags, began to wave. At New Buffalo we first came in sight of Lake Michigan. The dreary sandhills of this place were strangely in contrast with the scenery which we had been passing all along. The next point of interest was Michigan City, where we arrived at 1 o'clock P. M., and were treated to hot coffee by the barrel.

Left this place at 2½ P. M., and soon entered a broad
prairie, the first which many of us had ever seen. We soon
came to the junction of the Illinois Central Railroad, and,
taking that railroad, made Kankakee Station just at dark.

APRIL 24.—Morning, made Mattoon, at which place we
drew rations of bread and waited a train again. Here we
bought all the eatables that we could find at the bakeries, and
were not satisfied at that. The prairie, which we had not yet
left, was higher and better here. Took the Terra Haute and
St. Louis Railroad, run through several small stations, and
arrived at Bunker Hill (no hill at all) at 1 o'clock P. M., halted
only about twenty minutes. Here we left the prairie and
passed through some good farming country. Arrived at
Illinois town, opposite St. Louis, at 7 o'clock P. M., marched to
the Gladiator, and took our places—right wing on the hurricane deck, left wing on the middle and lower decks, and the
sick in the cabin. We now found that we were not to go to
St. Louis, but that an order had been received for us to go to
Pittsburg Landing instead. Most of us felt well pleased at
the change. We expected to move next morning at 10 o'clock,
but waited for the loading of ammunition, commissary, and
quartermaster's stores, until 4 o'clock P. M., when we loosed our
hold and were off for the scene of action. While lying at
Illinois Town, large numbers of the officers and men visited St.
Louis and enjoyed themselves well. Some a little too well, for
they were intoxicated with their pleasure or something else.
An amusing scene occurred at the boat. A citizen, who was a
little "boozy," not complying with the orders of the O. D.
(Capt. Pierson), and being noisy and disorderly, was ordered
ducked in the Mississippi, and he was soon floundering in the
river. After soaking in the drink awhile, he was started off,
not to come back again under penalty of being *left* in the river
next time.

While moving down the river we were deeply interested in
the scenes constantly presented, ever in new, pleasing, and
wonderful variety. The "bluffs," about which so much has

been written and said, claimed a good share of our attention, and served to shorten the weary hours.

## EXCITEMENT.

We arrived at Cairo, Illinois, at 12 o'clock and 20 minutes, April 26th. Here exciting rumors said that a fight was going on at Pittsburg Landing at that time; that boats were being fired into by guerrillas a little above Cairo; that our whole force was engaged, etc. These reports naturally excited us some, but the river was high and we could keep a good look-out, and we felt as though we were ready for them. Arrived at Paducah, Kentucky, at dark, stopped a short time, during which we heard many and contradictory rumors from the fight which was said to be raging at Pittsburg Landing. Rumor also said that the river above was filled with the dead bodies of drowned soldiers, etc.

April 27.—Weather clear, as it had been most of the time since our starting. Trees leaved out and spring time all about us. A short transition from winter to spring—almost summer. Passed a dead body of a soldier floating in the river at half-past 8 o'clock A. M., and a body dressed in citizen's clothes at 11 o'clock A. M. At half-past 11 o'clock passed Fort McHenry, now a desolate looking place. Awhile before coming up to the Fort a body of two hundred picked men were placed on the hurricane deck, and all others ordered below. These picked men were to keep a sharp lookout for the rebels, and were prepared to give them a warm reception if they made their appearance. During the night twenty of us were stationed at different points on the hurricane deck at a time, and relieved every hour, to watch for the guerrillas; but we saw nothing, although we thought we heard some signals. The picked men slept on their arms all night. At 3 o'clock P. M. to-day, a member of Company K. fell overboard, but was soon rescued, a slight ducking being the only disaster.

April 28.—Moved up the river with no ill fortune, passing many interesting, and many desolate scenes. Landed at Hamburg, Tennessee, four miles above Pittsburg Landing, at 6 o'clock P. M., and remained on board the "Gladiator" until morning.

APRIL 29.—This morning, when daylight appeared, a mixed mass of Tennessee mud, cavalry men, foot soldiers, mules, transport wagons, ambulances, etc., met our gaze, the whole presenting a most lamentably ludicrous scene. We left the boat at 8 o'clock A. M., and marched toward the front, through mud and water, and over mortar-mixed roads, at times wading almost waist deep. Indeed, our first introduction to marching was marching almost leg deep through a sort of bayou, caused by high water. We thought it rather *rough*, and, loaded as we were with heavy knapsacks, it proved so, too. We were dressed in new uniform, and, passing by some of the old troops, were complimented on our good appearance, for, besides having new clothes which made a good appearance, most of the regiment were men of large size, healthy and strong. As we passed along we were greeted often with comments like the following : " Won't wear them big knapsacks long." " You'll drop your fine feathers in a few weeks," etc. We were styled "the band-box regiment." Our knapsacks collapsed soon, as was predicted, and we found that *Tennessee* mud did not help us to keep clean.

We marched about five miles and came to higher ground. Bivouacked for the night in a piece of woods where there was plenty of leaves, and felt glad that we had room once more to straighten out, for we found it impossible on the cars or on the boat.

APRIL 30.—A part of our tents came up to-day. There was some excitement about transferring men, for some of the companies were over-full, and were obliged to transfer all above the maximum of those companies not up to a maximum. Rumor said that we should march out to meet the enemy next day, and we were busy making all preparations to be in readiness. Reports that our cavalry were constantly driving the enemy, reached camp every few hours.

MAY 1.—Marched five miles to the front, drew up in line of battle, and biveuacked for the night. We were obliged to leave a large amount of commissary stores behind, in charge of a guard, and it was fifteen days before these stores reached us.

MAY 2.—Retraced our march of yesterday for the distance of one mile, and then moved some two miles to the right of where we lay the night previous. This move carried us toward Farmington, Mississippi. Bivouacked in a hollow in the woods, near a small stream of water. Here sheep, calves and poultry were found, " possessed of secession sympathies," and hence were " confiscated."

MAY 3.—At 10 o'clock A. M. marched with twenty-four hours' rations, and no luggage, save blankets. This day several who were unable to walk were left behind. A rapid march was made, by a circuitous route, nearly to Farmington, Mississippi. The rebel pickets were driven back for several miles. The designed reconnoitre being completed, the force fell back a short distance. Our brigade bivouacked in a cornfield three miles in rear of Farmington, having marched sixteen miles. It rained during the night and for two succeeding days, and the cornfield became a mudfield, and the camp was appropriately named *Mud Camp*. Our tents reached us on the 5th, and we pitched them on, or rather in, the mud. Here we remained encamped until the 17th. Were called into line of battle several times on false as well as real alarms.

MAY 8.—March to Farmington; drove the rebels out of the town after some hot work, and followed them up closely until they reached a point within two miles of Corinth. Here a masked battery opened upon us and we were under fire some time. The shells flew above and around our regiment, but no harm was done. Some of them come close enough for comfort, however. But the men showed no signs of fear or alarm, although this was new business to them. This reconnoitering force was under command of Gen. Payne. Our brigade was commanded by Col. James D. Morgan, 10th Illinois Infantry, our demi-brigade by Col. Lum, and our regiment by Lieut. Col.

Dickerson. After thus rubbing the noses of the rebs by marching close to their stronghold, the force returned to camp with the loss of but one killed. Maj. Appleton, belonging to one of the regiments in the command, was struck by a shell and killed instantly. Marched ten miles.

MAY 9.—The enemy repossessed Farmington and made a dash upon our camps, but were repulsed; still they pressed on us so close that our sick were sent out of camp, and one of our batteries planted close to the hospital. Only two or three of their shells reached or came into our camp. We slept on our arms that night, about one-quarter of a mile in front of the camp.

MAY 10 AND 11.—Sick sent back to Hamburg Landing in ambulances.

MAY 15.—Marched half a mile front and a little to the right of our camp, and formed in line of battle on a hill, expecting to have a skirmish, at least, but, after waiting for the enemy two hours, and the danger being over, we returned to camp.

MAY 17.—Marched one and a half miles towards Farmington, and laid in a low swamp some three hours, under a broiling sun, and returned to camp disappointed, for we expected some fun *sure*, this time. At 4 o'clock P. M. we were called out without sound of bugle or drum, and marched to Farmington. Our forces possessed the place and immediately began to fortify. By daylight next morning Farmington was a strong point for the rebs to run against. Marched six miles.

MAY 18.—Notwithstanding we had worked in the trenches all night, we were placed on picket in front to-day.

MAY 19.—Pitched our camp in the village, and on this line our forces remained, without molestation, until the evacuation of Corinth. Picket and camp duties constituted our work here most of the time.

MAY 21.—Regiment called out to aid in supporting the Sharpshooters while they drove in the rebel pickets, as we wished to throw our pickets out further from camp.

MAY 26.—Our regiment on picket. To-day we met with a great loss. Adjt. S. D. Cowles, who was out on the picket lines, was shot dead by a rebel sharpshooter. When struck, he threw his hand upon his breast and exclaimed, "I have it here," and fell and expired immndiately. This was a loss we felt could not be replaced.

MAY 28.—Our forces advanced toward Corinth and threw up breastworks. Our works are about one mile in front of our camp. This afternoon three days' rations were ordered and prepared. Something decisive will be done soon, it is thought. Since occupying Farmington, and up to this time, picket firing and some heavy skirmishing has been going on most of the time.

MAY 30.—Rebels blew up their magazines, set fire to what stores remained in Corinth, and skedaddled. Our forces moved immediately in pursuit. The 10th started at 4 o'clock P. M., and moved with the column. Bivouacked some nine miles from Corinth, in an old cornfield, on a side hill.

MAY 31.—Laid in camp until about 11 o'clock A. M., when we were called out with an Illinois regiment to the support of the Sharpshooters, three miles in advance of our bivouac. While here we buried several dead horses and rebels while under fire of the rebel batteries and skirmishers. Had a hot time of it. Marched back several miles and bivouacked near the Mobile and Ohio Railroad, having marched ten miles.

JUNE 1.—Marched to Rienzi, Mississippi, in the direction of Boonville. We supposed we were bound for Jackson, Mississippi. Bivouacked for the night in an open field, having marched thirteen miles.

JUNE 2.—Marched at 7 o'clock A. M., arrived at Boonville at 3 P. M., having marched ten miles. Here we saw the wreck of rebel property which a cavalry expedition, sent out for that purpose, had burned.

JUNE 3.—Marched with the rest of the command to make a reconnoissance in force in front of Boonville. 'Found the enemy heavily entrenched some five miles out, and returned to camp late at night, tired and hungry, having been ordered back upon double quick. Rations very short, and of poor quality.

JUNE 4 AND 5.—Lay at Boonville. All quiet.

JUNE 6.—Fell in at 1 o'clock P. M., lay on our arms until half-past 4 o'clock P. M., then moved back and to the right of Boonville some three miles, and took up a new position. Bivouacked for the night in a fine piece of woods, but the water was very poor and scarce, all we could obtain being that which we found in stagnant pools in the bed of the river.

JUNE 7 AND 8.—Lay still at this bivouac.

JUNE 9.—Ordered to move. Fell out and formed ready for a start, and the order was countermanded.

JUNE 11.—Marched toward Corinth twelve or fourteen miles, bound, as rumor said, for Western Virginia. Very dusty and a great scarcity of water and provisions.

JUNE 12.—Started at light, marched three miles, halted and lay by in the shade until nearly noon, when we moved on, and at night bivouacked near the Mobile and Ohio Railroad, four and a half miles south of Corinth, near Clear Creek. Marched about twelve miles. Here we heard that the force of which we were a part, were to stay on Clear Creek thirty days, to rest and refresh, and if soldiers ever needed rest and refreshing, we did, for all through the march to Boonville and back it had been hot and dusty, and rations scarce and poor, and even when we stopped we were too tired to care to prepare what we did have to eat.

JUNE 13.—Began clearing up the ground preparatory to pitching tents, with expectation of staying a while. Camp at Farmington broken up to-day, and baggage brought up to this place.

JUNE 15.—Moved camp half a mile northward, in order to get a better encampment. Here we remained until July 20th. We set to work hard, and soon had one of the finest camps I ever saw, but it took a great deal of very hard labor. The underbrush were cut out, and the camp was kept so neatly and thoroughly swept and cleaned that the most fastidious belle need not fear dusting her silks in walking all through the regimental grounds. It was one of the first duties of the morning to police the whole camp thoroughly. This camp was named Big Springs, from the large springs near it, and from which we obtained water. Bowers were constructed to make more shade than the woods furnished, cellars at hospital and head-quarters were constructed to keep hospital stores and the "eatabilities," and particularly the "*drinkeralities*," of the field and staff in, and we resorted to all efficient means of keeping "cool." The 4th of July was celebrated in military style by our demi-brigade. A national salute was fired by our guns, and in the afternoon Col. Lum's command was congregated, or massed, at his headquarters, and he read the Declaration of Independence, and appropriate, enthusiastic and patriotic speeches were made by Lieut. Col. Dickerson and Maj. Scarritt, and, save the presence of the ladies, it was all "O. K." It was "bully," to say the least.

While remaining here many of our comrades sickened and had to go North to recruit their health in hospitals. Some of them found here their last resting place.

At last we were called to leave this beautiful camp, which we shall remember with sorrow and pleasure combined.

JULY 18.—Received orders to be ready to move soon.

JULY 20.—Companies E, K, G and B moved to the railroad and went on the train to Corinth. Reached Iuka the next day, and on the 22d arrived at Tuscumbia, Alabama, their destination.

JULY 21.—The remaining companies marched at 8 o'clock A. M., in the direction of Tuscumbia, Alabama. After marching thirteen miles, halting but once, we took dinner. Some of the men chose to carry their knapsaks, but as it was very warm they were soon willing to leave them and trust them to the train. Bivouacked at Burnsville, Mississippi, having made eighteen miles. The men who fell out during the heat of the day—and they were many—were arriving at all times during the night, and many of them were so completely worn out that they did not seek their companies at all, lying down at the first convenient place.

JULY 22.—Marched at 11 o'clock A. M., passed through Iuka—a fine town, celebrated for its mineral springs—and bivouacked just beyond it, in an open field. As the train had been delayed and did not come until next morning, we could not pitch tents if we would, and did not have any blankets or overcoats, which are very essential in that country in the nights, which are cold, even in the hottest weather. A heavy rain fell during the night, so that all were thoroughly drenched, and many, on waking, found themselves in pools of water from two to four inches deep. Rations, too, were short. An example will show. Two Lieutenants (Collins and Wheeler) of Company C., had one biscuit between them for their supper, which they divided and retired to rest. Marched eighteen miles.

JULY 23.—Column moved at 9 o'clock A. M. Marched through a fine country, well wartered, forded Clear and Bear Creeks, and encamped near the Alabama line, having marched twelve or fourteen miles.

JULY 24.—Left camp at 8 o'clock A. M., marched through a beautiful country, mostly planted to corn. Passed a large fountain spring, at which we drank the best water we had tasted since coming to "Dixie." Bivouacked at Little Bear Creek, four miles from Tuscumbia, Alabama, having marched twenty miles.

JULY 25.—Marched at 8 o'clock A. M., companies A and J remaining to guard the bridge at that point, and arrived at Tuscumbia at 10 o'clock A. M. Here we found the four companies of the left wing, who had come through by rail. Company I left Little Bear Creek at 2 o'clock P. M., and arrived at Tuscumbia at 4 o'clock P. M.

Company D being detailed to guard a ford and act as Provost Guard at Florence, four miles out, proceeded thither and entered at once upon their duties.

JULY 26.—Companies F, I, O and H, under command of Lieut. Col. Dickerson, were sent to guard Town Creek bridge, fifteen miles east of Tuscumbia. They started at 8 o'clock A. M., and marched to Leighton, where Company I was left to guard a railroad station and water tank. The remaining three companies arrived at Town Creek bridge at 6 o'clock P. M. Company I joined them on the morning of the 29th, having marched at midnight from Leighton.

Company A remained at Little Bear Creek, and companies E, K, G and B remained at Tuscumbia.

All passed off pleasantly except at Town Creek, where one or two incidents occurred to destroy the quiet of the camp. Still, all agree in saying that the best part of their soldiering in "Dixie," was in Alabama. By trading off rations—of which we had plenty and a surplus—we could obtain of the negroes everything we needed, at a cheap rate, and melons, peaches, chickens, milk, etc., disappeared with astonishing rapidity.

## TOWN CREEK—FALSE ALARM.

At Town Creek, on the night of July 31st, there was something of a scare and a run, and, although some seem disposed to find fault, yet, when the facts are known, no blame will rest on any, we think.

Intelligence, considered reliable, had been received at brigade headquarters that the enemy were collecting in the vicinity and threatening our position. Accordingly, Col. Smith, commanding the brigade, issued General Order No. 18, warning all "to be ready to move at a moment's notice;" ordering that all baggage not absolutely necessary, be disposed of by destroying or turning over to the proper departments;" adding, "the utmost *vigilance* and *activity* is enjoined upon all in our present position." This order was issued July 30, 1862. On the same day Col. Lum sent the following order to Lieut. Col. Dickerson, at Town Creek:

HEADQUARTERS 10TH REGIMENT MICH. VOLUNTEERS, }
TUSCUMBIA, July 30, 1862. }

To LIEUT. COL. ▓KERSON:

I have received reliable information that there is a large force of infantry, cavalry and artillery forming in your front. Your entrenchments are not sufficiently strong to resist artillery. If you should ascertain, from what you consider reliable sources, that an attack in force is to be made on your command, you will retreat towards this point by the road north of the railroad. You will see the necessity of constantly keeping your teams loaded, and your command ready to move at a moment's warning. The cavalry must see to it that you are kept informed of the movements of the enemy, as far as possible. If you should find it impossible to retire in this direction, you will retreat to the north side of the river, and join the forces at this point. A night movement is preferable, as it conceals your direction. Keep me fully informed of everything that transpires in your vicinity. If forced to move, it may be necessary to destroy some property. Do so rather than have it fall into the hands of the enemy. Inform the cavalry if forced to move.

CHARLES M. LUM,
*Colonel Commanding.*

LIEUT. GEO. TURNER,
*Acting Adjt. 10th Regt. Mich. Vols.*

This order was approved by Gen. Morgan. The next day information was received, through two "contrabands" who came in, that a large force of the enemy, consisting of cavalry and artillery, were coming down from the mountain on the right. The "contrabands" reported that a rebel Lieutenant entered their master's house, and told him that they had several thousand troops, and were going to make a move that night on our camp. This information was not received by Lieut. Col. Dickerson until evening, when he immediately sent out a cavalry force, under competent officers, to reconnoitre and report the strength of the enemy. This force returned at 11 o'clock P. M., and reported that they went near enough to make a proper reconnoissance; that they heard the enemy talking, and saw them stirring about in their camps, and, judging from the extent of ground covered by their camp fires, and from other things, they should calculate that their force consisted of at least ten thousand. Of course it would have been useless for four companies of infantry and two of cavalry to try to resist them. A counsel of company and cavalry commanders was called, and the result was that an immediate move was unanimously decided upon. We moved through a cornfield to the road, and as it was very dark and muddy, there was no little grumbling and muttering as one after another measured his length in mud and water.

A squad of cavalry were left behind with instructions to stay until the enemy took possession of the camp, and then come up with the command. If the enemy did not come by sunrise next morning, two only were to come forward and notify Lieut. Col. Lum at that time, the rest remaining.

The command moved so hurriedly that the officer of the guard (Lieut. Collins), and the guards were left behind. This was on account of the non-commissioned officers having been placed on the picket posts with their men, and hence most of the posts had to be notified by the officer of the guard in person. But they brought up the rear in good order and without confusion. They found some of the men lying by the roadside within two or three miles of "Town Creek," but they were so utterly prostrated that they could not be urged on. Next morning, after one of the most hurried and terrible of forced marches, the cavalrymen brought information that the enemy had moved to Leighton, and burned a water tank and railroad station, and moved away, not visiting our camp at all. A march would immediately have been made back again to "Town Creek," had it not been that the men were utterly unable to do it. As it was, we marched into Tuscumbia, rested until afternoon, took a train of cars to the bridge, and found all as we left it, save that a good share of the clothing and rations which had been left was gone, but the most of this was brought back to us next day by the negroes who had taken ● m.

## A SAD INCIDENT.

When we had marched six miles out from Town Creek, Peter White, Lieut. Hart's waiter, asked permission to go back and see if he could not find a favorite horse belonging to Lieut. Hart, which could not be found when they left camp. The Lieut. replied no, he must not go. But Peter was so loth to lose the horse that he asked a second time. Lieut. Hart then told him to ask Lieut. Col. Dickerson. He did so, and reluct antly he was permitted to return, the Lieutenant Colonel furnishing him with a mule to ride. On arriving at Winston's —a rich planter, on whose land we were encamped—he made known his business, and went on to camp three-quarters of a mile from this house. Winston and his "overseer" ordered horses, and coming up with Peter at camp, proposed to accompany him in his search. They learned at camp that a planter (Weims) living three miles from camp, had taken the horse. Peter then crossed the creek, and, accompanied by Winston, Stanley the overseer, and a negro named Jake, who is with the regiment now, set out for Weim's plantation. All proceeded together three-quarters of a mile up the road leading to said plantation, and at this point Peter wanted to turn to the left (east), but was ordered by Winston to turn to the right and recross the creek. Negro Jake winked to Peter and pointed to the left, to indicate that that was the right road. Winston again ordered him to go across the creek, when he began to cry (he was but a mere lad), and said if they were going to take him prisoner all right, but he did not want to be killed. Winston told him he was going to take him prisoner. They then crossed the creek and marched him nearly five miles up the creek, and leaving Jake in the rear, moved on out of sight, and then shot Peter through the head and rolled him down the bank of the creek. Through the information of negro Jake, who accompanied him, and acted as a guide, Lieut. Hart found his remains August 7th. He had his clothes, canteen, haversack and cup on, just as when he left the regiment. As he rolled down the steep bank some twelve or fifteen feet, he lodged on a sort of table-land formed by the washing of the creek at high water. Here he lay on his back, but decomposition had so far progressed that he could not be moved. The Lieutenant dug earth out of the bank with his hands, and covered him as well as he could with it, then cut some brush and threw over all—this being the best that could be done. Peter was an orphan, of Irish descent. No parents will mourn his loss, but his comrades never think of his sad fate but with sorrow.

This is another of their fiendish acts to record against our enemy. Immediately after committing this crime, Winston sought refuge in the rebel army.

## CONFISCATION.

Winston's whole plantation, and all his crops, were then declared confiscated, and Capt. Pierson was appointed administrator. This furnished a large addition to our rations, as he had several cows and a large peach orchard full of peaches, to say nothing of the chickens, melons, etc.

## HO! FOR NASHVILLE.

SEPT. 1.—The detachments of the regiment joined at the military ferry on the Tennessee River, and awaited orders. They came next day, and at 8 o'clock A. M. our brigade marched. Our regiment was the rear guard. We marched twelve miles through a good farming country, crossed Shoal Creek and bivouacked for the night in a piece of woods.

SEPT. 3.—Started at daylight and marched eighteen miles by 2 o'clock P. M. No halt was made in all this distance. Passed through Rogersville, a small and apparently very old town, and bivouacked for the night on the bank of Elk River.

SEPT. 4.—Marched at 5 o'clock A. M., forded Elk River, a stream some twenty rods in width, about knee deep, and very rapid, halted at 1 o'clock P. M., having marched twelve miles.

We were here within four miles of Athens. As it was reported that the enemy were in some force, a reconnoitering party was sent out to feel about the place and find the truth of the matter, but there was found to be no danger.

SEPT. 5.—Marched six miles, passing through Athens, and bivouacked two miles beyond the town. Athens is the county town of Limestone county, contains several fine buildings, among which are three churches, a court house, and several hotels. Population about 1,100. It is situated forty miles from Florence, fifteen from Decatur, and one hundred and ten from Nashville, Tennessee.

SEPT. 6.—Marched back as far as Athens, and took the Nashville "Pike," and bivouacked two miles out, in a cornfield. In fifteen minutes after halting, what corn was in the field had been well secured, and the stalks and leaves converted into beds. It takes Uncle Sam's boys to harvest and secure a crop in a hurry. Up to this time the 22d Illinois Infantry was all that had been with us of the 1st Brigade. At Athens we were joined by the balance of that brigade, and the Division was not separated again on their march through to Nashville.

SEPT. 7.—Our regiment formed the advanced guard, and marched at 5 o'clock A. M. The first ten miles was almost an unbroken forest. We then descended into a ravine between mountains high and steep, on either hand, close by the road, for the ravine was very narrow. After marching some distance in the ravine we came to a fine spring, and, as the men were thirsty, a halt was made to drink. As this was a fine place for guerrillas, Col. Lum allowed only one company to go to spring at a time, and then moved immediately on out of the range of the place. Our regiment had moved on and the 16th Illinois, who were next, not taking as much precaution as we, stacked arms and broke for the spring in a body. Just then a band of guerrillas fired a volley of musketry from a hill almost overhead, wounding four of that regiment. The regiment reseized their arms and charged furiously up the hill, after having returned the fire, but, upon gaining the top, found that the rebels had skedaddled. We marched on and passed through the village of Elkton, encamped, or rather bivouacked, at 4 P. M., having made twenty-eight miles since morning.

SEPT. 8—Marched at 5 A. M. Our regiment was rear guard. Passed through Pulaski, a town of about 2,000 inhabitants. As the rear of the train was leaving the town it was fired upon by a squad of fifteen or twenty men, apparently citizens, and about 4 o'clock P. M. a force of four or five hundred rebel cavalry made a dash upon our rear, and picked up a few stragglers—only one of our regiment. Marched eighteen miles.

SEPT. 9.—Marched at 5 o'clock A. M. Passed through Lynnville, a small town of two or three hundred inhabitants; also, passed through Columbia, a flourishing town of 2,500 inhabitants, situated on Duck River. As the rear guard were entering the town they were fired upon, killing one man of the 42 Illinois Infantry. Bivouacked for that night just north of Columbia. Marched eighteen miles.

SEPT. 10.—When the order came to move, and just as we were falling in, a flour mill which the "blue coats" had kept running all night for their own benefit, was set on fire and burned. As the column moved a body of thirty or forty rebels appeared near the mill, and fired into the train, killing one mule and wounding two or three others, causing considerable confusion for a few minutes. The rear guard returned the fire, and the rebels retreated into a building close at hand. A section of battery opened on the house and killed several of the rebels and routed the rest. Passed through a small village named Spring Hill. Marched eighteen miles.

SEPT. 11.—Advanced guard started at 5 o'clock A. M. Passed through Franklin, a town of 1,000 inhabitants, marched 22 miles, and bivouacked within two miles of Nashville, Tennessee. Here we laid until the 15th, doing picket duty, then marched into and encamped just south of Nashville.

## HEAVY DUTY—SHORT RATIONS.

Immediately upon entering the city we begun to fortify it, for it was constantly threatened by the enemy, who were hovering about in its vicinity. The river was low, so that no boats could come nearer than Clarksville, and the Louisville and Nashville Railroad was thoroughly destroyed at several points, so that communication was entirely cut off. Here we remained for months, without receiving any mail (and soldiers had rather go without any other rations than mail rations). In addition to this we could receive no supplies, and what we had was only enough for less than quarter rations to last until communication might be opened; hence we were obliged to forage on the surrounding country. Guerrilla bands infested the region about the city in all directions, and it was necessary to furnish large guards whenever a forage train was sent out. A section of battery was always in attendance, too. In this way we kept ourselves very well supplied with meat and bread, and forage for our teams; but coffee, sugar, beans, peas, salt, and candles, were more than short. A strong picket line had to be kept up all around the city, and the duties of picketing, foraging and fortifying were a triple dose. But there was little grumbling, and soon we considered the city was safe from any attack which might be made against it. The enemy continued to grow more and more bold, and many were the nights when our men, tired with hard duty, were called up at 12, 1 or 2 o'clock, to fall in on the color line. At last the enemy got so bold that they demanded the surrender of the city. In the meantime our troops were ready and harrassing them at different points.

OCTOBER 7.—The enemy were attacked by our troops—who marched from Nashville—and most gloriously whipped, at Lavergne. Our regiment was not sent out in time to help in the engagement, arriving at the scene of action just after the rebels had surrendered the town. Marched twelve miles.

Nov. 5.—The enemy having planted some batteries on hills a short distance from the town, commenced shelling our pickets, occasionally throwing a shot nearer town. But our guns on Fort Negley (a part of the fortifications we had constructed) soon silenced them. There was a great deal of excitement, however, and some anticipated a general attack. Our regiment marched out some three miles and returned without meeting the enemy.

Nov. 6.—All quiet. This evening a large number of men who had been sick in Northen hospitals, and officers who had been absent sick, joined our brigade—something like seventy joining our regiment. They had been collecting at Portland, Kentucky, under Maj. S. B. Raymond, of the 51st Illinois Infantry, and had marched through with Rosecrans' army. Leaving the army nine miles north of Nashville, this body of convalescents marched in. They were known as the First Independent Battalion, Army of the Mississippi, and self-styled " Mackerels."

Nov. 7.—A portion of Rosecrans' army arrived, thus opening communication with the North. And now that the Union troops were here in large force, the stars and stripes began to appear in all parts of the city, displayed by citizens. Heretofore they had been "few and far between."

Nov. 8.—As communication by railroad was open from Louisville to Mitchelville, thirty-five miles from Nashville, a large train was sent out by our brigade to get rations. Our regiment was sent as train guard. We reached Mitchelville at Night. As there was a rumor in Nashville that Bragg, with all his forces, threatened the town, the 30th Indiana Infantry was sent to occupy our camp this night, and when they left next morning, they took several articles of clothing, cooking utensils, etc., to remember us by(?) we suppose.

Nov. 9.—Marched from Mitchelville towards Nashville, arriving within ten miles of the city that night, having marchd twenty-five miles. We met no guerrillas, although there were rumors of squads of them in the vicinity of the road we traveled.

Nov. 10.—Returned to-day from Mitchelville, after what is generally considered as hard a trip as we ever made, tired and dusty and worn out. But we drew rations of bacon, sugar and coffee, and, after making us some coffee, and frying some bacon, and partaking thereof, we felt very much refreshed, for these were luxuries which we had not been used to for a long time.

Nov. 11.—Gen. Negley's and Palmer's Divisions were reviewed to-day by Gen. Rosecrans. The review was said, by those who witnessed it, to be splendid. Maj. Gen. Rosecrans seemed to be glad to see his old troops again, and greeted us warmly. But the review was tough on the 10th Michigan, for we had not been permitted to rest much since our return from Mitchelville.

Nov. 13.—The brigade marched to Stone River crossing, on the Lebanon "Pike," encamped on the left of the road on the bank of the river. We were a long time marching that eight miles, for we had to go out of our way a great deal to avoid a crossing where a bridge had been destroyed. At another creek we had to construct a "dug way" before we could cross. We were stationed here as an outpost, and to build bridges across Mill Creek, five miles out, and Stone River, eight miles out from Nashville.

Nov. 29.—At 2 o'clock P. M. the 60th Illinois, accompanied our regiment, and we started on a three days scout to visit a place known as Baird's Mill, twenty-six miles from our camp. Marched five miles. Made forced marches, and rations were short.

Nov. 30.—Started early and marched rapidly over very rough, new roads. When about two-thirds of the way out, Company B. which formed the rear guard, saw a body of rebel cavalry advancing on them. Capt. Richman, in command of the company, threw his men into line and stood ready to meet them, but they thought it best not to make an attack, for they disappeared. When we arrived at our destination the bird had flown. We found some rebel camps, apparently just deserted, and it is supposed they were a part of Morgan's guerrilla force. A forage train was sent out, in charge of Liet. Levy, with a guard of twenty-five or thirty men. They soon met what appeared to be a large force of rebel cavalry. Lieut. Levy arranged his men as best he could and waited for them

3

to advance. They asked who he was. He told them. They said, "for God's sake don't shoot, we are the 4th Michigan Cavalry." At night our men took lumber and made themselves comfortable places to sleep. Pickets were thrown out and were attacked by the enemy. The cavalry which Lieut· Levy met, and which came by another road, had joined us, were sent out and repulsed the attack. The heaviest of the attack was made on Company G. We sustained no loss, however, and took a few prisoners.

DEC. 1.—Returned to camp pretty well tired out. Considering the condition of the roads, which were very bad, the state of the weather, and the distances marched (twenty-five miles), the expedition to Baird's Mill may be safely set down as a big and hard march.

DEC. 3.—We had a battalion drill, commanded by Capt. Burnett, of Company A. It has been a long time since we have had a battalion drill before. It reminds us of old Camp Thomson times.

DEC. 8.—At 12 o'clock, midnight, we received marching orders, with only two hours notice to be off. The right wing was on duty and some tall hurrying had to be done. We marched toward Nashville as far as Mill Creek, and encamped in a muddy field, where we expected to remain, as our bridges were not completed. Accordingly we had our fireplaces built, our beds constructed, and our camp in good trim by night for occupation.

DEC. 10.—This morning we were finishing some arrangements about our camp when we were ordered to be ready to move at 9 o'clock A. M. Marched into Nashville and encamped on our old ground, and again began our old duties of foraging, picketing, etc. One very essential duty was to fall out nearly every night, under arms, on account of some false alarm, " or any other man."

DEC. 15.—Received our pay from Maj. Fell.

DEC. 31.—Our regiment formed part of a guard for an ammunition and provision train to go to Murfreesboro, where Maj. Gen. Rosecrans was fighting the terrible battle of Stone

River. Guerrilla parties are constantly harrassing his trains of supplies, which have to be sent from Nashville. Yesterday a large train was captured and burned. Marched rapidly twenty miles and rested and took dinner. Saw a great many wounded who had been brought from the battlefield. About 6 o'clock P. M., moved on seven miles and bivouacked on the field where a few hours before our lines had been struggling with the enemy. The dead and wounded were close by and around us. At 2 o'clock next morning we started on the return to Nashville, marched twelve miles and took breakfast, then marched on, arriving in camp at 11 o'clock A. M., having made twenty-seven miles. A few miles of the way most of the men rode in wagons of a train which was coming in. We neither saw nor heard of rebels, but this afternoon a train was attacked and a portion of it captured, and some of the guards were taken prisoner. We shall long remember that New Year's day. This was probably one of the longest marches made since the war broke out—being fifty-four miles in thirty-three hours.

JAN. 2.—Col. Lum was presented by the regiment with a fine horse, and Lieut. Col. Dickerson with a splendid sword. Presentation speeches were made respectively by Lieut. Hart and Capt. Richman. Replies were made by the recipients of the gifts.

JAN. 3.—Companies A and D were detailed to form part of a guard for an ammunition and provision train to Murfrees-boro. The whole guard consisted of a force equal to three regiments of infantry and one of cavalry. The train had got out about seven miles when it was attacked by a force of about 3,000 rebel cavalry, under "Wheeler." They made a dash upon the center of the train calculating to cut it in two. Most of the cavalry guard had passed, but the remaining few, seconded by the infantry, acted with so much promptness that the guerrillas were repulsed. That part of the infantry guard in which companies A and D were was wheeled out into the field or moved out, and, firing into the rebels, sent them skedaddling back to their reserve. Our loss was a cavalry

Sergeant Major killed, and one man wounnded. Their's was ten killed, and fifteen or eighteen taken prisoners. This was the first time companies A and D had had a chance to fire at the rebels, and they went into it with a will.

JAN. 25.—An affair of some interest took place on the Nashville and Chattanooga Railroad. A guard, detailed from our regiment, were stationed on this railroad, in charge of a construction train. The guard consisted of two corporals and twenty men, commanded by Sergt. Branch (now Lieut. Branch), of Company I. Here is Sergt. Branch's report of the affair:

MILL CREEK, NASHVILLE AND CHATTANOOGA R. R., January 27th, 1863.

COLONEL:

In accordance with your order, which received this day, I will proceed to write a statement of facts relative to the skirmish which took place near here on the 25th inst.

The engine, with a number of cars, started in the direction of Lavergne. There were from twenty-five to thirty men on the cars, acting as train guard. In a short time after the train moved I heard firing up the track. Supposing it to be an attack upon the train, I ordered my men to fall in. In three minutes we were moving on a double quick up the track. We came upon a rebel picket (mounted), who ordered us to halt. We replied by sending a number of shots after him. He ran and we saw no more of him. I now ordered twelve men to move forward as skirmishers until they came opposite the train, then rally and move toward the road. The balance of my men moved up towards the track on the right of the skirmishers. When we came within a few yards of the train we could distinctly hear the rebels at work burning the train. Some one halloaed "Tom, hurry up, the devils are burning the train." We were now opposite the train, and I gave the command, rally on the right file. We soon got into line and moved up within range, when we gave them a volley. They jumped from the cars and run for their horses, which were tied to a fence about sixty rods from the train. We gave one yell and charged on them, or, I should say, after them, for they had got quite the start of use. We drove them into the woods until we saw at least two companies of cavalry in line, waiting for the car-burners, which were about forty in number. They retreated over a hill and we left them. We now devoted our attention to putting out the fires which they had kindled on the train with rails. Some of the fires had got pretty well to going and one car was partly burned up. After putting out the fires we ran the train into our camp. We captured two horses, with equipments, and several guns. How many we killed I know not. The paroled prisoners, who were captured on the train, say they know we killed two and wounded several. These are the facts, as near as I can state them.

THOMAS BRANCH,
*Sergeant Company I, 10th Michigan Infantry,*
*Com. Guard to Construction Train on N. & C. R.*


## DUTY AND QUIET.

After this we had nothing to excite or annoy us more than common duty. All was quiet save occasionally we were called up in the night to stack arms on the color line, and we also received orders to be very vigilant, etc. But these are just commonalities which we don't mind so much since we have learned to be soldiers. Our duty is generally enough to keep us busy, and at times is very arduous. At one time, when a part of the brigade were called out, we had for several days to do the picket duty of three regiments, the right wing relieving each other every 48 hours.


## IN LINE IN TEN MINUTES.

MARCH 25.—Just as most of us were ready to eat our dinner an order came for the regiment to fall in on the color line in ten minutes, with sixty rounds of ammunition. A good many of the men were sleeping, and, although orders had to be given to the separate squads, twenty extra rounds of ammunition drawn and distributed to the men, and accoutrements to be put on, the regiment were moving at the end of ten minutes, with colors flying, and in high hopes of finding the rebels this time. But no! when the 10th Michigan go to seek them it has so far been like seeking a phantom vision, which flies ever from you. After marching eighteen miles in six hours, we returned to camp, somewhat weary. After halting and fronting in line of battle, Col. Lum said: "I never felt more like fighting in my life," and proposed, as there was no one to cheer us just then, "that *we* give three cheers for the old 10th, always ready in ten minutes." The cheers were given, and three more for Col. Lum, and with a will, too, that showed how we love our Colonel. The Colonel, in the meantime, rode along the line with raised cap, in acknowledgment of the tribute. The battalion was then dismissed, what the Colonel had said and done having cured the aching feet and weary limbs wonderfully.

## TEN DAYS PICKETING.

APRIL 7.—The most of the brigade were called out again, and the 10th Michigan had to shoulder their garrison duty. The right wing went on picket on the morning of April 7th, and the left wing were detailed for train and " down town " guards, and hence there were no troops to relieve the right wing, and they were obliged to remain there until April 17th. The left wing, at the same time, was doing other guard duty constantly.

## A FIGHT.

APRIL 01—A detail of companies H and E being guard on a passenger train to Murfreesboro, met with a sad accident as it was attacked on its return. When the train had passed Lavergne some three miles on its way to Nashville, upon nearing a point of cedars which came up close to the railroad, volley after volley of musketry was poured into the train and guard, by a body of rebel cavalry in ambush. The train was stopped on some account, and the cavalry made great slaughter with the guard. Our boys jumped from the cars and fought until the rebels were almost on to them, and with eight times their number, when they made the best of their way for safer quarters. Lieut. F. M. Vanderberg, of Company E, in command of the guard, was hit at the first volley, but he rallied his men, when he was hit a second, then a third time, when he fell. After he fell the guard fought from whatever cover they could find, until they were nearly surrounded. Our loss, compared with the number of the guard, was great. Out of forty-four guards five were killed, ten wounded, and three taken prisoners. Making a loss of eighteen men.

## LOSS IN COMPANY E.

Killed—Freeman Young, shot through the head; Frank Tacy, shot in the head; Geo. W. Bartlett, shot in the abdomen; Wm. Jones, shot in the head. Wounded—Lieut. Vanderburg, mortally, in abdomen, shoulder and hip; Sergt. Chapman, mortally, head; James Murphy, mortally, abdomen; Sergt. J. M. Corrington, forehead, wrist and finger tip; Patrick Lane, hips; Robert Pigne, foot; Urias Pigne, hips and hand; John Harris, thigh, slightly. Prisoner—Peter O'Neil, paroled.

## LOSS IN COMPANY H.

Killed—Benj. Wallace, shot in the head. Wounded—John Lashbrook, hip; David Henry, thigh. Prisoners—Wm. G. Harris, Miron M. Hungerford. Both escaped without being paroled.

Lieut. Vanderburg telegraphed immediately for his father, who arrived a few days before he died. His death occurred on the 18th. His remains were taken home by his father.

Sergt. Chapman, who was hit in the head (the ball penetrating the skull), was insensible until he died, on the 14th. James Murphy lived but two days, dying on the 12th.

After the above sad occurrence nothing happened to destroy the monotony of camp life except rumors of moving, until

MAY 15.—At his time it became the duty of the regiment to execute one of their number. Julius Milika, of Company E, was tried by a general court-martial, and convicted of desertion. The case was an aggravated one, as he had deserted several times, and from different regiments. He was found in Louisville, Kentucky, by accident, as it were, arrested, and brought to his regiment in irons, shut up in prison until he had his trial, and was sentenced "to be shot dead." The sentence to be carried out May 15th, 1863. The detail of twelve men to perform the execution, was made from our regiment. It was as follows:

Harrison H. Wheeler, Lieutenant commanding Detail.

Stephen Moore, of Company D, Sergeant.

| | |
|---|---|
| James Atherton, Co. D, | Morgan D. Mercer, Co. F, |
| Wm. Westbrook, Co. B, | Marion M. Grow, Co. G, |
| John Clark, Co. C, | Abram Harris, Co. H, |
| Charles Sissman, Co. D, | Archie Madison, Co. H, |
| Eugene Chase, Co. E, | Primins Klock, Co. I, |
| Luther Allen, Co. E, | Thomas Holton, Co. K. |

Before the regiment moved out to witness this sad scene, and at the time the detail received their guns, which had been loaded by the Adjutant, Col. Lum addressed the detail in an earnest, feeling manner, explaining the necessity of so painful a duty, and closed by asking them to have mercy enough on their comrade to take cool, deliberate aim at his *heart*.

All the troops in the division off duty were required to be present. At half-past 10 o'clock A. M. the troops began to assemble in a large green field west of the city, which had been selected as the place for the execution. Milika's grave was dug by his comrades. The troops were formed in three fronts of a hollow square, with the grave in the centre. A lone tree stands close to his grave, and marks his last resting place. At a few minutes before 12 o'clock the ambulance containing Milika and his coffin, drove slowly into the inclosure and up towards the grave. It was strongly guarded with cavalry. When Milika alighted he was recognized by his comrades, and his calmness made our hearts but beat the sadder. He shook hands with the officers and then they all retired, leaving only the Chaplains to talk and pray with him. He sat down on his coffin while prayer was offered, and when these ceremonies were ended, he waved an adieu with his hand to his comrades, and, laying his hand upon his breast, said, " comrades, aim here, farewell." The bandage was then placed over his eyes, and he sat very erect, giving a good chance to the detail to do its duty. Then, as the commands were given, we saw the guns brought to a shoulder. Ready—aim—then every heart was still—not a breath stirred the silent air, and all at once burst forth the volley. We knew that the men had remembered what the Colonel said to them, for we heard, as it were, but one gun, and Julius Milika was no more. He fell backward over his coffin, and died without a struggle. All six of the balls hit him, five of them in the breast. May we never be called upon to perform another so painful a duty. May Milika's fate be a sufficient warning to save all from that terrible end.

JUNE 7.—Late in the evening an order came for the regiment to be ready to move the next morning early, and, until near midnight, all was stir and confusion, getting camp and garrison equipage packed ready for transportation. This order was not received with as much good grace as most orders to move are by our regiment. For this there were several reasons: 1st. We had been here a long time and had begun to think—may be—that we had a right to stay a long time yet. 2d. We had just got our camp in the best of order, having "stockaded" the tents with brick and laid brick floors in most of them, a thing which we had neglected all winter and spring, expecting to "move soon." 3d. Most of the members of the regiment had formed acquaintances with the people of Nashville, and the result had been, in many instances, that very strong attachments had been formed, and, indeed, several of the soldiers had married there. 4th. The officers had, several of them, sent home and had their wives come to Nashville, and they were very loth to part with them again so soon.

June 8.—Early in the morning surplus stores were turned over, and all was ready for the move—still, we all hoped the order would be countermanded. In fact, strong influence was said to be at work, both military and civil, to get it countermanded. The good bye visits to their "new homes" had been made by the soldiers, and the partings

"Such as rend the life from out young hearts."

all made, when lo, here comes the countermand. Again the camps were put in shape, and we went to work to live again. Still, we could not expect to stay long, for it was well known that our General (Morgan), or at least believed, was at work to get his brigade ordered to the front.

June 11.—The brigade was reviewed by Gen. R. S. Granger, commanding the forces at this post, at 4 o'clock this P. M.

June 16.—We received two months pay from Uncle Sam, and the usual amount of excitement consequent on such additions to "pocket change" was prevalent in camp during the afternoon, and late at night.

June 21.—A man, supposed to be a spy, was shot by Corpl. Richmond, of Company C, while he was attempting to get away from him, as he was detailed to take him from the picket line to the headquarters of the post. This produced considerable excitement, some condemning and others approving. The Corporal was commended for it by the General commanding the post.

June 26.—Gov. Blair, of Michigan, visited us to-day. The regiment was formed in hollow square, on the parade ground, and the Governor made us a short speech, full of encouragement. He had been on a trip through the Army of the Potomac and our own army, to visit Michigan regiments. He said our regiment was as large as some whole brigades in the Army of the Potomac, and thought we were ready and willing to do whatever we were called upon to do. He said Michigan was proud of her troops, as she had reason to be, and that they had always discharged every duty assigned them with honor.

We were glad to see our Governor, and were encouraged by his words, and we believe he is heart and soul in the work of crushing the rebellion.

June 29.—Three companies of the regiment were ordered to relieve a like number of the 2d Brigade, who were guarding "contrabands," and the right wing was ordered to remain on picket until further orders. Fortunately it was only two days that this duty was to be performed.

July 4.—The companies which were not on duty had "dinners," the money for the purchase of which was donated by the officers of the regiment. The Nashville markets were well stocked with soldiers that morning from the "10th," and "greenbacks" were not used stintingly, either. Some rich dinners was the result of the effort, and this showed that soldiers do know how to cook as well as eat, if they have half a chance. Those companies who were on duty postponed their dinners a day or two. At some of the dinners, speeches were made by the field as well as line officers, and everything went off, as "dixie" had it, "right pert."

July 6.—Received two months pay from Uncle Sam, by the hand of Maj. Sperry, Paymaster for our brigade.

July 17.—The forces at this post, except those who were on duty, were reviewed by Maj. Gen. Rosecrans. The review was an interesting one. All felt an interest to do "their best," as "Rosy" was to be the reviewing officer. The General expressed his entire satisfaction at the appearance of the troops. He was received with a hearty welcome by one and all, and the Army of the Cumberland will always venerate and esteem Gen. Rosecrans.

July 18.—Received notice that we would move soon, and accordingly began preparations.

July 19.—Busy all day, preparing to march in the morning. Again the good byes had to be repeated, and this time it was in good earnest.

July 20.—Regiment marched out early, just after daybreak, and there was almost as much solicitude expressed by the friends of soldiers—considering the numbers—as when we left Flint. Many affecting, as well as ludicrous scenes, were enacted. It was surprising to see how many anti-union and demi-rebel persons had smothered their sentiments and swallowed their indignation for "Yankees" so much as to form so strong attachments.

Just outside of the town the whole brigade was collected and moved on. The day was very warm and we suffered considerable with the heat. As we were not used to marching it was the worse for us. Marched seventeen miles and a half and bivouacked in a clover field, near good water. It rained considerable during the night.

A member of the 10th Illinois Infantry committed suicide in the afternoon, by blowing his brains out with his musket. He said he was tired of "soldiering."

July 21.—Marched to Murfreesboro, Tennessee, a distance of twelve miles and a half, which we made by 11 o'clock and forty minutes. Made camp about a quarter of a mile north of the Lebanon "Pike." During our stay here we fixed up very comfortable and pleasant quarters considering that we had nothing but "dog tents" for covering. The rebel camps were stripped of lumber as were also the former camps of our own troops and appropriated to our own use. The regiment was drilled some here while the weather was very warm. For instance, August 14th, when the regiment started for the drill ground the thermometer showed ninety-six deg. Fah. in the shade, and in the sun the mercury rose to one hundred and six deg. Fah.

Our duty here was lighter than it had been at Nashville, for, the latter part of the time there we were on picket duty two days and off two, while here it was about one day in six.

Aug. 18.—We received orders to march to Columbia, Tennessee, and the day was mostly spent in preparing to march next morning.

Aug. 19.—As our transportation, which had been sent to Nashville for forage, had not yet returned, we could not start this morning. They did not arrive until 10 o'clock A. M., and, as some of the horses had to be shod, and other matters had to be attended to, so that we did not get started until 4 o'clock P. M., and yet, unused as we were to marching, we made thirteen and a half miles that afternoon, to a point opposite Fosterville. The country over which we passed was sterile and rocky, growing but little save a few stunted cedars. The only water we could obtain was stagnant and brackish. The men were very tired as our march had been rapid.

Aug. 30.—Marched fifteen miles, to a point three and a half miles beyond Shelbyville. Just beyond Shelbyville the regiment was halted—in fact the brigade halted—and, as it was on the bank of Duck River, and the men being very warm and dusty, many of them went in swimming. To-day many of them gave out on account of sore feet. One man fell by sunstroke, and others had to fall out on account of the heat. Water was scarce, too. Most of the country to-day was quite good, and we passed several fine farms in the vicinity of Shelbyville. Made bivouack at 5 o'clock P. M.

Aug. 21.—Started at 5 o'clock A. M., marched seventeen miles, to within a mile of Lewisberg, where we arrived at 1 o'clock P. M. Bivouacked in a cedar grove on the right of the road. Most of the regiment pitched tents. A heavy rain came on about half-past 3 o'clock P. M., wetting those who had not got their tents pitched, most piteously. Two large cornfields close by were entirely stripped of corn, and the way mutton, chickens, etc., had to suffer was a caution to disloyal quadrupeds and feathered bipeds. The boys said " they were not going to run the risk of them great fat sheep biting them, and, after they had killed them, it wasn't right to throw them away." Hogs, too, were accused of being possessed with fighting principles, and hens and chickens who wouldn't " crow for the Union " were declared " secesh."

Aug. 22.—Marched at 5 o'clock A. M. Most of the road was very rough, and in some places almost impassable, \on account of the mud. Marched eighteen miles and bivouacked within six miles of Columbia. This forenoon the 16th and 60th Illinois regiments joined us. Heretofore the 10th Illinois was all that had been with us. Just at night four guerrillas were captured by our advance. It was reported that they were trying to burn a bridge at Fountain Mills, over which we were to pass. We had expected to have met with more such before this time. Our bivouac was near Fountain Mills. Some corn, fowls, etc., were "confiscated."

Aug. 23.—The brigade marched through Columbia and encamped about half a mile beyond the town. What few rebels occupied the town skedaddled in the morning. Not a Union flag was flying in all the town, and the people received us in the coolest manner possible. While some looked surprised others wore vexed countenances, and still others looked as though they would liked to have murdered us. Now and then, to be sure, amid the disappointed crew, you would see the merry sparkle of an eye which told what the heart dared not utter in any other way. "By the "contrabands" we learned as soon as the people found the "Yankees" were coming they closed their houses of worship and the congregations hurried home.

Our regiment did not pitch camp, as four companies, A, F, G and B, were detailed as Provost Guard, and it was thought the remainder of the regiment would be put upon some other than ordinary duty. Here we expected to remain for some time, and promised ourselves we should do something towards converting the inhabitants to "Yankee" faith. But our destiny was not to remain.

The town of Columbia is supplied with water by a strange method, and one which I can not expect to describe understandingly. Suffice it to say, it is by means of a force pump, worked by a water power which is obtained by means of an undershot water wheel being placed in Duck River, more than one-fourth of a mile from the pump. The motion is communicated from the crank of the water-wheel to the pump, by a continuous lever, which is composed of wooden rods or poles,

spliced together for the whole of this distance. In the distance the motion is changed at right angles twice—once at
the river bank, from a perpendicular to a horizontal, and once
near the spring where the pump is placeed. The lever which
connects the pump with the water wheel is carried over very
rough ground, now suspended by chains from poles set over
it in the shape of an inverted V, again resting only on top of
a cross bar placed across two uprights, resting on the ground,
and still again resting on a rock. Indeed, the kinds of sup-
ports were about as various as the number, and they were
placed at a distance of about every fifteen feet for the whole
distance, and there that lever worked, back and forth, night
and day, doing a valuable service to the town, with but a trifle
of expense, and next to no care. The whole machine was very
rude and elicited a great many remarks and queries from the
soldiery, who would have thought it nothing very strange if
they had seen it North, but to find such ingenuity displayed in
Tennessee, was a "stumper."

Aug. 25.—Moved a little nearer town, and began pitching
camp, and before night had a respectable looking camp, with
comfortable quarters, in an advanced stage of completion,
when lo! here comes an order to march "to-morrow morning,'
with all the rations we could transport, and one hundred and
twenty rounds of ammunition per man.

Aug. 26.—Moved out of camp at 2 o'clock P. M. We were
delayed on account of drawing rations and ammunition. We
marched eight and a half miles and bivouacked in a piece of
woods on the left of the road.

Aug. 27.—Marched at 5 o'clock A. M. Reached Lynnville
at half-past 8 o'clock A. M. Passed through Pulaski at 4
o'clock P. M. Many of the buildings were burned. The inhabitants seemed somewhat surprised to see so many "blue
coats" in their town. We bivouacked one mile beyond (or
south), of Pulaski, making a march of twenty-three and one-
half miles.

Aug. 28.—Marched eighteen miles, which took us some five
miles south of Elkton, Tennessee, and very near the Alabama

line. Captured a few guerrillas and several hundred pounds of bacon, which was intended for the "rebels." Our camp this night was close to where the brigade was fired upon by the guerrillas last year, when marching through the same "gap" towards Nashville. Encamped near one of the large springs for which Northern Alabama is so famous. This was very comfortable, for water had been scarce on the march for the last two days.

Aug. 29.—Marched at 6 o'clock A. M. Reached a point two and one-half miles north of Athens, Alabama, at 11 o'clock A. M. Here we halted until Gen. Morgan went ahead and looked out a camping ground. Went through the town at half-past 2 o'clock P. M., and made camp about a quarter of a mile south, having marched sixteen miles.

Aug. 31.—We moved our camp a little more to the south-west of, and nearer the town. Received orders to march in the morning.

Sept. 1.—Marched early for Huntsville, Alabama, distant twenty-five miles, which we reached and marched through about 5 o'clock P. M. Made camp, or, rather, bivouacked, about three-quarters of a mile east and south of the town. This is conceded by all to be the most lovely and picturesque town we have seen in all the South. The streets are clean and well laid out, the inhabitants looked cheerful and intelligent, and greeted us with as hearty a welcome as could be asked in so southern a town. We were hopeful that we might stay here some time, and, indeed felt sure we should, but again we were deceived. Our destination seems ever on. To.day's march was twenty-six miles, mostly through uncultivated, and much of it wild land.

Sept. 2.—Marched to Brownsville, a little place on the bank of Flint River, Alabama, situated on the railroad which runs from Stevenson to Huntsville, distant from Huntsville ten miles. The road over which we marched was exceedingly rough and monotonous, so that many thought that that ten miles was harder than the twenty-six of the day previous. A telegraph operator detached the wires and in a few minutes we had communication with Gen. Rosecrans. Mail reached us by cars, which came from Stevenson. This was only the third mail which we had received since leaving Murfreesboro. Here again we commenced building quarters, expecting to stay some time. This camp was known as Camp at Flint River, Alabama.

SEPT. 4.—Marched in the direction of Stevenson, Alabama. Started at half-past 12 o'clock P. M., marched eleven miles and bivouacked at half-past 4 o'clock P. M. just north of the Huntsville and Stevenson Railroad. The country over which we passed was very hilly.

SEPT. 5.—Started at 5 o'clock A. M. The country was still rough and hilly. After marching twenty miles made camp at 4 o'clock P. M., at Larkinville, Alabama. Here we found some rabid "secesh." Sweet potatoes, and geese, and "fresh" of all kinds suffered some. Several of our sick were sent through on the cars.

SEPT. 6.—Started at 4 o'clock and forty-five minutes A. M., passed through Scottsville at 7 o'clock A. M., and reached Belle Fonte 10 o'clock and twenty-five minutes, making thirteen miles in five hours and forty minutes, over a rough country and very bad roads. Near Belle Fonte the country was less rough. Here we found the town entirely deserted except by two or three families. Gen. Bragg told the inhabitants when he retreated that the Yankees would close the houses as fast as they came to them, and burn them, inmates, contents and all. By this piece of worse than scandal he induced all who could, to follow him across the Tennessee River. Large libraries were scattered upon the floors of deserted buildings, and pianos left to the tender mercies of the soldiers. There were many nice books carried away from that town by our men. We bivouacked near another of those famous springs of Northern Alabama. Again the farmers of that section suffered loss in fresh meats and vegetables. We think the Russell House, of Detroit, could not have furnished a greater variety than did our camp that night.

4

SEPT. 7.—We started at 5 o'clock A. M. and marched slowly, halting and resting several times. Twice we had to ford a stream of water of considerable size. The roads were very dusty, as they had been for two days past. As the road lay through woods where no wind could come, the dust rose in such masses as to nearly smother those who were marching in the ranks. It is literally true that many times a man could not be seen at a distance of twelve or fifteen feet, any more than in the darkest night that ever settled upon this mundane sphere. We reached Stevenson at half-past 2 o'clock P. M., marched some distance beyond the town, and encamped in an open field, near a small stream. Stevenson is a war-stricken place indeed. We have not seen a more desolate, woe-begone town since our first soldiering, and, indeed, never anywhere its equal. It is literally killed and needs a resurrection before it can thrive again. Marched fourteen miles.

SEPT. 8.—Companies A, F, I, E and B were detailed to-day as Provost Guard in Stevenson. Company H was sent out on the railroad four miles to guard Widow Creek bridge.

SEPT. 10.—Company H returned to-day from Widow Creek bridge.

SEPT. 11.—Company G detailed on Provost Guard duty at Stevenson, as the five companies already there were not enough. The remaining four companies moved camp into the woods and put up comfortable quarters. Heretofore they had been expecting to be detailed on some guard duty or to march, and had put up no quarters.

SEPT. 17.—Received pay by Paymaster Maj. Sperry.

SEPT. 20.—This afternoon we received orders to be ready to move at 8 o'clock the next morning. About dark we were ordered to be ready to march at 1 o'clock, instead of 7 o'clock A. M.

SEPT. 21.—We started at 2 o'clock A. M. for Bridgeport, Alabama. It was very dark and dusty, and although the road lay through woods, and in many places was rather blind, we were fortunate enough to keep it all right, and arrived at Bridgeport at 6 o'clock and fifteen minutes A. M., having marched thirteen miles. Crossed the river and encamped on the island north of the railroad. Here we remained until Oct. 1st. This was very unhealthy, and many became sick here who had never been sick before, and our number of men for duty was getting less every day. Several exciting rumors were put in circulation of the enemy being about to make a demonstration against that point, and we threw up fortifications on the border of the island.

Sept. 26.—Company G was detailed as guard to accompany some artillerymen who were to take two 32-pounder Parrott guns to Chattanooga. They went up the Sequatchie Valley as far as Anderson's Cross Roads, and then climbed up the mountain. In ascending the mountain there are several short turns to be made, where not more than two teams can draw at all, and here the men were obliged to draw these large pieces of ordnance by hand, and they were liable to be surprised at moment by bands of guerrillas which were infesting the mountain near by. But, after much hard toiling, on short (yes, more than short) rations, the huge guns were transported across the mountain and safely landed at Chattanooga. But in going down into the "gulch" about half way across the mountain, as well as down the side of the mountain towards Chattanooga, the guards were obliged to hold them back by ropes attached to them. They returned by another route, just in time to avoid a raid which was made by the rebels and by which they destroyed a great deal of property. The poultry, hogs, sheep, etc., of the country were confiscated in large quantities, or the boys must have starved. They were highly complimented by Gen. Rosecrans for the dispatch with which they performed the work assigned them. The company returned to Bridgeport, which they reached October 4th, three days after the regiment had left.

Oct. 1.—It had been raining nearly all day and the night previous, and just at night an order came for the regiment to march immediately to Jasper, as a force of rebel cavalry had come upon our supply trains near there and were making sad havoc. The roads were full of running water, to say nothing of the mud which had been cut up and worked up to the depth of from six to eighteen inches. The regiment started just after dark (and it was dark, too), and the rain still poured, still on we struggled, over rocks, and roots, and through mud, until we were all exhausted. Shoes were lost and clothes torn and spoiled, as one after another measured his length in a puddle of the yellow clay. At length, covered with mud from head to foot, and wet to the skin, tired and exhausted, we halted within five miles of Jasper, until daylight, having made seven miles, and it seemed as though it was twice that number.

Oct. 2.—Marched at half-past 7 o'clock A. M., and arrived at Jasper at 10 o'clock A. M. After leaving Jasper we received orders to keep a sharp lookout on our right, where a ridge of mountains rose from near the road, as it was supposed a band of guerrillas was hovering in that region. We had orders, also, to load our guns and increase the number of cartridges per man, which being done, we moved on, but met with no interruption, and bivouacked nine miles beyond Jasper, in a northeasterly direction. Made fourteen miles.

Oct. 3.—Started at 6 o'clock A. M., and, after marching five miles, came to where the rebels had been burning a supply train of ammunition, clothing and rations, which were being sent to Chattanooga, Tennessee. Marched five miles further, finding ruins of wagons and army stores burning every little distance. Some three hundred Government wagons and their loads of supplies were this time destroyed by Forest and his thievish band. Large amounts of sutler's stores were also destroyed. Encamped at Anderson's Cross Roads, Tennesse, having marched ten miles—or, we should more properly have said, bivouacked, for there were no tents at all, except two or three "dog tents," which some of the boys had "toted" on their backs. Fortunately, there was plenty of straw and corn-stalks close at hand, and huts, such as only the Army of the Cumberland could improvise, sprung up like magic, and, although the weather was cold and stormy, we were compara- tively comfortable. Fences disappeared from the surrounding country in proportion as huts appeared, and hogs, sheep and cattle, with a good sprinkling of poultry, helped to splice out our short rations.

Oct. 6.—The camp and garrison equipage was ordered up from Bridgeport, and reached the camp about 5 o'clock p. m., the next day (Oct. 7th), and we immediately set about preparing comfortable quarters and fortifying our position. A line of breastworks was thrown up close by our camp, and a long, irregular line of brush and small trees piled up through the open fields, to break a cavalry charge if one should be made, as some thought it might be, for it was rumored that Forrest was still hovering about. All the lumber in the vicinity soon found its way into our camp, and in a few days very commodious quarters were erected, and we expected, or at least hoped, we might stay some time. Our camp was near the bank of the Sequatchie River, in a very pleasant valley, with the Waldron Ridge on one side, and a smaller one on the other. Our duty consisted in picketing and helping trains up the mountain. The people of Sequatchie Valley were very ignorant and seemed to possess no other ambition than to own slaves enough to raise crops which would suffice to keep them from one year to another. Thrift and enterprise were entirely absent. Here was a rich tract of land, a good fruit country, and yet scarcely a fruit tree of any kind. No schools, and many of the inhabitants who had reached the ages of eighteen or twenty years, had never been outside of the valley, which was in most places less than one mile and a fourth in width, and scarcely exceeding two miles at any point. One family being asked if they had a time piece, replied no! and asked of what use it would be to them, as none of them could tell the time by it. The oldest of their number was not less than sixty years. Some of them did not know what tea or coffee was—at least so they asserted. There were some exceptions to this low state of intelligence, of course, and some families were quite respectably situated and well educated, but they were few.

Oct. 18.—Received orders to march immediately, with no luggage save what the men carried with them. A few teams went to carry rations and ammunition. Marched at 11 o'clock A. M. Some were out getting lumber to improve their quarters, but they threw down their loads after carrying them a long way, and cheerfully donned the habiliments of war, and, in a cold, unpleasant rain, marched on. We moved up the valley nine miles and bivouacked at the foot of Waldron Ridge, at what is known as Barnett's Gap. It was rainy all day, and as the roads had been softened by previous rain, it was very slow work moving up the valley. The 60th Illinois Infantry and the 10th Wisconsin Battery accompanied us.

Oct. 19.—Started up the mountain at half-past six o'clock A. M. The mountain road was so very muddy and cut up with trains passing, that we were all day in rising the mountain, a distance of only three miles. The battery teams were almost wholly useless, as they were entirely inadequate to move the guns up the terrible road. Long ropes were attached and we were ordered to help drag them out of the mud. So at it we went with a desperate will, and with a sturdy heigh, ho! out they came, and in this way we moved slowly along. Officers as well as men catching hold of the ropes and lifting with a determined will. Certainly there were some who feared to soil their delicate hands or spot their uniforms, but let it be remembered that the soldiers mark all such, and will not forget them. Just at night we reached the top of the mountain, and a pitiable looking set we were, covered with mud from head to foot, and almost exhausted. We might easily have been mistaken for a lot of "butternuts," the mud having effectually changed the color of our uniforms.

Oct. 20.—Started at half-past 6 o'clock A. M., and, after going about six miles, found we could not descend the mountain by the road we were traveling, on account of large wagon trains coming up, and the mountain road not being wide enough to admit of passing. So we marched back a mile and a half and took another road. In descending the mountain the road was so steep and rocky that it was found impossible for the battery teams to hold back enough to steady the guns, and again the ropes were attached to the carriages, and we helped to ease the "critter" down. Every once in a while the carriage came to a place almost perpendicular, and, in spite of the combined efforts of teams and soldiers, down it would go, shoving the teams ahead of it and dragging the men hold of the ropes into the mud with no more care than as though Uncle Sam didn't have to pay us thirteen dollars per month, and the unlucky ones, who happened to get well "jerked," would pick themselves up, and, with a "here's your mule," or "plumb battery," or "that's what's the matter," grab the rope again, resolved to give it another trial. These are scenes at the same time deplorable and laughable. Marched ten miles and bivouacked in Tennessee Valley.

Oct. 21.—Started at half-past 6 o'clock A. M., and marched through rain and mud to Dallas, Tennessee, on the bank of the Tennessee River, some thirteen miles above Chattanooga. We reached Dallas at 11 o'clock A. M. Had one of the heaviest thunder storms we have ever experienced. The distance marched to-day was nine miles. While in camp at this place rations were very short—as high as 25 and even 50 cents were offered for a single hard tack by our men.

Oct. 23.—Orders to march were received and countermanded.

Oct. 24.—Moved at 7 o'clock A. M. for a march of forty miles (it was said), and we had no rations except meat and parched corn, nor any means of procuring any; but, upon reaching Gen. Spear's Brigade we were fortunate in being able to borrow ten boxes of hard tack, and this saved us from starving. Marched ten miles and bivouacked in the woods. It is needless to remark that to-day, as well as all through this march, a great deal of "drawing" rations on "personal requisitions," was done.

Oct. 25.—Started at half-past 6 o'clock A. M., and marched through a very good farming country, reaching Washington, Tennessee, at 12 o'clock, noon, passed through and bivouacked two and a half miles beyond, or northeast of Washington, having marched seventeen miles. Washington has been a thriving little town, nearly on the Tennessee River. Many of the inhabitants had now skedaddled, and it was a desolate looking place. Orders were given when we halted to-night to the effect that no individual foraging would be allowed, as quite an amount of meat had been lawfully confiscated near Washington. But, notwithstanding that guards were posted all around, a great deal of "fresh" found its way into camp, and helped to splice out rations. It would be tedious to undertake to explain the many different ruses used to convey it through the guard lines, and we will not undertake it. It is enough that we got it.

Oct. 26.—At 7 o'clock A. M. we were again *en route* for ——. After marching five miles we reached Smith's Ferry, seven and a half miles above Washington, and fifty-five miles above Chattanooga. We found this was our destination for the present. It was a very important post, on the extreme left of the Army of the Cumberland. Only a short time since we were on the extreme right, in Alabama. A detachment of the 10th Wisconsin Battery was stationed here with us. Again we supposed we might remain some time, and immediately went to work to put up winter quarters, as it was very late in the fall. In a short time we had erected very comfortable quarters. They were made of logs, and well "chinked" and mudded, so as to be very warm. There was a fire-place in each house. Some of the officers built large houses and covered them with "shake," or, rather, their men did for them. Many of the company quarters were covered in the same manner. Upon our first arrival at the ferry, the rebel pickets on the opposite side of the river were quite quarrelsome, and fired at us whenever opportunity offered. They boasted loudly of what would be our fate in a short time—predicting that our army would all be across the Cumberland River in less than three weeks; that Bragg's headquarter's would be at Louisville, etc. Our pickets were ordered not to return the fire of the enemy, but once or twice a rebel picket bit the dust by the sharp shooting of our pickets, for it was more than human

nature could stand to be a mark without retaliating, and their
firing soon ceased, their manner towards us changed, and we
used to converse with them. At the time of the change of
commanders of the Army of the Cumberlaod, we asked them
how they liked it. The reply was that " Grant dug too much."
And just here it will not be improper to say that the Army of
the Cumberland felt very deeply sorrowful when " Rosy " was
taken from them. We heard but few oaths, as usual on such
occasions, but a deep sorrow seemed to be felt by all, as though
a loved parent had been taken away, and although we placed
great confidence in Gen. Thomas, still we felt as though "Rosy"
was the man.

OCT. 25.—The camp and garrison equipage, which had been
behind since we left Anderson's Cross Roads, and also the
knapsacks, was started for the regiment. As our teams were
in poor condition, and the roads very bad, it took two days to
get to the top of the mountain, and here was only a part of
the equipage at that, and it was seven days before it reached
the regiment. The rest was brought up at two different times,
the last reaching the regiment the day before it left. It was at
this time, or a little before, that six of our teams and wagons
were taken from us, and hence our transportation was very
short. While in camp here (Smith's Ferry, Tennessee), our
Lieutenant Colonel, C. J. Dickerson, showed his willingness to
do for his men, and his care for their welfare, by confiscating
from noted rebels all the subsistence we needed. Wheat and
corn were taken in large quantities, and, as our teams could
not haul it fast enough, teams belonging to citizens were pressed
into our service, and a mill was also pressed and run by men
detailed from our regiment—Lieut. Papst in charge—so that
we had plenty of corn meal and flour, and the inhabitants
brought in potatoes and apples and sold them very reasonable.
Poultry, and, in fact, everything we could wish was brought in
from the surrounding country at very fair rates. A scout,
consisting of several men, detailed from the companies was
also formed and mounted on pressed animals, to scour the
country for guerrillas, and to go out and drive in sheep, cattle

and hogs from the stocks of noted guerrilla leaders and other rabid secessionists. They were denominated the "Burnett Scouts," and were under command of Capt. Burnett, of Company A, then detailed as Major. Sergt. L. E. Davie, of Company I, was the only non-commissioned officer. He often went out with them alone, and they were known, in camp terms, as Davie and his ten thieves. They rendered valuable service, and made some hard scouts, lying on the ground all night, with no blankets, when the weather was very cold. But they were determined fellows, and bound to do their duty, and, as they were placed in an important position, felt the necessity of using the more diligence to perform what was assigned them. Although we could draw but little from the Government, we lived on the top shelf while in camp at Smith's Ferry. All through the camp were chickens, geese and turkeys, running in every direction, and cock-fighting was resorted to as a pastime, and, indeed, it was carried to that extent that bets of large amounts of money were made upon it, and some of the best "gamers" have been kept with the regiment ever since. We were very comfortable all the time we remained here. For a few days we were entirely without salt, and, as our meat was all fresh, it was rather unwholesome and unpleasant.

Nov. 11.—Gen. Jeff. C. Davis visited our camp and all were eager to see our Division Commander, for we had lately been transferred to his division.

Nov. 19.—We were paid by Maj. Sperry, our Brigade Paymaster, to whom we are very much attached, as he is so gentlemanly, showing that the officers and men can be harmoniously combined.

Nov. 20.—We received orders to march the next morning to near Chattanooga. This was throwing cold water on all our "fine fixins," but still a willing disposition was shown by all, and immediate preparations were made to be off. But owing to the lateness of the order reaching us, and to a rain storm which set in just at that time, the march was delayed until next morning.

Nov. 21.—Marched at 7 o'clock A. M., the weather being cold and rainy. It continued to rain until the afternoon, and the small streams which we might otherwise have crossed dry-shod, were now swollen and turbulent, and fording became necessary. Upon approaching one larger than those already forded, the advance hesitated an instant, but, as there was no other way, they sprang in and the column followed on, shouting, laughing, and making the best possible grace of the matter, as they had done scores of times long before. The distance marched was eighteen miles. We bivouacked near a nice spring, tired enough to enjoy rest, for we had marched fast and hard, the roads being in very bad condition.

Nov. 22.—This morning was cold and frosty, but the day grew warm and pleasant. We started at 6 o'clock A. M., and marched twenty miles and bivouacked at the foot of Waldron's Ridge at half-past 3 o'clock P. M. Forded Sail Creek, a clear, cold stream, about eighteen inches deep and four or five rods wide. During the day heard heavy cannonading, supposed to to be at Chattanooga.

Nov. 23.—Started at half-past 6 o'clock A. M., and marched fourteen miles, reaching Camp Caldwell, four miles above Chattanooga, where other regiments of our brigade were stationed. Here we were halted between the high hills which skirt the river, with orders not to ascend the hills or build much fire, as that would show our whereabouts to the enemy, who still held possession of the heights on the opposite side of the river. Here we were obliged to lay inactive, listening to the conflict which was progressing but a short distance from us.

Nov. 24.—We received orders to fall in at half-past 5 o'clock A. M., and at 6 o'clock we stacked our arms and waited until 12 o'clock M., before starting, although heavy bodies of troops had crossed the river on a pontoon bridge which had been thrown over during the night. Ferry boats, too, had been employed, so that by daylight the Yankees had two lines of earth-works under the very noses of the rebels. Our brigade crossed at 2 o'clock P. M., and formed in line of battle, as the troops which had already crossed were also formed. An advance was made, slowly at first, by one body after another passing ahead of others and deploying constantly in line of battle. In this way our brigade advanced and formed three lines of battle in different positions. About 3 o'clock P. M. a heavy force moved forward with fixed bayonets and colors flying, and the enemy soon fell back to Mission Ridge without much fighting. All the afternoon a heavy column of cavalry passed on our left, and advanced up the Knoxville and Chattanooga Railroad. At night we slept on our arms, one mile from the river."

Nov. 25.—Early day found us stirring, and again we were doomed to be idle spectators of the great drama which was being enacted before us. Forming a new line of battle, we stacked arms and remained all day. Heavy and terrible was the fighting, and stubborn and willful the enemy. But our troops were inspired with bravery and courage and full of faith that they were to be victorious, and, with an unyielding will and an undying energy, they pressed the enemy back, back, step after step, and held every inch of the blood-stained ground which they had fought so hard to gain. All day, and far into the night the wounded were carried past our division.

Nov. 26.—At half-past 12 o'clock P. M. our division fell in and moved up the Tennessee River, crossing the Chickamauga at its mouth on a pontoon bridge, and, after going two and a half miles further up the river, halted and received orders not to build any fires. As it was very cold we were obliged to keep stirring in order to keep warm. War dances were held around the great trees, and various were the methods adopted to keep the blood in circulation. After two hours orders were received to build fires and get breakfast. During the time we lay here we could distinctly hear the rebels chopping, hammering, etc., and preparing to skedaddle. At daylight we moved on, and came upon the rebel skirmishers after marching about four miles, having visited their deserted camps nearly two miles further back, where we found their camp fires still burning. The 21st Regiment of Kentucky Infantry, which were temporarily attached to our brigade, were deployed as

skirmishers, and the remainder of the brigade stacked arms
and waited the result. The rebels moved obstinately, and the
10th Illinois infantry were sent to reinforce or relieve the 21st
Kentucky. At this the enemy broke and run, as the 21st
made a furious charge upon them, not being of a mind to give
it up so.

About two miles farther on we came suddenly upon two
forts filled with live rebels. They opened fire upon us with
two small field pieces, and threw some shells very close to us,
one nearly striking our Lieutenant Colonel, C. J. Dickerson,
and a small piece of another lodging lightly in the hair of a
member of Company C. But, seeing the large force opposing
them (for our division was drawn up in three lines of battle in
rear of each other, and there were more still in the rear of
them) they beat a hasty retreat, our artillery helping them
amazingly.

One man of Company F was slightly wounded by a spent
ball striking him in the back.

At about 2 o'clock P. M. our brigade entered Chickamauga
Station, the 10th Michigan marching in and taking possession
of the works immediately in the place. Here we captured two
large siege guns, several wagons and ambulances, and a large
amount of corn meal and hard bread. Two large commissa-
ries were burned, destroying a large amount of stores. Five
men were found dead and unburried, whom the rebels had left
in their hasty retreat. Others were dying, and, altogether, it
was a lamentable spectacle.

Here we rested about an hour, and then took up the pursuit again. Just at dark we found some signs of the butternuts,
but night closed in quickly, and we bivouacked, having made
twelve miles.

Nov. 27.—Reveillee waked us as usual, long before the
break of day, and when the first gray streakings of light showed themselves, we started again after the fleeing rebels. We
soon came up to where they had abandoned two pieces of
artillery and thrown away cooking utensils, sacks of meal, etc.,
which had encumbered their flight.

At noon we arrived at Grayville and halted one hour, where the 11th Alabama Cavalry passed us.

In the afternoon we marched in line of battle considerable of the time, and at 5 o'clock we halted and bivouacked for the night within two miles of Ringgold, Georgia. So we were in Georgia for the first time.

A drizzling rain set in in the afternoon and continued until some time in the night. While at this point we heard that Ringgold was in the possession of our troops, and a large number of prisoners taken with it, and, the fighting which we had heard during the day having ceased, confirmed it in our minds.

Rations were very short—next to none. Marched twenty miles.

Nov. 28.—Started at 7 o'clock A. M., marched three miles, halted, and remained the rest of the day. At night we drew two days rations, which were quite acceptable, as we had started in the morning with only one hardtack each. What little transportation we had with us was at this point turned back, and we had to "tote" everything we used.

Nov. 29.—At 7 o'clock A. M. we started towards Knoxville, where Longstreet had laid siege to the garrison defending that place. The 4th, 11th and 15th Corps were dispatched to raise the siege, and our division accompanied them. In the forenoon we marched in nearly a northerly direction, and crossed White Oak Ridge about eight miles out. In the afternoon we bore more to the east, and bivouacked at night in a piece of pine woods one mile south of Cleveland, having marched twenty miles. Several Union flags were displayed by citizens, who welcomed our army in its march of victory.

Nov. 30.—Again at 7 o'clock in the morning we were on our way, and, leaving Cleveland on our right, we marched towards Charleston. Here some four or five hundred rebels seemed opposed to our troops taking possession of the town, which is situated on the Hiawassee River, and which we had to cross before entering the town. But seeing our large force the rebels diplayed their "Southern hospitality" by giving up their quarters to us, but rather unbecomingly destroyed the pontoon bridge which they had built across the river. Our regiment bivouacked within one mile of the town, and here we received some rations of fresh beef. Our march this day was fourteen miles.

DEC. 1.—Passed through Charleston early in the forenoon, having started at 8 o'clock. The railroad bridge being in repair, it was planked for the artillery to cross on, and the column passed over in the same way. Thus the unchivalrous rebels did not bother us long.

We made only ten miles to-day, and at night drew rations for one day.

DEC. 2.—At daylight we marched on with nothing of uncommon interest occurring. At noon we passed through a small town containing a cotton manufactory. At half-past 4 o'clock P. M. we bivouacked in a nice grove, having marched twenty-two miles.

DEC. 3.—Again, at 7 o'clock A. M., the "fall in" ran along the lines and we were soon moving. We passed through a fine farming country, in which were good buildings, and thrift and enterprise seemed to mark the country by well cultivated fields. Very little slave labor was employed. Passed a fine church in a pleasant grove.

Our forces drove one thousand rebels out of Londen, and took one hundred prisoners. The enemy ran two locomotives and a large amount of ammunition into the Tennessee River to keep it from falling into our hands. We marched to-day eighteen miles and bivouacked near Londen.

DEC. 4.—Marched at half-past 6 o'clock A. M. The air was cold and piercing. At 8 o'clock we passed through Londen, marched towards Morgantown, and bivouacked in the woods, one mile from Morgantown, having marched twelve miles. Our rations were still short and there was no prospect of their being more plenty. Parched corn formed a great part of our sustenance.

Dec. 5.—We were delayed to-day by the building of a bridge across the little Tennessee River, which we had to cross at this point.

At half-past 2 o'clock in the afternoon we "fell in" and marched to the bridge, but were delayed in crossing by a wagon breaking through. No great damage was done, however; and at sundown we crossed, and passing through Morgantown we marched out five miles from where we stopped the night before and bivouacked at 8 o'clock.

Dec. 6.—At 7 o'clock this morning we started again and expected in a day or two to meet the rebel forces under Longstreet, and force them to raise the siege. We were marching through a fine country, when, at 10 o'clock A. M. we were halted and word passed along the lines that Longstreet had skedaddled, and that there was no further need of our services. We ought to have been glad that our purpose was accomplished so easily, but there was scarcely a soldier who did not feel disappointed that we did not have a chance to teach that noted rebel a serious lesson.

While we were halted thus, a procession of ladies appeared bearing a splendid Stars and Stripes. Passing along our lines, they halted by our brigade, and shout after shout, and peal after peal of applause rang through the air, and rank and file joined in one great overwhelming shout of welcome to the fair bearers of our country's emblem. Immediately a large crowd gathered about to learn the history of that flag, for it was a curiosity to find here, where the enemy had so long held their iron sway, so gorgeous a banner, but orders to march interrupted the scene, and our armies moved back, leaving the ladies, with their flag again without our lines. There were about a dozen of these ladies who thus boldly displayed their patriotism. The flag was borne by a Miss Dunn, by whose efforts it had been made. Indeed, her own hands had wrought almost the whole work, and, during its construction, these patriotic ladies were forced to resort to many methods for concealing it. At times they were forced to wear it about their persons to keep it from the prying eyes of the rebels who were on the alert to find out anything of the sort which might chance to be going on.

What a rebuke is this to the poor, cold patriotism of many of our more favored citizens in the North. What faith it showed in the minds of this tyrannical people. Let it be an earnest lesson to our own home folk.

After turning back, our forces crossed the Tennessee River and our regiment bivouacked at the same place it did on the night of the 4th inst. Marched fifteen miles.

Dec. 7.—At 9 o'clock A. M. we were again moving on the road we had so recently traversed in an opposite direction, but we soon changed our route, continuing south of the railroad instead of recrossing it at London. We passed through Madisonville—a small town, but big with secession—at 3 o clock P. M., and made our bivouack in the woods, having made sixteen miles.

Dec. 8.—The morning broke cold and cloudy, but at half-past 6 o'clock we were on the move. At 10 o'clock it began raining and continued all day. Rations had been very short all along; and now they were entirely gone, and, in fact, we might have said the same many a day before this. At night we bivouacked within one mile of Columbus, having marched twenty miles.

Dec. 9.—Marched to Columbus and halted. Here we remained until December 15th. While here we built a bridge across the Hiawassee River. Columbus consists of one house. Years ago it is said it was quite a country town for the South, but a freshet destroying a large share of the houses one man bought the place and lived in a goodly house until shortly before the arrival of our troops. He is reported as having been actively engaged in collecting commissary stores for the rebels. We found large quantities here and supplied ourselves with rations from them.

The weather was very cold, and, as we were very destitute of blankets, it was with the greatest difficulty we kept from suffering severely. Many of the men were by this time wholly

5

or nearly barefooted, and our condition was pitiable in the extreme, but all were brave hearted and no complaints were heard.

Dec. 14.—We received orders to march at 10 o'clock this morning, and made preparations to do so, when lo! the order was countermanded.

Dec. 15.—At half-past 6 o'clock this morning we marched toward Charleston, through which we passed at noon, and at half-past 5 o'clock p. m. bivouacked in a field of wheat stubble, having marched twenty-three miles.

Dec. 16.—As we were the advanced guard yesterday, we were the rear guard to-day. As the roads were very muddy the division could march only slowly, and, although we started at 7 o'clock in the morning, we did not make camp, or rather, bivouac, until after dark, making only seventeen miles. Several Union flags were displayed on to-day's route, and the people seemed possessed of a great deal of patriotism and devotion to the Union.

Shortly after halting a terrible thunder storm came up and pelted us unmercifully, as we were without shelter, and the rest obtained that night was but poor, and, like the Irishman's riding the plough beam, "if it had not been for the name of it would as soon walk;" so we, had it not been for the name of resting, would as soon have marched.

Dec. 17.—The morning was cold and extremely unpleasant. Our blankets were wet and heavy, as were our clothes, our stomachs empty and woe to the rebels who had chanced to meet us that morning. At 7 o'clock we "shoved out" and passed through McDonald's Gap in the White Oak Mountains, or Ridge, at 9 o'clock. Here we halted and waited for our division wagon train to come up. In the afternoon we marched on the railroad for nine miles, which, by the by, is the most tiresome and laborious kind of marching. Our bivouac that night was in a piece of woods near the railroad. Marched twelve miles.

Dec. 18.—During the night orders came to march to Grayville, Georgia. But that order was countermanded and we were to proceed to Chattanooga, and go into our old camps. Again taking the railroad at 9 o'clock next morning, we marched to Chattanooga, pushing through the tunnel, which is over forty rods in length and arched over most of the way with brick, being built up the sides with stone. This tunnel passes through Mission Ridge.

We arrived at Chattanooga not far from noon, but here we were doomed to wait for the passage of other troops over the pontoon bridge until late in the afternoon, and just as we were about to cross the bridge was broken by some driftwood floating down the river. While lying here a little hard tack was obtained for us. Many of us had not tasted a mouthful of food all that day, and not a few had no supper the evening previous.

At last we were ferried over in a swing ferry, which was moved by the current of the river alone. In this way two companies crossed over, and it was 9 o'clock at night when we reached our camps, having marched twelve miles.

This was the hardest march we have ever made, and we doubt its being often excelled in any respect. The rations we received on the whole march would not exceed a limited supply for ten days, and here we had been out twenty-eight days, and marching almost constantly. During the whole time we had no chance to change our clothing, and by constant exposure it had become tattered and filthy, so as to be almost unwearable. Nothing but the ground for a bed, and many times muddy with rain storms, which had wet us as well, for we were entirely unsheltered. Many were entirely barefooted, and, marching over frozen ground, their feet were lacerated and bleeding. To remedy this evil in part, blankets were cut up and bound on to the feet, a piece at a time, thus depriving the owners of the necessary use of that article at night, when the temperature of the atmosphere was almost universally at or below freezing.

Still, no word of complaint escaped these brave defenders of our liberties. Is not this valor and patriotism equal to any shown in the history of the world?

For many days we marched on the strengh we derived from eating parched corn, and even this we could obtain only by picking it out of the troughs or off the ground where the mules were feeding, or by picking it up where it was scattered along the road. Many a poor mule was obliged to share his scanty mess with a starving soldier. Some times we could get it in larger quantities out of some farmer's granary, but our officers were very strict about straggling, so our chances were very slim for "foraging." It was no more than right that they were thus strict, for by a great share of the army moving on that march, great depredations were committed, and the strong Union people were very unhappily disappointed in our army, which, instead of relieving them of their distress, plunged them deeper into misery by plundering and stealing almost the last mouthful.

It is sad to relate this of our army, but it is no less sad than true.

In our division, or at least in our brigade, there was a roll call every time we halted, and all who were absent were reported to headquarters, and they had to answer for being absent in some satisfactory manner, or suffer punishment. This, in a great degree, prevented straggling.

While our soldiers are suffering like this, some of our patriotic (?) brothers at home are unwilling to let their shoulders bear their portion of the burden. Poor, selfish patriotism.

Dec. 19.—We moved camp about one-half mile, in order to have more wood and to lay out a regular camp for the regiment. At this place we did not put up any quarters any more than to stretch our "dog tents," to protect us from the rain, for we did not expect to stay only to draw some new clothing, and then move into Georgia and take up winter quarters.

We remained here until the 26th of December, nothing of note occurring. There was some excitement about re-enlisting, and investigations were made to see if we could, but it was found that we could not until after February 6, 1864, and, as the time for paying large bounties extended only to January 5, 1864, the subject was dropped.

DEC. 26.—At half-past 7 o'clock this morning our brigade moved to take its position near Rossville, Georgia. Crossing on the pontoon bridge at Chattanooga, we moved across Missionary Ridge, and at half-past 4 o'clock P. M. halted in a piece of woods about one and a half miles from Rossville, Ga., and nearly eight miles from Chattanooga, Tennessee, having marched twelve miles. The day was rainy, cold and unpleasant, and the men had to "tote" their knapsacks containing their clothing, blankets and tents.

Arrived here, we began immediately to construct winter quarters and soon had fine log houses built, with a fireplace in each house, so that, had our rations been plenty, we should have been comfortable. But rations were very short, being in all only half rations, and, when a soldier works at chopping and carrying logs day after day, and building houses, fireplaces and the like, on half rations, I'll wager he will swear he is getting no more than quarter rations, and, let a citizen or raw recruit do the same and he will swear he is starving to death.

Our transportation had, a good share of it, been sent up to Smith's Ferry, some sixty miles from here, for forage, and, not returning as soon as was expected, our camp and garrison equipage could be brought up only slowly, three trips being made to bring it up. In the meantime our animals were entirely without anything to eat, and it was horrible to hear their howlings, and they would bite into the dry dust and leaves in sheer agony of starvation. Many of them starved to death, but, on January 4th, 1864, early in the morning, the teams which had gone to Smith's Ferry for forage had returned well loaded, and the starvation of our animals was arrested.

Shortly after this the railroad was completed from Bridgeport to Chattanooga, Tennessee, and rations and forage became plenty, and about the 20th of January we began to draw full rations, and again we saw "better times."

Jan. 4.—In the evening we had a fall of about one-fourth of an inch of snow, the first we had seen this winter. And again, on the night of the 14th, just enough fell to whiten the ground, but disappeared when the morning sun showed its rays.

About the middle of January, sunny, pleasant weather commenced, and continued, with but little interruption, for a month. A good share of the time it was so warm that we needed no fires in our tents the greater part of the day, and coats and jackets were doffed as being too warm and burdensome. Many of the days were such as we enjoy in Michigan the latter part of May or the first of June. Out-door games, such as ball, quoits, etc., were enjoyed with a relish by us almost every day.

Near the middle of February it became a little cooler, but yet pleasant and comfortable.

Jan. 13.—At dress-parade in the afternoon the following orders were read, which will show how well we conducted ourselves on the great march we had so lately completed:

HEADQUARTERS DEPARTMENT OF THE TENNESSEE,
CHATTANOOGA. December 18, 1863.

GEN. JEFF. C. DAVIS, Chattanooga:

DEAR GENERAL—In our recent short, but useful campaign, it was my good pleasure to have attached to me the corps of Gen. Howard and the division commanded by yourself. I now desire to thank you personally and officially for the handsome manner in which you and your command have borne themselves throughout.

You led in the pursuit of Bragg's army on the route designated for my command, and I admired the skill with which you handled the division at Chickamauga, and more especially in the short and sharp encounter at nightfall near Grayville.

When Gen. Grant called on us unexpectedly and without due preparation to march to Knoxville for the relief of Gen. Burnside, you and your officers devoted yourselves to the work like soldiers and patriots, marching through cold and mud without a murmur, trusting to accident for shelter and subsistence.

During the whole march, wherever I encountered your command I found all its officers at their proper place, and the men in admirable order. This is the true test, and I pronounce your division one of the best ordered in the service. I wish you all honor and success in your career, and shall deem myself most fortunate if the incidents of war bring us together again.

Be kind enough to say to Gen. Morgan, Gen. Beatty and Col. McCook, your brigade commanders, that 1 have publicly and privately commended their brigades, and that I stand prepared at all times to assist them in whatever way lies in my power.

I again thank you personally, and beg to subscribe myself

Your sincere friend,

(Signed)                   W. T. Sherman,

*Major General.*

HEADQUARTERS 2D DIVISION 14TH ARMY CORPS,  
CHATTANOOGA, Tenn., Dec. 22, 1864.

To Gens. Morgan, Beatty and Col. McCook:

To you, as brigade commanders, I have the honor to transmit the above flattering testimonial of Maj. Gen. Sherman to the efficiency and soldierly bearing of the troops, and skill of the commanders as evinced in our recent campaign in East Tennessee.

The remarks of Gen. Sherman are highly complimentary, and when we consider the high rank and great experience of this officer in conducting campaigns, and the trying circumstances under which these complimentary observations were elicited, I am sure they will not fail to be highly appreciated by us all, and from an additional incentive to future exertion and success.

Please permit me to unite with Gen. Sherman in expressing my admiration of the conduct of the troops, and to thank you, gentlemen, as brigade commanders, for your zealous co-operation during this short and eventful campaign.

Very respectfully, your ob't serv't,

(Signed)            · JEFF. C. DAVIS,

*Brigadier General Commanding Division.*

<br>

HEADQUARTERS 1ST BRIG. 2D DIV. 14TH ARMY CORPS, }
December 23d, 1863. }

The General commanding takes great pleasure in communicating the above flattering testimonial of Gens. Sherman and Davis to the good conduct of his command during the late successful campaign, and embraces the present opportunity of adding his own thanks to the commissioned and non-commissioned officers and privates of his brigade, for their prompt obedience to orders, and their soldier-like conduct during the time referred to.

Soldiers who can march over two hundred miles in winter, many of them barefooted, poorly clothed, without camp or garrison equipage, frequently on short rations, without complaint, but, on the contrary, with cheerfulness, deserve not only the thanks of officers but of the whole country.

(Signed)            JAMES D. MORGAN,

*Brigadier General Commanding Division.*

<br>

HEADQUARTERS 10TH REGIMENT MICH. VOL. INF., }
1ST BRIGADE 2D DIV. 14TH ARMY CORPS, }
December 23d, 1863. }

### GENERAL ORDERS—NO. 21.

On the morning of the 21st ultimo, at daybreak, in the midst of a severe rain storm, the 10th regiment, in accordance with orders previously received, commenced a forced march from Smith's Ferry, fifty miles above Chattanooga, to a point on the Tennessee River opposite the mouth of the South Chickamauga.

On the 24th it crossed the river on the pontoon bridge four miles above Chattanooga, and constituted a part of Gen. Sherman's reserve in the operations of our forces against the enemy on Lookout Mountain and Mission Ridge.

Being with the advance in the pursuit of Bragg's army, it had the honor of first occupying the enemy's works at Chickamauga.

Called upon to march with Gen. Sherman's army to Knoxville, to the relief of a besieged and brave garrison, all devoted. themselves to the performance of the task with cheerfulness and without a murmur. By the advance of our army the enemy were compelled to raise the siege of Knoxville, and, on the evening of the 18th, after having performed a march of three hundred miles, under the most difficult and trying circumstances, in the winter season, having slept for twenty-eight successive nights without any kind of shelter, upon the frozen earth, often suffering from hunger, trusting almost entirely to chance for subsistence, the regiment returned to its camp opposite the mouth of the South Chickamauga.

As an evidence that our services have been appreciated, the Lieutenant Colonel commanding takes great pleasure in publishing to the regiment the foregoing testimonials from Maj. Gen. Sherman and Brig. Gens. Jeff. C. Davis and James D. Morgan, and embraces this opportunity to tender his own thanks to all the commissioned, non-commissioned officers, and privates under his command, for the gallant and soldier-like manner in which they discharged their duty throughou the late campaign.

(Signed)                                C. J. DICKERSON,
                                *Lieutenant Colonel Commanding.*


JAN. 15.—We received notice that we could re-enlist as veterans if we chose, as the time for paying high bounties had been extended. So we immediately set to work to make out the necessary papers.

JAN. 19.—Received notice that we could not re-enlist until after February 6th, two years from date of muster-in. If at that date three-fourths of the regiment chose to re-enlist, they should be paid their old bounty and monthly wages up to date, clothing settled for, and an installment of sixty dollars of the veteran bounty, together with one month's pay in advance, and be furloughed in a body for thirty days, from some point in our own State. New papers or blanks were procured, and we went to work anew, dating enlistment papers and muster rolls February 6, 1864.

Jan. 23.—The regiment marched out on to the Chickamauga battle-field (all of them who chose to), and visited some of the most interesting parts of it. There were a great many relics obtained, and a great deal of curiosity satisfied in regard to it. We found marks of severe struggles, where the trees were riddled from both sides, and the earth torn by the death-dealing missiles, and in imagination could see the contending lines surging backwards and forwards as the death hail fell fatally among them and thinned the almost exhausted ranks of friend and foe. Here the dead were burried with scarce enough earth to conceal them from view, and here, in wild confusion, they lay all around us, with a few shovels full of earth thrown upon them as they fell, or perhaps with none at all, their bones bleaching on the southern plain. Bragg had kept his word not to bury any Yankees in Georgia. But since our possession of the territory details had been busy burying our brave comrades who fell in that fearful struggle.

Jan. 27.—In the evening we received an order to march the next morning, with three days rations in our haversacks and sixty rounds of ammunition.

Jan. 28.—At daylight the regiment was on the move and marched immediately to Ringgold, or rather to within one mile of the place, where we arrived at 1 o'clock in the afternoon and formed in line of battle, and halted for one hour, while a bridge was being built across a creek over which we wished to pass.

As soon as the bridge was completed we moved on, and marched through Ringgold, which was only a mass of ruins, most of the buildings having been burned by our forces in the last battle. We marched through a gap in the ridge of mountains just beyond Ringgold, and halted one and one-half miles beyond the town until dark, during which time the cavalry attached to the reconnoitering •force had some sharp skirmishing with the enemy.

At dark we marched back through Ringgold and bivouacked for the night, as we supposed, one mile in rear of the town, and we had just got our coffee and bacon nicely cooking when we were ordered to fall in. Again we marched to Ringgold and bivouacked near a bridge close to the town to guard it during the night. By the time we reached this point it was 9 o'clock in the evening, and we were very tired, having marched twenty miles, carrying blankets and three days rations with "sixty rounds."

JAN. 29.—At daylight we were on the move again, and again were marched back to one mile in rear of Ringgold and halted until our division passed, leaving us as rear guard. The object of the reconnoitre having been accomplished we marched back to our camp near Rossville, starting at 10 o'clock A. M. and reaching camp at half-past 3 o'clock in the afternoon. The day was very warm and almost sultry. We marched fifteen miles to-day and felt satisfied without its being a greater distance.

From this time until the 4th day of February we were busy and excited about getting ready to muster as veterans. Enlisting was rapid and most of the companies had the required three-fourths re-enlisted, and the papers almost entirely completed.

But we were doomed not to get off so easily. On the evening of the 3d day of February we received orders to take seven days rations and proceed to Chickamauga Station to do picket duty there. The 60th Illinois accompanied us. This was a sort of outpost, and troops doing duty there were kept out a week at a time.

FEB. 4.—Our regiment started at about 6 o'clock A. M., and marched slowly to Chickamauga Station, Tennessee, on the Chattanooga and Dalton Railroad, eight miles from our camp.

Here the duty was not very heavy, at least not so hard as we had performed, as we had to furnish the picket guard every other day, which took half the regiment, and consequently brought each man on every four, days. The weather was quite pleasant most of the time, and we were comparatively comfortable, for most of us had fixed up some sort of shelter.

But we were probably thinking of home more than we had done in a year before, because we hoped to be on our way there before we were yet mustered, and the time passed rather slowly.

The seven days passed, and, owing to a portion of our division having been sent away, and another brigade receiving pay, we were not relieved, and it was not until the tenth day made its appearance that we could leave that duty and return to camp.

FEB. 14.—The morning broke cloudy and threatening. At 11 o'clock we received orders to fall in to be relieved. In half an hour we were moving for camp. We made a rapid march and that eight miles soon wore off, and in the early part of the afternoon we reached our old camp.

When we found that our delay at Chickamauga Station could not be avoided, we sent to camp and got the "veteran rolls" and went to work to complete them. Arrived again in camp they were soon done, and the mustering officer visited us on the 16th day of February, and again we took the oath to serve for three years. Three hundred and eighty men were mustered out and mustered in, and a few others at a later period, who were not eligible because they had not served two years.

Those who mustered in and pledged themselves to do so as soon as eligible, amounted to four hundred and sixteen on that day.

This muster dated back to February 6, 1864, just two years from the date of our former muster.

If not the largest, this is certainly one of the largest veteran regiments yet mustered in the field.

We thought now to soon get started for home, but again a new cause for delay became apparent.

The Paymaster was out of funds and again the old Camp Thomson story began to get in circulation, viz: "that the Paymaster had gone to work at sawing wood by the cord to earn money to pay us."

And various rumors about our starting for home were put in circulation, and promulgated with true Mrs. Grundy energy. Our duty at this time was still picketing every other day, as a great share of our division was gone from this post.

## DISTANCES MARCHED.

| DATE. 1862. | | MILES. | | DATE. 1862. | | MILES. | |
|---|---|---|---|---|---|---|---|
| April 29 | - - | 5 — | 5 | Sept'r 6 | - - | 4 | |
| May 1 | - - | 5 | | 7 | - - | 28 | |
| 2 | - - | 3 | | 8 | - - | 18 | |
| 3 | - - | 16 | | 9 | - - | 18 | |
| 8 | - - | 10 | | 10 | - - | 20 | |
| 15 | - - | 6 | | 11 | - - | 22 | |
| 30 | - - | 9 | | 15 | - - | 2 — | 160 |
| 31 | - - | 10 — | 59 | Oct'r 7 | - - | 12 — | 12 |
| June 1 | - - | 13 | | Nov'r 5 | - - | 6 | |
| 2 | - - | 10 | | 9 | - - | 35 | |
| 3 | - - | 10 | | 10 | - - | 25 | |
| 6 | - - | 3 | | 11 | - - | 10 | |
| 11 | - - | 13 | | 13 | - - | 8 | |
| 12 | - - | 12 — | 61 | 29 | - - | 5 | |
| July 21 | - - | 18 | | 30 | - - | 21 — | 110 |
| 22 | - - | 18 | | Dec'r 1 | - - | 26 | |
| 23 | - - | 13 | | 8 | - - | 3 | |
| 24 | - - | 20 | | 10 | - - | 5 | |
| 25 | - - | 4 — | 73 | 31 | - - | 27 — | 61 |
| Sept'r 2 | - - | 12 | | 1863. | | | |
| 3 | - - | 18 | | Jan'y 1 | - - | 27 — | 27 |
| 4 | - - | 12 | | Mar. 25 | - - | 18 — | 18 |
| 5 | - - | 6 | | July 20 | - - | 17½ | |

| DATE. | | MILES. | | DATE. | | MILES. | |
|---|---|---|---|---|---|---|---|
| | 1863. | | | | 1863. | | |
| July 21 | - - | 12 1-2 — | 30 | Nov'r 21 | - - | 18 | |
| Aug. 19 | - - | 13 1-2 | | 22 | - - | 20 | |
| 20 | - - | 15 | | 23 | - - | 14 | |
| 21 | - - | 17 | | 26 | - - | 12 | |
| 22 | - - | 17 | | 27 | - - | 20 | |
| 23 | - - | 7 | | 28 | - - | 3 | |
| 26 | - - | 8 1-2 | | 29 | - - | 20 | |
| 27 | - - | 23 1-2 | | 30 | - - | 14 — | 121 |
| 28 | - - | 18 | | Dec'r 1 | - - | 10 | |
| 29 | - - | 16 — | 135½ | 2 | - - | 22 | |
| Sept'r 1 | - - | 26 | | 3 | - - | 18 | |
| 2 | - - | 10 | | 4 | - - | 12 | |
| 4 | - - | 11 | | 5 | - - | 5 | |
| 5 | - - | 20 | | 6 | - - | 15 | |
| 6 | - - | 13 | | 7 | - - | 16 | |
| 7 | - - | 14 | | 8 | - - | 20 | |
| 21 | - - | 13 — | 107 | 15 | - - | 23 | |
| Oct'r 1 | - - | 7 | | 16 | - - | 17 | |
| 2 | - - | 14 | | 17 | - - | 12 | |
| 3 | - - | 10 | | 18 | - - | 12 | |
| 18 | - - | 9 | | 26 | - - | 12 — | 194 |
| 19 | - - | 3 | | | 1864. | | |
| 20 | - - | 10 | | Jan'y 23 | - - | 11 | |
| 21 | - - | 9 | | 28 | - - | 20 | |
| 24 | - - | 16 | | 29 | - - | 15 — | 46 |
| 25 | - - | 17 | | Feb'y 4 | - - | 8 | |
| 26 | - - | 5 — | 100 | 14 | - - | 8 — | 16 |

Total distance marched when the whole regiment was together, is 1,335 miles. By computing the distances marched by detachments on detailed duty, and by the regiment while on foraging expeditions, etc., and averaging it for the whole regiment, it would amount to about three hundred miles, making 1,700 miles marched in less than twenty-two months service, ten of which were spent in garrison duty at Nashville, Tennessee, leaving only twelve months of field duty.

## BRIGADED AND COMMANDED.

Upon arriving at Hamburg, Tennessee, we were assigned to Maj. Gen. Pope's command, and brigaded with the 14th Michigan Volunteer Infantry and 10th and 16th Illinois Volunteer Infantry, and six companies of Yates' Sharpshooters.

At " Mud Camp " the 60th Illinois Volunteer Infantry was added to our brigade. These five regiments of infantry have most of the time constituted our brigade since. The 14th Michigan were detached in 1863 for a while, and occasionally on some expedition or scout some regiment or regiments have been temporarily attached.

Until the latter part of November, 1863, a battalion of sharpshooters or section of battery was also attached, but this part of the brigade has been changed several times.

We were in the 2d Brigade, 4th Division Army of the Mississippi, until the latter part of August, 1862, when our division was transferred to the Army of the Cumberland, and our brigade was made 2d of the 7th Division of the 14th Army Corps. The number of the division was changed to the 4th, December 1st, 1863, and the number of the brigade to 1st, January 20, 1863.

The 13th day of June, 1863, we were transferred to the Reserve Corps, commanded by Maj. Gen. Gordon Granger, in which our brigade was 1st of the 2d Division, and by an order dated October 9, 1863, were again transferred to the 14th Army Corps, Commanded by Maj. Gen. Thomas, the number of the division not being changed.

At the present time we belong to the same organization, viz : 1st Brigade, 2d Division 14th Army Corps.

When we first entered the field our brigade was commanded by Col. J. D. Morgan, and the division by Brig. Gen. Payne.

When we reached Tuscumbia, Alabama, Col. (now Brigaaier General) J. D. Morgan commanded the division, and, also, the post, and Col. B. F. Smith, of the 16th Illinois Volunteer Infantry, commanded our brigade. Brig. Gen.

Morgan was relieved of command of the post at Tuscumbia, Alabama, by Brig. Gen. Payne, who had been absent sick, but returned before we left that place.

When we reached Athens, on the march from Tuscumbia to Nashville, Tennessee (September 6, 1862) the division, which had been separated, met at that place, and Gen. Palmer took command of the division—Gen. Morgan remaining in command of our brigade.

The command was not again changed until after we returned to Nashville, Tennessee, from Stone River, when Gen. Morgan took command of the division, and Col. Smith of the brigade.

May 28, 1863, Gen. Morgan took command of the post of Nashville, and Col. Smith of the division, while Col. Lum was placed in command of the brigade, where he remained until June 15th. The brigade was under his command, also, from April 10th to April 25th.

June 15th Col. Smith again took command of the brigade, and Gen. Morgan of the division.

At Murfreesboro, Tennesse, and Columbia, Tennessee, Gen. Morgan had command of the post and division, and Cols. Smith and Lum being absent (Col. Smith on court-martial at Nashville, and Col. Lum on leave of absence), Col. Tillson, of the 10th Illinois, commanded the brigade.

In the early part of September, Col. Smith again took command of the brigade.

While we were at Bridgeport, Alabama, Col. Smith commanded the post, and, upon the removal of the brigade, Col. Tillson again took command and kept it until after our arrival at Anderson's Cross Roads, where Col. Smith again assumed the command.

The changes have been so frequent that correct dates could not be obtained without consulting the brigade or division records.

Nov. 4.—Gen. J. D. Morgan took command of the brigade, Gen. Jeff. C. Davis having been placed in command of the new division October 9th, by orders from department headquarters.

At the present date (February 20, 1864) Gen. Morgan is temporarily in command of the division, Gen. Jeff. C. Davis having been called away a short time since, and Col. Anderson, of the 60th Illinois Infantry, commands what remains of the brigade. The 10th and 16th Illinois Infantry, and four companies of the 14th Michigan, having gone home on furlough as veterans, and the remaining six companies of the 14th Michigan being detached, leaves only the 60th Illinois Infantry and the 10th Michigan Infantry in the brigade.

# Historical Sketch of the Officers.

## COL. CHARLES M. LUM

Is now about 33 years of age. He was born in the pleasant
town of Canandaigua, New York, and while yet very young
he removed with his parents to Detroit, Michigan. His father
was an architect and well known in the State. While quite a
boy Charles went as clerk in a dry goods establishment, where,
owing to his uniform good conduct and attention to business,
he remained for several years. He then entered a drug store,
as clerk, where he remained a short time only. This was not
his place nor calling. He had from earliest youth exhibited a
strong passion for drawing and painting, and was now sent to
Newark, New Jersey, to follow out his inclinations by studying
the profession of a painter. Here he remained three and a
half years and then removed to Troy, New York, where he
lived the same length of time. In 1852 he returned to his
home in Detroit, Michigan, being about 20 years of age. Here
he opened his studio, where he sat by his easel until the breaking out of the rebellion. It is said he wrought in his profession with great success, and did credit to himself and to his
calling. Indeed, judging from what we have seen, now and
then, of a stray artistic sketch from his pen, we would conclude
that his genius was happily set in the character of an artist.
At the breaking out of the rebellion he was Orderly Sergeant
of the Detroit Light Guard, one of the best military organiza-

tions in the whole West, and which, by the way, has more officers now in the field, which went from its ranks, than almost any other similar organization. On the 17th day of April, 1861, a meeting of the company was called to take into consideration the Proclamation of President Lincoln, calling for 75,000 men, and the offering of the services of the company for three months, the company unanimously volunteering. Col. (then "Orderly") Lum, was that night elected its Captain, and with them went immediately into the field in the 1st Regiment, (Col. O. B. Wilcox) a regiment which did its whole duty from the time of its departure from Fort Wayne, Detroit, until its return home. A regiment of which our State is, and may well be, proud—and so she may be of all her "sons of thunder."

Capt. Lum's company was assigned as Company A—the highest in the regiment, which speaks well for his conduct as an officer. When the regiment marched into Alexandria, Virginia, on the morning of May 24, 1861, the morning on which Col. Ellsworth was killed, Capt. Lum had the pleasure of leading his company first into the town.

About the middle of June he was sent with his company to take charge of the extreme outpost at Cloud's Mill, on the Fairfax road, four and a half miles from Alexandria, which he held until the whole body of troops then gathered at Alexandria, moved forward towards Manassas. On the 1st of July he was detailed on the first court-martial convened in that department. The court held its sessions in Alexandria, whither the Captain went every morning and returned every evening to his command.

About the 15th day of July the regiment moved, with many others, to Cloud's Mill, and remained there a few days, preparatory to moving to Centerville, when Company A again took its place in the line.

Col. Wilcox was in command of a brigade composed of the 1st Michigan Volunteer Infantry and Ellsworth's Fire Zouaves, and, the Lieutenant Colonel being absent on recruiting service

leaving the Major in command of the regiment, he relieved the
Captain of the command of his company and placed him in
the position of Acting Lieutenant Colonel.

On the morning of the 21st of July, at 2 o'clock, the whole
of Gen. McDowell's army commenced moving from Centerville.
After halts, delays, and reconnoissances, arrived at the battle-
field about 10 o'clock in the forenoon, when knapsacks, overcoats,
and everything not needed in an engagement, were thrown off,
and piled along the roadside.

Gen. McDowell, in person, ordered the regiments forward
into action. About three-quarters of a mile from where the
order was given, shot, shells and balls were flying thick and
fast, yet on the Captain's regiment went, in good order and
full of courage.

While crossing the field two riderless horses came dashing
towards the head of the column, and both were captured by
the boys of Company A, and one of them presented to the
Captain, the one upon which he was already mounted being old
and badly lamed by an accident. A few minutes after this the
regiment was in the midst of the fight, doing its whole duty,
nobly and well, as all Michigan regiments have done since the
commencement of the war.

Having performed the duty assigned it, and being almost
surrounded by the enemy, the Captain was ordered by the
Colonel commanding the brigade, to face the regiment about
and march it off the field. It had moved about thirty yards
when the Captain stopped to give his personal attention to
some of the wounded, and while thus engaged, about twenty of
the enemy, not more than one hundred and fifty feet from him,
made their appearance at the edge of the cedar clump, which
the regiment supposed they had "cleaned out" entirely, and
leveled their pieces directly toward him and fired, killing his
horse instantly, and knocking a pistol from the Captain's hand,
but leaving him uninjured. By the time he could pick up his
pistol, which was hurled by the shot some twelve feet from
where his horse fell, another volley was fired at him by the

same group, one shot wounding him severely in the knee. He
with great difficulty retired to a clump of low cedars, where
he bound up his knee with his handkerchief and the strap of
his canteen. Being yet able to walk, he started to go from the
field, lying down several times to shield himself from the
shower of bullets and for the purpose of resting. He passed
in this way between two opposing regiments, without further
injury. He was soon seen by Lieut. Throop, of Company A,
(now Lieutenant Colonel 1st Michigan Infantry), and private
Higgs, of Company I, who went to his assistance. He stopped at the first hospital on the field, and remained until shelled
out by the enemy. After walking about a mile further he was
placed in an ambulance, with five others—three men lying on
the bottom (the Captain in the middle). In this way he got
along very well until going down the long, gradually sloping
hill that crosses Cub Run. At this time the enemy commenced
shelling the road, thus carrying the panic to its highest pitch.
Every man in the ambulance left it, except Capt. Lum, who
managed to get to the front and sieze the lines the driver had
left. Turning the horses into the field on the right, he drove
down towards the Run. On reaching the stream he found the
stone wall on its bank partly demolished, and in attempting to
drive over it one horse fell and could not get up again, because
of being entangled in the harness. The Captain cut the
horses both loose from the ambulance, and was assisted by a
soldier to mount on an artillery horse close at hand, on which
he rode forward and reached the hospital at Centerville about
8 o'clock in the evening. Here his wound was dressed by Dr.
Frank Hamilton. He remained at Centerville until about
midnight, and then started for Alexandria, which place he
reached about 11 o'clock Monday morning, July 22d. He was
removed to Washington on Tuesday, the 23d, in the afternoon,
where he was obliged to remain two months, receiving every
care and attention which could be given to any, by Dr. Valentine Harbaugh and family. After recovering sufficiently he
returned to his home in Detroit. On account of the nature of

his wound, it was a long time in healing and recovering entirely. Capt. Lum was thus confined rather closely to his home for some time.

In the fall of 1861 he was appointed Colonel of the 10th Michigan Volunteer Infantry, with rank and commission from November 20, 1861. Previous to this time there had been a considerable excitement in camp at Flint, among the members of the regiment, as to who should be their Colonel. There were several candidates, among whom was Lieut. Beach, of the 5th Infantry, and "Col. Thomson." All had their supporters, and their "just and proper merits" were descanted upon at length by the newly fledged soldiery, in debate and harrangue. November 25th it was announced that Capt. Lum was appointed Colonel, and that he would shortly be in camp. The boys were wide awake to see and to make the acquaintance of "our Colonel." About the middle of the afternoon he reached camp. He was received with the best military honor we then knew how to bestow. All the men who were armed being drawn up in open order at the gateway leading into the camp, and faced inward. We received him with arms presented, and as he passed through the opening between the two ranks in an open carriage, with Col. Thomson, he removed his cap in token of respect. The two ranks were separately filed to left and right, and followed the vehicle to the middle of the camp ground, and were then marched to their quarters. The Col. soon won the esteem of his men. He was with his regiment constantly until its departure from the State, and has had a leave of absence but once since.

Shortly after the regiment reached Mississippi he was placed in command of a demi-brigade. This took place May 2, 1862, and he was continued on that duty until July 23d, when he again assumed command of his regiment. On the 20th of September he was detailed on court-martial, as President, in Nashville, Tennessee. In the latter part of October he again returned to his regiment, and November 28th was detailed to act on the Court-Martial Board, as President, which duty he performed until February 24, 1863. After this he was placed in command of the brigade from April 10th to April 26th, and from May 28th to June 15th. August 2d he obtained a leave of absence for a few days and started for home. On his return, when he had got as far as Nashville, he was detailed as the President of the Military Examining Board, for examining candidates for offices in colored troops. Here he remains at the present writing (Jan. 30, 1864).

As an officer, we think we are safe in saying he has not a superior among our volunteers. He is thoroughly versed in drill, from the manual of arms to the evolutions of the brigade or of the division. He handles the musket with all the ease and grace possible, and understands the many different kinds of "manuals," and the bayonet exercise perfectly. If all our commanders were as thorough, we might expect far less blunders. In the exercise of military power vested in him, he is firm, yet humane. He is willing to do all in his power for the good and comfort of his men, and is willing to grant all favors to men and officers under him, which it is possible to allow; and the better soldiers perform the duties assigned them, the greater favors they will receive at his hands when opportunity offers.

As a man, he is well liked by all who become acquainted with him. In conversation he speaks rapidly and in rather a low tone. His eye is quick and keen, and catches every scene within its scope in an instant. He generally knows everything that is going on in camp, whether night or day. He often passes through camp at night, to see that all is right. His liberality is well known by all who are acquainted with him, and, aside from subscribing largely for donations, gifts, etc., he has made several fine presents to members of his own regiment, who, he considered, had, by their application and thorough discharge of duties assigned them, earned some distinction. He is beloved and respected, both as an officer and a man, by his regiment, and receives the praise of all who are thrown into his society. May we always have a Charles M. Lum for our Colonel.

# LIEUT. COL. CHRISTOPHER J. DICKERSON.

Was born September 30, 1828, at Lewiston, Niagara county, New York. In 1838 his father, John Dickerson, emigrated with his family to Michigan, and settled in Almont, Lapeer county. That portion of Michigan was then comparatively an unbroken wilderness. School houses were few, and such as had been erected were of the rudest kind. Fortunately for Lieut. Col. Dickerson, his father had received a good education and he spent much of his spare time in imparting to his son the rudiments of an education. The first school which he attended in Michigan was taught in a log school house, in the now prosperous and beautiful village of Almont.

In 1841 his father died, and as he was the eldest child, and his mother's health being poor, the responsibility of providing for and protecting the interests of the family devolved upon him.

By hard and constant labor he performed this double duty of guardian and son, with much credit, and received the highest praise, from friends and neighbors, for his energy and perseverance.

He lost no opportunity of attending school during the winter season. The winter previous to his seventeenth year he began his labors as a school teacher, in Dryden, Lapeer county. Having met with good success, he was employed in the same school for three successive winters.

A portion of the summer of 1844 he spent in attending the branch of the Michigan University at Romeo, under the charge of Prof. Nutting. About this time the Rev. Mr. Parker, an able scholar and fine gentleman, opened an academy in Almont, as a preparatory department to the Michigan University at Ann Arbor. He was a student in this school during the years 1846-47—except winters. At the expiration of which time he was prepared to enter the University, and he went to Ann Arbor for that purpose, but was persuaded by a friend to enter upon the study of the law instead.

He commenced his legal studies with Governor O. D. Richardson, at Pontiac, in the spring of 1848. After having been in his office about six months, he was compelled, for want of means, to lay aside his studies and again teach school. In the spring of 1859 he was employed as Principal in the Hills-dale Union School, and continued in charge of the same nearly one year. In those days a Union School was a "big thing," and he did not fail to support the dignity of his calling. He was deservedly popular as a teacher, and, having many warm friends in Hillsdale, he determined on making that his home.

He again commenced the study of the law, with Judge E. H. C. Wilson, where he completed it, and was admitted to the bar in April, 1851. He immediately secured a good practice, and, as might readily be judged from his former energy and perse-verance, he acquired a reputation as a lawyer of which any young man might be proud. The records of the Courts of Hillsdale county show that for the last five years he has had one side of almost every case of any importance that has been tried in that county. He was practicing law in Hillsdale county at the breaking out of the rebellion. Though pleas-antly situated, doing a profitable business in his profession, and surrounded by the endearments of a beautiful home, he determined that he could not remain an idle spectator, and, throwing aside books and pleas, and bidding adieu to wife and children, he left his home to encounter the trials and hardships of a soldiers life. He was commissioned as Lieutenant Colonel on the 20th day of November, 1861. He soon became familiar with the infantry tactics, and remained with the regi-ment at Flint until three days before it marched, when he proceeded, under orders of April 19, 1862, to St. Louis, Missouri, to provide ordnance stores and make arrangements for transportation.

May 3, 1862, Col. Lum being assigned to the command of a demi-brigade, he took command of the regiment, remaining thus until July 26, 1862, when the regiment was broken up, and he took command of four companies of infantry and two of cavalry, at Town Creek bridge. On the 20th day of September, 1862, Col. Lum being detailed on court-martial, the command again devolved upon him, and, with the exception of some twenty days, he was in command until February 24, 1863, and once or twice since, the command has devolved upon him for a few days at a time, viz: from April 10th to April 26th, and again from May 28th to June 15th—Col. Lum being in command of the brigade both of these times. Col. Lum received leave of absence August 2d, and the command of the regiment has since been in Lieut. Col. Dickerson's hands, as Col. Lum was detailed, upon his arrival at Nashville, on his return, as President of the Military Examining Board, where he has since remained.

As a man, Lieut. Col. Dickerson is highly esteemed, being sociable and gentlemanly at all times. As an officer, he is well drilled, being thoroughly acquainted with military tactics. He is kind, but firm, and attentive to the wants of his men. He is always ready to speak to his men and hear their complaints, and, if possible, remedy their wrongs. He has always shown a deep interest in the welfare of the regiment, and has been with it constantly and under all circumstances, with the exception of a few days while we were encamped at Nashville, when he got a furlough to go home, but returned cheerfully at the expiration of the time to his duties. He is always cheerful and buoyant, thus doing much to keep up the spirits of the officers and men.

## MAJ. JAMES J. SCARRITT.

Was born in the year 1822, in Connecticut. He moved to Michigan and was pastor of a Baptist church at Jackson for some time. Afterwards, leaving his pastorate, he engaged in the book business at the same place. In the year 1858 he moved to Port Huron, Michigan, where he edited a paper known as the "Port Huron Press." In 1860 he was elected Judge of Probate. He received authority to raise five companies for the 10th Michigan Volunteer Infantry, in the fall of 1861, and immediately set to work to recruit the required number of men. He was commissioned as Major of the 10th Michigan Infantry, November 20, 1861, and was with the regiment up to November 26, 1862, when he was detailed as Provost Marshal at Gallatin, Tennessee. He remained on that duty there until the brigade commenced its campaign, when he was made Provost Marshal of the brigade, and many is the soldier who remembers Maj. Scarritt. He was faithful, and even rigid, but no more than was right in the discharge of his duties. His services did much to prevent straggling on our marches, and at any post where the brigade was stationed the secessionists and demi-rebels were made to feel the weight of military law. There was no sneaking out from under his hand. He made the best kind of a Provost Marshal, and was continued on that duty until he was taken violently sick at Anderson's Cross Roads, Tennessee. He started immediately for home, but was too ill to proceed further than Nashville, Tennessee, where Col. Lum took him to his own rooms and took the best of care of him, bestowing his time and efforts in endeavors to restore him to health, until he became sick himself, but all to no avail. The Major died on the 16th day of November, 1863, and his remains were sent to his friends in Michigan.

## STAFF OFFICERS.

Chap. John O'Brien was appointed January 15, 1862. He was an Episcopalian minister, of Pontiac, Oakland county, Michigan. He resigned March 20, 1862, on account of his advanced age, which would not admit of his being exposed to the fatigues and hardships of the duties of the field.

Adjt. Sylvester D. Cowles was a native of South Butler, Wayne county, New York, where he was born in the year 1834. He moved to Michigan in 1852, and was married in Pontiac, Oakland county, Michigan, in 1855, being in his 21st year. Before entering the service his occupation had been farming, in which his indomitable energy must have made him successful. He entered the military service in Pontiac, April 18, 1861, as 2d Lieutenant in a company which was at that time forming for the 5th regiment, but as the services of only one regiment were accepted at that time, the company was disbanded, except the officers, who entered a drill school. When the 5th regiment was called out and organized, he failed to obtain a position in it, and was detained from accompanying it by the death of his child. He then entered the 9th Michigan Infantry at Detroit, and, during its formation, rendered signal service as Drill Master. Failing here to get the position he sought, he made still another effort, and when the 10th Infantry was rendezvoused at Flint he joined them in the early part of the formation, and rendered valuable aid in drilling the officers and men. He was commissioned 1st Lieutenant, and Adjutant, November 8, 1861. By his firmness he soon won the respect both of officers and men, and by his uniform kindness and accommodating nature secured their good will. But all too soon we lost him. May 26, 1862, when the regiment was on picket near Corinth, he went out on to the lines, and, although the rebel pickets were constantly firing upon our men, he walked along the line fearlessly, at the same time cautioning others to keep out of sight. When standing in an exposed position he was struck by a ball from a rebel sharpshooter, and throwing his hand upon his breast, he exclaimed, "I have it here," and fell, expiring immediately. His remains were carried to Hamburg, Tennessee, and there interred.

QUARTERMASTER EDWIN A. SKINNER was born October 23, 1822, at Lebanon, Warren county, Ohio. At 15 years of age he moved to Butler county, Ohio, and engaged in the dry goods and pork packing business at Hamilton. In 1842 he engaged in the pork-packing business in Cincinnati, Ohio. He was married at Hamilton in 1848, and moved to Detroit, Michigan, in April, 1851, and was conductor on what was then called the Detroit and Pontiac Railroad, under command of N. P. Stewart. In 1853 he was Express Messenger for the American Express Company, on the Great Western (Canada) Railway, from Detroit to Buffalo. From 1854 to 1858 he was employed as conductor on the Michigan Central Railroad from Detroit to Chicago, and was employed as Receiver on the same

Railroad from 1858 to 1860. He was commissioned as 1st Lieutenant and Quartermaster of the 10th Michigan Infantry, November 8, 1861, in which capacity he was employed in the regiment until April 2, 1863, when he was detailed as Brigade Quartermaster, where he remained until the latter part of December. He took charge of the Quartermaster's Department of the regiment January 1, 1864, which position he still fills.

## MEDICAL STAFF.

Surgeon John C. Wilson was appointed December 7, 1861, and resigned March 2, 1862. He was, before entering the military service, a regular practicing physician in Flint. After leaving the 10th, he was appointed Surgeon of the 8th Michigan Infantry.

1st Asst. Surg. Franklin B. Galbraith was born in Sanilac county, Mich., Dec. 25th, about the year 1834. He entered the Medical Department of the Michigan University in the fall of 1858. Passed examination for the degree of M. D. in the spring of 1860, but, on account of having studied only two years, the degree was withheld for one year, as the regulations of the Department required that three years study should be given before that degree could be conferred. In the summer of 1860 he entered the College of Physicians and Surgeons in New York City, and graduated as M. D. at the close of the term. He was commissioned as Assistant Surgeon December 19, 1861. He proved himself worthy of his position—yes highly worthy—but, on account of long-continued ill health, he was obliged to resign. His resignation was accepted, to date from February 7, 1863.

## NON-COMMISSIONED STAFF.

Frederick S. Stewart, *Sergeant Major*, was born January 25, 1836, in Rome, Oneida county, New York. When about three years of age his father moved to Michigan with his family, and for two years resided in the village of Auburn, at

the expiration of which time he (Frederick) moved to Pontiac,
where he lived, with his parents seven years, when circumstances caused by the death of his uncle, called his father to the
city of Cincinnati, Ohio, in the early part of 1848. Here he
resided with his parents some four years, during which time
his father was engaged in the wholesale dry goods trade, and
in 1851 in an extensive rolling mill. In the spring of 1852 he
moved to Detroit, Michigan, where he resided two years, when
he went to Rochester, New York, and in the fall of 1854
entered into co-partnership with John R. E——, in the wholesale and retail grocery business, but in consequence of hard
work and close confinement his health was so much impaired
that he was obliged to give up his business in the summer of
1855, when, upon medical advice, he sailed for Europe, where
he remained some six months, and returned again to his native
country, with health entirely restored. He was married
December 3, 1856, in the City of New York. December 22,
1856 he took up his residence in Rochester, New York, where
he lived until the breaking out of the war. He entered the
service of the United States as Sergeant Major of the 10th
Michigan, November 27, 1861. He filled that position until
May 28, 1862, when he was promoted to Adjutant, *vice* Cowles,
killed. His health failed soon after, and he was thus kept
from duty some time. At another time he suffered some five
weeks from broken bones received by the falling of his horse,
qut is at present at his post, performing his proper duties with
willingness and energy.

GEORGE ALLEN, *Quartermaster Sergeant,* was born in Macomb county, Michigan, in 1835. When quite young he moved
with his parents to Clarkston, Oakland county. After arriving
at a suitable age he began attending school there, and most of
his time was thus spent until 1859, thereby obtaining a good
education. Between his school terms, he being possessed of a
desire to see the world, made visits to different parts of the
State. In the fall of 1859 he went to Hazelhurst, a small town
on the New Orleans and Great Northern Railroad, in Mississippi. Here he was employed as a bookkeeper until the last

Presidential election, in the firm of Stewart & Pratt. He
enlisted in Capt. Burnett's company October 20, 1861, and
served in the capacity of Sergeant until January 20, 1862,
when he was appointed Quartermaster Sergeant. His name
not appearing on Company A's records, he is not noticed there.
He was promoted to 2d Lieutenant of Company C, *vice*
Wheeler, promoted), March 31, 1863, and was detailed as
Regiment Quartermaster April 2, 1863, in which capacity he
served until January 1, 1864, when he was relieved and took
his place in his company.

JOHN S. ROUSE, *Hospital Steward*, was born April 11, 1830,
in Ontario county, Canada West, where his parents still reside.
After leaving the farm John first learned and worked at the
carpenters trade for several years in Michigan, where he moved
in 1854. He then began the study of medicine under Dr. C.
Earle, of Orion, Oakland county, Michigan, and, after reading
here some months, he passed through a course of study at the
Michigan University, and commenced the practice of medicine
at Hadley, Lapeer county, Michigan, in the spring of 1861.
February 1, 1862, he was appointed Hospital Steward of the
10th Michigan, in which capacity he has served his country
faithfully. We think we are safe in saying that not one in one
hundred of our Hospital Stewards have rendered the faithful
service that he has. He was promoted to Assistant Surgeon
of the 14th Michigan Volunteer Infantry July 1, 1863.

DAVID O. LUM, *Commissary Sargeant*, was born in Genesee
county, State of New York, in the year 1820. For several
years he was employed as a civil engineer in Detroit, Michigan,
and for more than six years he was thus employed at Eagle
River and Marquette, in the northern part of Michigan. In
Eagle River he was connected with the Cliff Copper Mine, and
at Marquette with the railroad survey, and afterwards was
appointed Surveyor of the Port. He was married in New
York City, in the year 1846. He was a brother of Col. Lum,
and entered the regiment while it was redezvoused at Flint,
and was appointed to rank as Commissary Sergeant from
February 1, 1862. While the regiment was at Camp Big

Springs he died of congestion of the brain, July 3, 1862. His remains were sent to Michigan. This was a heavy stroke for our Colonel, but he met it with fortitude, like a true soldier and brother.

EZRA B. MADISON, *Principal Musician*, Data already given in Company F.

CHARLES F. LACEY, *Principal Musician*. Data already given in Company B.

HIRAM E. BELCHER, *Color Sergeant*. Data already given in Company H.

CHARLES W. COWLES, *Chief Bugler*. Data already given in Company B.

## CHANGES IN, AND ADDITIONS TO, MEDICAL STAFF.

Shortly before leaving Michigan, F. H. Adams, M. D., of Clarkston, took the position of Surgeon, but was never regularly appointed, and, shortly after the regiment reached the field he left it.

Fred. W. Sparling was appointed Surgeon May 1, 1862. He has been detailed away from the regiment a great deal, and is at present at division headquarters, on duty.

DANIEL A. SPICER, *2d Assistant Surgeon*, (it was not until after the regiment had been in service some time that 2d Assistant Surgeons were allowed), was born in Ontario, New York, July 26, 1828. He studied medicine with Dr. Butler, of Andover, Alleghany county, New York, and graduated in the spring of 1852, at the medical department of the Western Reserve College, at Cleveland, Ohio, and commenced the practice of Medicine in Stuben county, New York, and afterwards practiced a few years in Chatauque county, New York. He moved to Michigan in 1857, and practiced medicine in Newaygo, seat of Newaygo county, Michigan, until the breaking out of the war. He entered the United States military service in September, 1861, as Hospital Steward of the 2d Michigan Cavalry. He received the appointment of 2d Assistant Surgeon of the 10th Michigan Infantry, September 23, 1862, and March 31, 1863, was promoted to 1st Assistant Surgeon, *vice* Galbraith, resigned.

DAVID M. VANDERBURGH, 2*d Assistant Surgeon*, was born in the City of New York, December 7, 1841. He pursued his medical studies at Port Huron and at Ann Arbor, Michigan. He entered the United States Army, as Medical Cadet, August 26, 1862, and served in Washington, D. C., in that capacity until March 31, 1863, and was appointed 2d Assistant Surgeon of the 10th Michigan Infantry, and received a commission as such from April 13, 1863.

## COMPANY A.

*H. S. Burnett*, of Byron, Shiawassee county, Michigan, received authority from the Governor of the State to raise a company to be assigned to some one of the regiments to be raised in the State. This authority was received October 4, 1861, and on the 28th of the same month he had the minimum of a company recruited. On the 2d of November, 1861, he received orders to take his company to the rendezvous of the 10th Michigan, at Flint. November 5th, 1861, the company arrived at the rendezvous with an aggregate of eighty-six men, being the second company in camp. Mustered into the United States service, with an aggregate of one hundred men, February 6, 1862. This company was raised principally in Southern Shiawasse and Northern Livingston counties, and known as the Byron Guards until the companies received their letters or numbers.

### COMMISSIONED OFFICERS.

*Capt. Henry S. Burnett* was born September 13, 1831, near Geneva, in the State of New York. He moved to Michigan, with his parents, in September, 1836. They settled on a farm, near Ypsilanti, Michigan, and two years after moved to Delhi, on the Huron River, between Ann Arbor and Dexter. In the spring of 1852, having previously studied civil engineering with Lieut. (now Gen.) H. P. Vancleve, he went to Ohio and engaged on the Springfield, Mt. Vernon and Pittsburgh Railroad. Stationed at Mt. Vernon. While engaged on this railroad he was married to Minerva, youngest daughter of Luther Boyden, of Webster, Michigan, in January, 1863. The work having been suspended on the Springfield, Mt. Vernon and Pittsburgh Railroad, for want of funds, in October, 1853, and the engineering corps discharged, he returned to Michigan and remained until the following spring, when he engaged on the Marietta and Cincinnati Railroad. Stationed at Athens, Ohio. He left this Railroad in January or February, 1855, and again returned to Michigan. His father (Wm. Burnett) died the ensuing fall, and he superintended the settlement of the estate. In the spring of 1858 he engaged in the hardware business in Byron, Shiawassee county, Michigan, and continued in that business until entering the military service. Immediately after the first call for three years men, he was elected 1st Sergeant of a company of home guards, organized in his village for drilling. The Captain subsequently resigned, when he was elected to fill the vacancy, and soon after received authority and recruited a company and joined the 10th. He is still with us ; has been detailed considerable of the time from his company as field officer, and on courts-martial. Promoted to Major, *vice* Maj. J. J. Scarritt, deceased, to rank from December 29, 1863. Commissioned by Gov. Blair, November 24.

*1st. Lieut. Robert F. Gulick,* was born December 9, 1831, at Pultney, Stuben county, New York. He moved to Michigan with his father (John Gulick) in May, 1843, who settled in Burns, Shiawassee county, on a farm, and died in September of the same year. After the death of his father he returned to his place of nativity in New York, and remained until 1851, when he again moved to Michigan with a good education which he had obtained by hard study at intervals between hours of labor and rest. Pursued the mercantile business at Byron, Michigan, until September, 1855, when he entered the office of S. T. Parsons, of Corunna, Michigan, to pursue a regular course of study, and was admitted to practice in all the courts of Michigan, October 28, 1856. He was married

August 12, 1858, to Miss Sarah C. Stewart, of Byron. He practiced law at Byron until October 1, 1861, when he received a commission as 1st Lieutenant of the 10th Michigan Infantry, and was assigned to Company A. February 25, 1862, was attacked with fever and congestion of the lungs, and, after a hard sickness partially recovered and was troubled with hœmorrhage of the 'lungs, and on account of continued ill health resigned May 23, 1862.

*2d. Lieut. Bradford Cook* was born in Orleans county, New York, January 29, 1835. He moved to Michigan, in 1837, in the month of June. Settled in Calhoun county, and went to Livingston county in 1839, when that part of the State was almost an unbroken wilderness. He always lived and worked on a farm until 20 years of age, when he taught school winters and followed the plow in the summer season. October 1, 1861, he received a commission as 2d Lieutenant. He was promoted to 1st. Lieutenant, *vice* Gulick, resigned, May 25, 1862. Promoted to Captain of Company E., *vice* Hartsuff, promoted.

### NON-COMMISSIONED OFFICERS.

*H. Walter Nichols, 1st Sergeant*, was born in Michigan, county of Washtenaw, in the year 1838. His father died when he was about four years of age, and as he was a mechanic, depending upon his labor for the support of his family, they were left almost without any means of support. When Walter was nine years old he got permission of his mother and went to live with a farmer, with whom he remained several years, following that occupation. He enlisted October 7, 1861, and was appointed to rank as 1st Sergeant from that date. Promoted to 2d Lieutenant May 25, 1862, *vice* Cook, promoted, and March 31, 1863, was promoted to 1st Lieutenant of Company H, *vice* S. Ter Bush, promoted.

*Maxwell G. Cooley, 2d Sergt*, was born November 30, 1830, at Turin, Lewis county, New York. Attended school most of the time until 18 years of age, when he left home and learned the painters trade, which he followed until Oct. 8, 1861, when he enlisted and was appointed to rank as 2d Sergeant from date of enlistment. Was promoted to 1st Sergeant, May 25, 1862, and March 31, 1863, promoted to 2d Lieutenant, *vice* Nichols, promoted. Resigned December 28, 1863, on account of ill health.

*Samuel S. Tower, 3d Sergeant*, was born in Oakland county, Michigan. Enlisted October 24, 1861, at Byron. Was 20 years of age, and by occupation a blacksmith. Was appointed to rank as 3d Sergeant from January 20, 1862.

*Jay J. Parkhurst, 4th Sergeant*, born in Bennington, Vermont. Enlisted October 9, 1861, at Byron. Aged 23 years. By occupation a farmer. Appointed to rank as 4th Sergeant from date of enlistment. Died June 30, 1862, at General Hospital, near Farmington, Mississippi.

*Ira Brayton, 5th Sergeant*, born in Washington county, New York. Enlisted October 23, 1861, at Howell. Aged 43 years. A farmer. Appointed to rank as 5th Sergeant from date of enlistment. Discharged February 25, 1862, at Flint, Michigan.

*Ira I. Sweet, Corporal*, born in Springfield, Vermont. Enlisted October 17, 1861, at Vernon. Aged 28 years. A farmer. Appointed to rank as Corporal from the date of enlistment. Discharged January 14, 1863, at Evansville, Indiana.

*Wm. B. Pratt, Corporal*, born in Macomb County, Michigan. Enlisted October 18, 1861, at Byron. Aged 24 years. A farmer. Appointed to rank as Corporal from date of enlistment. Promoted to Sergeant May 25, 1862.

*Perry Trim, Corporal*, born in Oswego county, New York. Enlisted October 18, 1861, at Corunna. Aged 25 years. A blacksmith. Appointed to rank as Corporal from date of enlistment. Reported as deserter and dropped from the rolls December 23, 1863, by order of O. J. Dickerson, Lieutenant Colonel.

*Duane Coffin, Corporal*, born in Livingston county, Michigan. Enlisted October 11, 1861, at Byron. Aged 18 years. A farmer. Appointed to rank as Corporal from date of enlistment. Deserted August 2, 1862, from Little Bear Creek, Alabama.

*John J. Campbell, Corporal,* nativity unknown. Enlisted (and appointed to rank as Corporal from) October 9, 1861, at Byron. Aged 32 years. A cooper.

*James Devlyn, Corporal,* born in Livingston county, Michigan. Enlisted Octtober 11, 1861, at Cohoctah. Aged 19 years. A farmer. Appointed to rank as Corporal from date of enlistment.

*Marcus P. Andrews, Corporal,* born in Rensselær county, New York. Enlisted October 19, 1861, at Vernon. Aged 23 years. A farmer. Appointed to rank as Corporal from date of enlistment. Promoted to Sergeant April 3, 1863.

*Charles Rice, Corporal,* born in Wayne county, Michigan. Enlisted October 12, 1861, at Byron. Aged 22 years. A farmer. Appointed to rank as Corporal from date of enlistment. Promoted to Sergeant September 15, 1862.

#### MUSICIANS.

*Riley W. Litchfield, Bugler,* born in Washtenaw county, Michigan. Enlisted January 16, 1862, at Corunna. Aged 23 years. A harness maker.

*Wm. W. Barker, Fifer,* born in Onondaga county, New York. Enlisted October 18, 1861, at Newberg. Aged 44 years. A physician. Died June 27, 1862, at General Hospital Cincinnati, Ohio, of chronic diarrhœa.

*Peter Degraff, Drummer,* born in Montgomery county, New York. Enlisted January 23, 1862, at Flint. Aged 58 years, A carpenter. Discharged at Evansville, Indiana. Reported as a deserter and dropped from the rolls by order of Lieut. Col. C. J. Dickerson, December 23, 1863.

#### PRIVATES.

*James Atherton,* born in Genesee county, New York. Enlisted October 10, 1861, at Argentine. Aged 18 years. A farmer. Appointed Corporal July 15, 1863.

*Robert Agnew,* born in Cayuga county, New York. Enlisted October 11, 1861, at Antrim. Aged 18 years. A farmer. Discharged January 2, 1863, at Jefferson Barracks Missouri,

*Godfrey Abell*, born in Germany. Enlisted October 23, 1861, at Webster. Aged 24 years. Laborer.

*Jonas Botsford*, born in Monroe county, New York. Enlisted October 14, 1861, at Byron. Aged 27 years. Moulder.

*Jacob C. Bently*, born in Ontario county, New York. Enlisted October 17, 1861, at Mundy. Aged 27 years. Farmer.

*Henry Baird*, born in Shiawassee county, Michigan. Enlisted October 12, 1861, at Byron. Aged 18 years. Farmer.

*Martin Brayton*, born in Stuben county, New York. Enlisted Oct. 9, 1861, at Byron. Aged 21 years. Farmer. Discharged October 11, 1862, at Cincinnati, Ohio.

*Wm. Brown*, born in Shiawassee, Michigan. Enlisted October 29, 1861, at Vernon. Aged 23 years. Farmer.

*Albert Campbell*, born in Oakland county, Mich. Enlisted October 8, 1861, at Byron. Aged 18 years. Cooper.

*Charles Chatfield*, born in Lapeer county, Mich. Enlisted February 20, 1862, at Flint. Aged 18 years. Farmer.

*David C. Calkins*, born in Oswego, New York. Enlisted Oct. 14, 1861, at Venice. Aged 27 years. Farmer. Discharged June 24, 1862, at Detroit, Michigan.

*Silas Crawford*, born in Oakland county, Mich. Enlisted March 26, 1862, at Flint. Aged 18 years. Farmer.

*Alfred Cronkhite*, born in Monroe county, N. Y. Enlisted October 19, 1861, at Venice. Aged 18 years. Farmer. Died July 5, 1862, at General Hospital near Farmington, Mississippi, of typhoid fever.

*Phillip Chamberlain*, born in Hillsdale, N. H. Enlisted October 21, 1861, at Byron. Aged 43 years. Farmer. Discharged August 5, 1862, at Columbus, Ohio.

*Lyman V. D. Cook*, born in Livingston county, Mich. Enlisted October 16, 1861, at Cohoctah. Aged 19 years. Farmer.

*Gideon Cassady*, born in Chemung county, N. Y. Enlisted Oct. 30, 1861, at Conway. Aged 44 years. Farmer. Discharged March 2, 1863, at Keokuk, Iowa.

*Lanson Condon,* born in Genesee county, Mich. Enlisted October 22, 1861, at Argentine. Aged 18 years. Farmer.

*Horace S. Calkins,* born in Oswego county, N. Y. Enlisted October 25, 1861, at Venice. Aged 18 years. Farmer. Appointed Corporal April 3, 1863.

*Henry Clark,* born in Shiawassee county, Mich. Enlisted October 21, 1861, at Newberg. Aged 18 year. Farmer. Dropped from the rolls May 3, 1863, not having been regularly enlisted.

*Edward Cowles,* born in Wayne county, N. Y. Enlisted November 5, 1861, at Pontiac. Aged 18 years. Printer.

*Benjamine Colborn,* born in Wayne county, Mich. Enlisted October 29, 1861, at Conway. Aged 35 years. Farmer.

*George Coffin,* born in Point au Pelee Island, Lake Erie. Enlisted December 10, 1861, at Byron. Aged 22 years. Farmer. Discharged August 25, 1862, at St. Louis, Missouri.

*John Damon,* born in Saginaw, Mich. Enlisted December 4, 1861, at Gaines. Aged 36 years. Farmer. Discharged September 20, 1862, at Evansville, Indiana.

*Charles Darby,* born in Jefferson, N. Y. Enlisted October 16, 1861, at Gaines. Aged 20 years. Farmer.

*Shelden Dickson,* born in Auburn, Ohio. Enlisted October 9, 1861, at Byron. Aged 19 years. Farmer. Died July 22, 1862, at General Hospital, near Farmington, Mississippi, of typhoid fever.

*Andrew Effrets,* born in Prussia. Enlisted October 18, 1861, at Argentine. Aged 26 years. Farmer.

*Arthur Ellis,* born in Oakland county, Mich. Enlisted October 9, 1861, at Cohoctah. Aged 25 years. Blacksmith. Appointed Corporal May 25, 1862. Deserted August 2, 1862, from Little Bear Creek, Alabama.

*Israel Ellsworth,* born in Leeds county, C. W. Enlisted October 22, 1861, at Cahoctah. Aged 22 years. Farmer. Discharged March 10, 1862, at Flint, Mich.

*Albert Ervy,* born in N. J. Enlisted November 13, 1861, at Argentine. Aged 21 years. Shoemaker.

*Judson Ervy*, born in Sussex, Penn. Enlisted February 18, 1862, at Agentine. Aged 18 years. Shoemaker.

*Edward F. Fuller*, born in Macomb county, Mich. Enlisted October 29, at Antrim. Aged 18 years. Farmer.

*Wm. B. Forbes*, born in Niagara county, N. Y. Enlisted October 14, 1861, at Argentine. Aged 22 years. Farmer.

*Wm. B. Fuller*, born in Oakland county, Mich. Enlisted November 18, 1861, at Conway. Aged 18 years. Farmer. Died July 11, 1862, at General Hospital, near Farmington, Mississippi.

*Rufus Griswold*, born in Livingston county, Mich. Enlisted November 12, 1861, at Flint. Aged 19 years. Farmer.

*John H. Gilbert*, born in Canada. Enlisted November 25, 1861, at Flint. Aget 20 years. Farmer. Discharged January 7, 1863, at Detroit, Michigan.

*Wm. Gove*, born in Cayuga, N. Y. Enlisted October 28, 1861, at Byron. Aged 18 years. Farmer.

*Luman Harris*, born in Lapeer, Mich. Enlisted October 8, 1861, at Byron. Aged 21 years. Farmer.

*Geo. Harris*, nativity unknown. Enlisted October 31, 1861, at Byron. Aged 44 years. Farmer. Reported as a deserter and dropped from the rolls by order of Lieut. Col. O. J. Dickerson, December 28, 1863.

*Elbert Hawley*, born in Monroe county, N. Y. Enlisted October 18, 1861, at Deerfield. Aged 30 years. Farmer. Died January —, 1863, at his home.

*Edwin A. Hart*, born in Bradford county, Penn. Enlisted October 21, 1861, at Howell. Aged 19 years. Farmer. Discharged September 20, 1862, at Evansville, Indiana.

*Edmond Hart*, born in Tioga, N. Y. Enlisted October 21, 1861, at Howell. Aged 38 years. Mechanic. Discharged July 2, 1863.

*Wm. Hall*, born in Wyoming, N. Y. Enlisted October 19, 1861, at Cohoctah. Aged 20 years. Farmer.

*Sherwood Hart*, born in Bradford, Penn. Enlisted October 26, 1861, at Howell. Aged 18 years. Farmer. Died November 17, 1862, at Hospital No. 12, Nashville, Tennessee.

*J. Deloss Jewell,* born in Stuben county, N. Y. Enlisted November 4, 1861, at Byron. Aged 24 years. Joiner. Appointed Sergeant February 25, 1862. Promoted to 1st Serg't April 3, 1863.

*Henry H. Keys,* born in Orange, Vt. Enlisted October 19, at Byron. Aged 44 years. Farmer. Discharged July 9, 1862, at Camp Big Springs, Mississippi.

*Daniel B. Lacy,* born in Portage, Ohio. Enlisted February 25, 1862, at Mundy. Aged 21 years. Farmer.

*Henry Miller,* born in Ontario, N. Y. Enlisted December 9, 1861, at Burns. Aged 32 years. Farmer.

*Blake R. Miner,* born in Monroe, N. Y. Enlisted October 22, 1861, at Byron. Aged 26 years. Farmer. Appointed Corporal May 25, 1862.

*Orlando Mills,* born in Shiawassee, Mich. Enlisted October 15, 1861, at Byron. Aged 18 years. Farmer.

*Hugh McKeever,* born in Ireland. Enilsted October 27, 1861, at Howell. Aged 40 years. Laborer. Discharged July 21, 1862, at Detroit, Michigan.

*Thurlow L. Millard,* nativity unknown. Enlisted November 16, 1861, at Byron. Aged 30 years. Minister of the Gospel. Died May 17, 1862, of nostolgia, on board of steamer Empress. Buried at St. Louis, Missouri.

*Wm. J. Moseley,* born in Saginaw county, Mich. Enlisted October 28, 1861, at Byron. Aged 23 years. Printer. Discharged October 4, 1862, at Keokuk, Iowa.

*George Mills,* born in Oakland county, Mich. Enlisted November 4, 1861, at Byron. Aged 22 years. Farmer. Appointed Corporal September 15, 1862.

*Henry Marsh,* born in Washtenaw, Mich. Enlisted November 16, 1861, at Flint. Aged 19 years. Farmer.

*Ethan Marsh,* born in Oakland county, Mich. Enlisted March 7, 1862, at Flint. Aged 18 years. Farmer. Discharged March 10, 1862, at Flint.

*Albert Martin,* born in Washtenaw county, Mich. Enlisted December 2, 1861, at Flint. Aged 18 years. Farmer. Discharged August 5, 1862, at Columbus, Ohio.

*Melton J. Moore*, born in Hunt, Tenn. Joined the Texan Rangers of the rebel army June 10, 1861. Was at the battles of Springfield, Lexington, Shiloh, and Pea Ridge, and, at the time of the evacuation of Corinth, deserted from the Rangers and came to our lines. Enlisted August 26, 1862, at Tuscumbia, Alabama. Aged 29 years. Farmer.

*Geo. Miner*, born in Battle Creek, Mich. Enlisted December 17, 1861, at Flint. Aged 18 years. Farmer. Discharged September 29, 1862, at St. Louis, Missouri.

*Levi Norris*, born in Livingston county, Mich. Enlisted October 16, 1861, at Argentine. Aged 19 years. Farmer. Reported as a deserter and dropped from the rolls December 28, 1863, by order of Lieut. Col. Dickerson.

*Allen Morris*, born in Stuben county, N. Y. Enlisted October 16, 1861, Argentine. Aged 25 years. Farmer. Died March 9, 1862, in Hospital at Flint, Michigan.

*Alexander O'Rouke*, born in Whitboro, Oneida county, N. Y. Enlisted October 16, 1861, at Byrton. Aged 40 years. Farmer.

*Geo. Parker*, born in Livingston, Mich. Enlisted October 10, 1861, at Byron. Aged 18 years. Farmer.

*Munroe Putnam*, born in Livingston, N. Y. Enlisted October 14, 1861, at Argentine. Aged 20 years. Farmer.

*David Palmer*, born in Ontario, N. Y. Enlisted October 12, 1861, at Cohoctah. Aged 28 years. Farmer. Discharged July 22, 1862, at Columbus, Ohio.

*Christopher Palmer*, born in Livingston, Mich. Enlisted October 16, 1861, at Cohoctah. Aged 21 years. Farmer.

*John Peckins*, born in Washtenaw, Mich. Enlisted October 11, at Cohoctah. Aged 19 years. Carpenter. Died July 29, 1862, at Military Hospital, Cincinnati, Ohio, of chronic diarrhœa.

*Thomas J. Pettis*, born in Shiawassee, Mich. Enlisted October 26, 1861, at Byron. Aged 19 years. Farmer.

*Phillip Richardson*, born in Onondaga, N. Y. Enlisted November 28, 1861, at Byron. Aged 18 years. Farmer.

Died March 13, 1863, at Regiment Hospital, Nashville, Tennessee.

*Miles Rood*, born in Genesee county, Mich. Enlisted March 8, 1862, at Flint. Aged 19 years. Farmer. Discharged March 23, 1863, at Nashville, Tennessee.

*Abram Rigle*, born in Erie, N. Y. Enlisted October 14, 1861, at Byron. Aged 23 years. Farmer.

*Israel D. Russel*, born in Caledonia, Vt. Enlisted October 14, 1861, at Corunna. Aged 43 years. Carpenter.

*Auren Roys*, born in Wayne, N. Y. Enlisted October 18, 1861, at Newberg. Aged 25 years. Carriage maker. Appointed Corporal April 3, 1863.

*Charles Ryno*, born in Genesee county, Mich. Enlisted October 17, 1861, at Gaines. Aged 21 years. Farmer.

*Charles Robinger*, born in Baden, Germany. Enlisted April 20, 1862, at Flint. Aged 25 years. Laborer. Appointed Corporal September 15, 1862.

*Geo. Stroud*, born in Livingston county, Mich. Enlisted October 21, 1861, at Cohoctah. Aged 18 years. Farmer.

*Edwin R. Scully*, born in Wayne, Mich. Enlisted October 12, 1861, at Burns. Aged 26 years. Farmer.

*Allen Stevens*, born in Genesee, Mich. Enlisted October 21, 1861, at Newberg. Aged 18 years. Laborer. Discharged July 17, 1862, at Benton Barracks, Missouri.

*Lemuel J. Smedley*, born in Shiawassee, Mich. Enlisted October 11, 1861, at Vernon. Aged 23 years. Farmer. Appointed Corporal September 15, 1862.

*Charles F. Stewart*, born in Washtenaw, Mich. Enlisted December 16, 1861, at Corunna. Aged 19 years. Farmer. Discharged December 22, 1862, at Evansville, Indiana.

*Wm. J. Tower*, born in Oakland, Mich. Enlisted October 19, 1861, at Burns. Aged 18 years. Farmer.

*Geo. Tubbs*, born in Washtenaw, Mich. Enlisted October 8, 1861, at Webster. Aged 25 years. Farmer.

*Geo. W. Vincent*, born in Herkimer, N. Y. Enlisted February 18, 1862, at Flint. Aged 45 years. Blacksmith

Reported as a deserter and dropped from the rolls December 23, 1863, by order of Lieut. Col. C. J. Dickerson.

*Judd Vincent*, born in Shiawassee, Mich. Enlisted February 14, 1862, at Flint. Aged 20 years. Farmer.

*Charles Wrigglesworth*, born in Lancashire, England. Enlisted October 16, 1861, at Argentine. Aged 18 years. Farmer. Died July 2, 1862, at Military Hospital, West End, Cincinnati, Ohio, of typhoid fever.

*Marion Wittam*, born in Genesee, Mich. Enlisted October 17, 1861, at Mundy. Aged 18 years. Farmer. Discharged March 17, 1862, at St. Louis, Missouri.

*John Walworth*, born in Shiawasse county, Mich. Enlisted October 12, 1861, at Byron. Aged 23 years. Farmer.

*Edgar D. Welch*, born in Shiawassee, Mich. Enlisted October 17, 1861, at Burns. Aged 18 years. Farmer.

*Peter Wooliver*, born in Stuben, N. Y. Enlisted January 18, 1862, at Flint. Aged 21 years. Farmer.

*Andrew Williams*, born in Jerusalem, N. Y. Enlisted October 18, 1861, at Cohoctah. Aged 19 years. Farmer.

## COMPANY B.

The authority to raise this company was given to Charles H. Richman, of Saginaw, Michigan, September 6, 1861. He immediately began recruiting, and, although the country there, as elsewhere, was filled with officers recruiting for the Mechanics and Engineers, the Lancers, two regiments of cavalry and some for infantry, he entered camp at Fort Wayne, Detroit, September 20, 1861, with forty men. Because Capt. Richman would not consolidate, he did not enter the 9th Infantry, then forming at that place. After the 9th had left the camp he was ordered to take his company to Flint, and take command of the camp for the formation of the 10th Infantry. He moved from Detroit with 99 aggregate, November 1, 1861, and mustered February 6, 1862, a maximum company. This company was at first known as the Saginaw Rangers.

.Capt. *Charles H. Richman* was born September 28, 1831, at Canandaigua, Ontario county, New York. A company, known as the Mackey, Oakley and Jennison Company, of which his father was a member, having purchased a tract of land in Saginaw, Michigan, they emigrated there in 1837. This company, consisting of fifteen families, chartered the steamer " Gov. Marcy " at Buffalo, and, after a journey of two weeks and three days, arrived at their. destination—the site of the present City of Saginaw, then marked only by two small trading posts, one blacksmith shop, and two dwelling houses, and surrounded by a camp of 1,500 Chippeway Indians.' The city lots were immediately laid out, and improvements begun and carried on with great rapidity. From ten to fourteen years of age Capt. Richman was employed in his father's store, where an immense trade was carried on with the Indians, in furs, etc. He then returned to Canandaigua, New York, and attended school for two years, when he went again to Michigan, and pursued his studies for two years more in the Michigan University, at Ann Arbor. At the time of leaving here he was a member of the Junior Class. He then acted as a traveling agent for his father's trading house until nineteen years of age, at which time he entered into the employ of Gray & Lewis, at Detroit, Michigan, as chief in their extensive warehouse at the foot of Woodward avenue. He remained here two years, and then was employed as principal in the general trading house of W. L. P. Little & Co., at Saginaw. In 1853 he engaged in the lumbering business, then so largely carried on at Saginaw. In 1856 his father died, leaving a large estate for him to settle. This estate, cleared of incumbrance, was worth about $58,000, and fell to Capt. Richman and his mother and sister. In the spring of 1861 he received a strong recommendation from prominent men of Michigan for a foreign appointment. .This recommend found favor and he was appointed Consul to Cadiz, Spain, June 11, 1861. Owing to some official negligence in filing his Consular bond in proper time, he was thrown out of the appointment. He then entered the military service and received commission as Captain from October 1, 1861. · Owing to ill health he has been obliged to be absent considerable, but is at present with his regiment. June 12, 1862, he was appointed Brigade Inspector, in which capacity he is still acting.

1st *Lieut. Harvey Lyon* was born in Schenectady, New York, in 1823. He moved to Cleveland, Ohio, in 1843, and in the fall of 1846 enlisted in Capt. John S. Perry's Company 15th U. S. Regulars, as a private, under what was at that time known as the "new ten regiment bill," and was with the regiment during its glorious campaign in Mexico. At the storming of Chapultepec he received wounds, on account of which he was discharged in April, 1848. He had been appointed Ser-geant during his service. He was married in Cleveland, Ohio, in 1860. Previous to entering the 10th Michigan he was a carriage maker, and up to September 1, 1861, he received a pension, as his wounds received at Chapultepec had rendered him a cripple for five years. He received commission as 1st Lieutenant in the 10th Michigan Infantry from October 1, 1861. He was promoted June 28, 1862, to Captain of Com-pany F, *vice* Beach, resigned. Capt. Lyon resigned October 31, 1862.

2d *Lieut. Geo. Turner* was born in Genesee county, New York, January 29, 1835. He was married March 1, 1856, at the age of twenty-one years. From fifteen to twenty-one years of age he was in the service of the United States, in the north-west, upon government surveys, after which he made explora-tions in the north-west, for individuals, and at the time of entering the military service was County Surveyor of Midland County, Register of Deeds for said county, Notary Public, and State Swamp Land Road Commissioner, under the appointment from the Governor. In 1859 he passed examination before the Board appointed by the Surveyor General, under the direc-tion of the President of the United States, and was ordered upon the service as 1st Assistant. Upon entering the military service he received commission as 2d Lieutenant from October

1, 1861. June 23, 1862, he was promoted to 1st Lieutenant, *vice* Lyon, promoted. He was detailed as Officer in the Pioneer Corps, November 25, 1862, and reported to Capt. James St. C. Morton. In the organization was appointed Ajdutant 1st Battalion, and served as such during the terrible battle of Stone River. He then received the apppointment—from then Brig. Gen. James St. C. Morton—of Chief of Topographical Engineers of said battalion, and built, under direction of Brig. Gen. Morton, the fortifications at Murfreesboro.

### NON-COMMISSIONED OFFICERS.
#### *Sergeants.*

1st. *Almon D. Ellis* was born in Putnam county, State of New York, in 1835. Previous to entering the military service he was employed as a mechanic. He enlisted September 6, 1861, at Saginaw, Michigan, and was appointed to rank as 1st Sergeant from date of enlistment. June 23, 1862, he was promoted to 2d Lieutenant, *vice* Geo. Turner, promoted.

2d. *Wm. B. Walker,* born in Grafton county, New Hampshire. Enlisted September 6, 1862, at Saginaw. Aged 33 years. Mechanic. Appointed to rank as Sergeant from date of enlistment. Promoted to 1st Sergeant July 1, 1862.

3d. *Isaiah Windover,* born in Lenox county, Canada. Enlisted September 16, 1861, at Midland. Aged 34 years. Mechanic. Appointed to rank as Sergeant from date of enlistment. Discharged February 17, 1863, at Nashville, Tennessee.

4th. *Miron C. Woodward,* born in Jefferson county, N. Y. Enlisted September 17, 1861, at Saginaw. Aged 30 years. Mechanic. Appointed to rank as Sergeant from date of enlistment.

5th. *Wm. Sickles,* nativity unknown. Enlisted October 26, 1861, at Holly. Aged 21 years. Hotel keeper. Appointed to rank as Sergeant from date of enlistment. Discharged at Flint, Michigan, date unknown.

*Corporals.*

1st. *Wm. A. Stewart*, born in Wayne county, Michigan. Enlisted September 25, 1861, at Saginaw. Aged 20 years. Mechanic. Appointed to rank as Corporal from the date of enlistment. Promoted to Sergeant April 3, 1863.

2d. *Thomas Horner*, born in Lapeer county, Mich. Enlisted September 18, 1861, at Saginaw. Aged 23 years. Farmer. Appointed to rank as Corporal from date of enlistment. Promoted to Sergeant July 1, 1862.

3d. *Theodore V. Kelsey*, born in Jefferson county, N. Y. Enlisted October 3, 1861, at Saginaw. Aged 29 years. Laborer. Appointed to rank as Corporal from date of enlistment. Promoted to Sergeant July 1, 1862.

4th. *Samuel B. Andrews*, born in Nova Scotia. Enlisted October 18, 1861, at Saginaw. Aged 25 years. Sailor. Appointed to rank as Corporal from date of enlistment.

5th. *Leroy Horner*, born in Lapeer county, Mich. Enlisted September 18, 1861, at Saginaw. Aged 21 years. Farmer. Appointed to rank as Corporal from date of enlistment. Discharged August 19, 1862, at Detroit, Michigan.

6th *Wm. A. Copeland*, born in Cumberland, Penn., in 1831. His parents had come from Ireland and settled there some years prior to that date. His father died when he was five years old. Shortly after, the family moved to Seneca county, New York, where he lived two years, and in the year 1848, they moved to Oakland county, Michigan. When William was 9 years of age he was adopted by a wealthy farmer of Plymouth, Wayne county, Michigan. Here he lived until 18 years of of age. When he was 14 years old his mother died. He says " this was my first great sorrow." Leaving his foster parents much against their will and arguments, in the year 1859 he rambled through Northern Ohio, Indiana, Illinois, Wisconsin, Minnesota and Iowa. In November he was taken sick at Galena, Illinois, and on recovering he went into employment on the steamer Ben Franklin, where he remained until close of navigation. After spending the winter at St. Louis, Missouri, he engaged in the fur business in the country of the Crow and Blackfoot Indians. Returning again to St. Louis he visited the country of the Lower Mississippi, and in the spring of 1852 returned to Michigan and engaged in farming. In 1854 he went into the wild forests and began clearing a farm, keeping "bachelors" for one year. In the winter of 1855 he married Miss Helen Yerkes, of Wayne county, Michigan, and they went on to the " new farm," to " begin living ;" the war breaking out he enlisted October 16, 1861, at Midland. He was appointed to rank as a Corporal from date of enlistment. Promoted to 5th Sergeant February 26, 1862. Promoted to 3d Sergeant July 1, 1862. Promoted to 2d Lieutenant March 31, 1863, *vice* Ellis, resigned.

7th. *Isaac Hanson,* born in Canada. Enlisted September 18, 1861, at Saginaw. Aged 26 years. Tradesman. Appointed to rank as Corporal from date of enlistment.

8th. *John Mason,* born in Equath, N. H. Enlisted September 25, 1861, at Saginaw. Aged 21 years. Laborer. Appointed to rank as Corporal from date of enlistment.

### MUSICIANS.

*Wm. Brown, Drummer,* born in New York. Enlisted October 16, 1861, at Saginaw. Aged 18 years. Lumberman.

*O. B. Rogers, Fifer,* born in Wyoming, N. Y. Enlisted October 24, 1861, at Flint. Aged 40 years. Farmer. Discharged April 2, 1862, at Flint, Michigan.

*Charles Lacy, Drummer,* born in Oakland county, Mich. Enlisted September 16, 1861, at Saginaw. Aged 18 years. Jeweler. Appointed Principal Musician October 13, 1862.

*George R. Collier, Drummer,* born in N. Y. Enlisted October 16, 1861, at Midland. Age unknown. Moulder. Discharged April 21, 1862, at Flint.

### PRIVATES.

*James H. Arnold,* born in Lycoming county, Pa. Enlisted September 16, 1861, at Midland. Aged 20 years. Farmer.

*Alexander H. Allen*, born in Conn. Enlisted October 28, 1861, at Holly. Aged 24 years. Laborer. Appointed Corporal March 3, 1862.

*Luther Alexander*, born in Genesee county, Mich. Enlisted December 8, 1861, at Flint. Aged 25 years. Laborer. Reported as a deserter December 23, 1863.

*Robert Allen, Sen.*, born in Washington county, N. Y. Enlisted November 8, 1861, at Midland. Aged 42 years. Farmer. Discharged January 6, 1863, at Evansville, Indiana.

*Francis H. Andrews*, born in Livingston county, Mich. Enlisted December 20, 1861, at Danby. Aged 19 years. Farmer. Died January 17, 1864, at Chattanooga, Tennessee.

*Robert Allen, Jr.*, born in Warruby, N. Y. Enlisted March 25, 1862, at Flint. Aged 18 years. Farmer. Discharged September 16, 1862, at Evansville, Indiana.

*Ezekiel Bourbrina*, born in Monroe county, Mich. Enlisted April 9, 1862, at Flint. Aged 18 years. Laborer.

*Theodore B. Bacon*, born in Clayton, N. Y. Enlisted September 18, 1861, at Midland. Aged 23 years. Mechanic.

*Francis Bayno*, born in Canada. Enlisted September 26, 1861, at Midland. Aged 25 years. Farmer.

*Hiram Braley*, born in Saginaw county, Mich. Enlisted September 26, 1861, at Saginaw. Aged 20 years. Farmer. Appointed Corporal April 3, 1863.

*Geo. Brown*, born in Wayne county, N. Y. Enlisted September 26, 1861, at ——, Isabella county. Aged 18 years. Farmer.

*Abram Brock*, born in Midland county, Mich. Enlisted September 26, 1861, at Saginaw. Aged 22 years. Farmer. Died October 26, 1862, at Elizabethtown, Kentucky, of inflammation of lungs.

*Deloss W. Benjamine*, born in Onondaga county, N. Y. Enlisted October 4, 1861, at Saginaw. Aged 24 years. Teamster.

*Robert Byron*, born in Scotland. Enlisted October 19, 1861, at Saginaw. Aged 18 years. Laborer.

*Lee Baker,* born in Monroe county, N. Y. Enlisted October 25, 1861, at Detroit. Aged 25 years. Mechanic.

*Benjamin Buck,* born in C. W. Enlisted October 26, 1861, at Detroit. Aged 24 years. Teamster.

*Charles Bullock,* nativity unknown. Enlisted October 3, 1861, at Saginaw. Aged about 22 years. Laborer. Deserted October 24, 1861, at Flint.

*Stephen Beers,* born in Cayuga county, N. Y. Enlisted October 29, 1861, at Detroit. Aged 73 years. Laborer.

*Charles W. Cowles,* born in Hunterdon county, N. J. Enlisted January 9, 1862, at Flint. Aged 20 years. Farmer. Appointed Chief Bugler April 1, 1862. Transferred to Brigade Band September 1, 1862.

*Eugene Cole,* born in Delhi, Mich. Enlisted February 18, 1862, at Midland. Aged 19 years. Farmer.

*Abraham Conkwright,* born in Livingston county, N. Y. Enlisted September 12, 1861, at Saginaw. Aged 25 years. Farmer.

*Wm. Conkwright,* born in N. Y. Enlisted September 26, 1861, at Midland. Age unknown. Farmer. Died January 6, 1862, at Flint, Michigan.

*Wm. Chatfield,* born in Sanilac county, Mich. Enlisted September 22, 1861, at ——, Isabella county. Aged 22 years. Laborer.

*S. S. E. Cartwright,* born in Schenectady, N. Y. Enlisted October 3, 1861, at Saginaw. Aged 42 years. Laborer. Transferred to Company E, April 2, 1862.

*Edwin A. Cross,* born in Genesee county, N. Y. Enlisted October 16, 1861, at Midland. Aged 26 years. Farmer. Discharged July 11, 1862, at Detroit, Michigan.

*A. W. Crownover,* nativity unknown. Enlisted October 16, 1861, at Midland. Aged 38 years. Farmer. Discharged December 26, 1861, at Flint, Michigan.

*Franklin M. Cummings,* born in Wayne county, N. Y. Enlisted October 28, 1861, at Holly. Aged 18 years. Cooper.

*W. W. Cairns,* born in St. Johns, New Brunswick. Enlisted October 28, 1862, at Detroit. Aged 37 years. Farmer. Reported as a deserter and dropped December 31, 1863.

*Jefferson W. Crydamon,* born in Mich. Enlisted October 26, 1851, at Roxand. Aged 22 years. Farmer.

*Nathan Croff,* born in Eaton county, Mich. Enlisted November 15, 1861, at Rockland. Aged 19 years. Farmer.

*Robert Down,* born in Gloustershire, England. Enlisted January 27, 1862, at Flint. Aged 34 years. Mechanic.

*Wm. Dennis,* born in Norfolk, Canada. Enlisted October 19, 1861, at Saginaw. Aged 23 years. Laborer. Appointed Corporal July 1, 1862.

*Charles Duffany,* born in Quebec county, Canada. Enlisted October 23, 1861, at Bay City. Aged 26 years. Mechanic.

*Geo. Eldridge,* born in Mich. Enlisted October 18, 1861, at Saginaw. Aged 18 years. Farmer. Deserted from Flint, Michigan, December 8, 1861. Returned to duty June, 1862. Deserted December 25, 1862, from Hospital No. 5, Nashville, Tennessee.

*Benjamin Frost,* born in Washington county, Maine. Enlisted October 21, 1861, at Saginaw. Aged 42 years. Laborer. Discharged September 25, 1862, at Nashville, Tennessee.

*Horatio Gary,* born in Saginaw county, Mich. Enlisted September 10, 1861, at Saginaw. Aged 23 years. Farmer. Died July, 1862, at Jefferson Barracks, Missouri, of fever.

*James Gruit,* born in Bay county, Mich. Enlisted September 26, 1861, at Gratiot. Aged 19 years. Farmer.

*Robert J. Gibbs,* born in Chittenden county, Vt. Enlisted January 9, 1862, at Flint. Aged 24 years. Laborer. Died November 10, 1861, at Jackson, Tennessee, of typhoid fever.

*Wm. Greenwood,* born in Courtland county, N. Y. Enlisted Dec. 20, 1861, at Rockland. Aged 44 years. Farmer. Died June —, 1862, at Henderson, Kentucky, of fever.

*Scott S. Greenman,* nativity unknown. Enlisted October 31, 1861, at Detroit. Aged 21 years. Lumberman.

*Robert B. Hough, Sen,* born in Home District, Canada. Enlisted October 18, 1861, at Saginaw. Aged 44 years·

Mechanic. Discharged November 28, 1862, at St. Louis, Missouri.

*Lionel Harris*, born in Fairfield, Ohio. Enlisted November 4, 1861, at Flint. Aged 19 years. Farmer. Discharged May 20, 1863, at Nashville, Tennessee.

*Cyrus Hall*, born in Stuben county. N. Y. Enlisted October 22, 1861, at Roxand Aged 18 years. Farmer.

*John B. Herriman*, born in N. Y. Enlisted October 28, 1861, at Holly. Aged 22 years. Farmer. Appointed Corporal July 1, 1862.

*Elijah Hough*, born in Saginaw county, Mich. Enlisted November 8, 1861, at Saginaw. Aged 19 years. Laborer.

*Robert B. Hough*, born in Saginaw county, Mich. Enlisted January 8, 1862, at Saginaw. Aged 10 years. Laborer.

*Thomas Jarvis*, nativity unknown. Enlisted October 19, 1861, at Detroit. Age unknown. Laborer.

*Lewis Kelsey*, born in Lapeer county, Mich. Enlisted January 9, 1862, at Flint. Aged 20 years. Farmer.

*Henry Lavier*, nativity unknown. Enlisted September 27, 1861, at Saginaw. Aged 22 years. Laborer.

*Geo. Lixey*, born in Wayne county, Mich. Enlisted September 23, 1861, at —, Saginaw county. Aged 22 years. Laborer. Discharged April 21, 1862, at Flint.

*Baptist Laducia*, born in Lantamond, L. C. Enlisted September 27, 1861, at Saginaw. Aged 23 years. Laborer.

*Reuben Lawhead*, born in Fayette county, Pen. Enlisted October 30, at Roxand. Aged 41 years. Died April 28, 1863, at Nashville, Tennessee.

*Amos Miner*, born in Conn. Enlisted September 16, 1861, at Midland. Aged 43 years. Mechanic.

*Geo. H. Miner*, born in Vt. Enlisted September 16, 1861, at Midland. Aged 18 years. Laborer.

*Wm. Miner*, born in Bridgeport, Mich. Enlisted September 6, 1861, at Saginaw. Aged 18 years. Fisherman. Died November 28, 1861, at Flint.

*John Mason*, born in Acworth, N. H. Enlisted September

25, 1861, at Saginaw. Aged 21 years. Laborer. Died July 31, 1862, at Farmington, Mississippi, of fever.

*Newton Merrill,* born in Broome county, N. Y. Enlisted September 26, 1861, at —, Isabella county. Aged 21 years. Farmer. Died May 24, 1862, at Henderson, Kentucky, of fever.

*Alanson Marcy,* born in Cayuga, N. Y. Enlisted October 16, 1861, at Midland. Aged 40 years. Mechanic. Reported as a deserter and dropped from the rolls December 31, 1863.

*Stephen Munger,* born in Commerce, N. Y. Enlisted October 18, 1861, at Saginaw. Aged 20 years. Farmer.

*Neal McMillin,* born in Scotland. Enlisted October 21, 1861, at Bay City. Aged 37 years. Farmer.

*Philander H. Myers,* born in Susquehanah county, Penn. Enlisted November 4, 1861, at Midland. Aged 25 years. Laborer.

*Orin B. McNelt,* nativity unknown. Enlisted March 6, 1862, at Flint. Aged 38 years. Mechanic. Discharged August 17, 1862, place unknown.

*John McGroury,* born in Ireland. Enlisted November 4, 1861, at Saginaw. Aged 30 years. Farmer.

*Thomas McCarty,* born in Armagh county, Ireland. Enlisted December 7, 1861, at Midland. Aged 44 years. Farmer.

*Wm. Newton,* born in N. Y. Enlisted October 3, 1861, at Saginaw. Aged 19 years. Laborer.

*Wm. Patterson,* born in Saginaw county, Mich. Enlisted September 18, 1861, at Midland. Aged 21 years. Laborer.

*Erastus B. Paxson,* born in Erie county, N. Y. Enlisted September 16, 1861, at Midland. Aged 25 years. Mechanic. Appointed Corporal February 26, 1862. Promoted to Sergeant November 4, 1862. Promoted to. Sergeant Major July 15, 1863.

*Henry F. Pierce,* born in Saratoga county, N. Y. Enlisted October 18, 1861, at Saginaw. Aged 18 years. Laborer.

*Phineas F. Pierce,* born in Saratoga county, N. Y. Enlisted October 18, 1861, at Saginaw. Aged 20 years. Mechanic.

*John B. Parker*, born in Berkshire county, Mass. Enlisted October 30, 1861, at Roxand. Aged 29 years. Farmer.

*Charles Peters*, born in Shiawassee, Mich. Enlisted February 26, 1862, at Flint. Aged 19 years. Farmer.

*Geo. Peters*, born in Siawassee county, Mich. Enlisted February 26, 1862, at Flint. Aged 18 years. Farmer.

*Geo. Rodell*, born in Germany. Enlisted September 27, 1861, at Saginaw. Aged 18 years. Laborer.

*Laprise Rosell*, born in Ohio. Enlisted October 30, 1861, at Danby. Aged 18 years. Farmer.

*Wm. Russell*, born in Monroe county, N. Y. Enlisted October 31, 1861, at Detroit. Aged 18 years. Laborer. Died March 10, 1862, at Nashville, Tennessee, from an accidental shot.

*Joseph Stickney*, born in Genesee county, N. Y. Enlisted Septeber 16, 1861, at Saginaw. Aged 26 years. Teamster. Discharged September 12, 1862, at Columbus, Ohio.

*John Sparks*, born in England. Enlisted October 18, 1861, at Saginaw. Aged 35 years. Laborer. Discharged February 4, 1862, at Flint, Mich.

*James Spencer*, born in Kingston, Canada. Enlisted September 27, 1861, at Saginaw. Aged 31 years. Laborer.

*James L. Staples*, born in Sussex county, N. J. Enlisted September 27, 1861, at Saginaw. Aged 43 years. Laborer. Discharged October 30, 1862, at Louisville, Kentucky.

*Wm. Smith*, born in Tioga county, N. Y. Enlisted October 11, 1861, at Saginaw. Aged 39 years. Farmer. Discharged April 21, 1862, at Flint.

*Washington Saxton*, born in Ulster county, N. Y. Enlisted October 22, 1861, at Roxand. Aged 31 years. Farmer.

*Wm. H. Smith*, born in N. Y. Enlisted October 19, 1861, at Detroit. Age unknown. Boatman.

*Daniel Sanford*, born in St. Lawrence county, N. Y. Enlisted September 16, 1861, at Midland. Aged 37 years. Glover. Discharged at Detroit, Michigan, date unknown.

*John D. Sowles*, born in N. Y. Enlisted October 22, 1861, at Roxand. Aged 18 years. Farmer.

*Vandermark Story*, born in Oneida county, N. Y. Enlisted October 30, 1861, at Roxand. Aged 30 years. Farmer.

*Abraham Savage*, born in Cayuga county, N. Y. Enlisted November 15, 1861, at Roxand. Aged 45 years. Mechanic. Transferred to Company E April 21, 1862.

*Ira Sowles*, born in Eaton county, Mich. Enlisted March 28, 1862, at Flint. Aged 18 years. Farmer. Discharged January 25, 1863, at Nashville, Tennessee.

*Henry Taylor*, born in Oakland county, Mich. Enlisted September 16, 1861, at Midland. Aged 18 years. Laborer. Appointed Corporal July 1, 1862.

*John Taylor*, born in Ireland. Enlisted October 20, 1861, at Detroit. Age unknown. Laborer. Discharged January 28, 1862, at Flint.

*Lorenzo F. Taylor*, born in N. Y. Enlisted September 16, 1861, at Saginaw. Aged 45 years. Lumberman. Transferred to Company H February 5, 1862.

*Charles Truax*, born in Ontario county, N. Y. Enlisted September 6, 1861, at Saginaw. Aged 19 years. Laborer.

*Albert Turner*, born in Wayne county, Mich. Enlisted October 28, 1861, at Pontiac. Aged 18 years. Laborer. Died June 13, 1862, of fever, at General Hospital, near Farmington, Mississippi.

*Wm. A. Turner*, born in Ionia county, Mich. Enlisted October 22, 1861, at Danby. Aged 20 years. Farmer. Died, date and place unknown.

*Junius C. Turner*, born in Ionia county, Mich. Enlisted October 22, 1861, at Danby. Aged 18 years. Farmer.

*Orrin Tucker*, born in Eaton, Mich. Enlisted March 4, 1862, at Flint. Aged 18 years. Farmer. Discharged January —, 1862, at Flint.

*Henry Vanpatten*, nativity unknown. Enlisted September 9, 1861, at Saginaw. Aged 30 years. Farmer.

*Nathan Vanhousen*, born in Westminster, Canada. Enlisted January 9, 1861, at Flint. Aged 24 years. Farmer.

*Samuel Vanavery*, born in Lockport, N. Y. Enlisted October 26, 1861, at Holly. Aged 42 years. Joiner. Discharged August 25, 1862, at Detroit, Michigan.

*Ralph Vosburg*, born in Oakland county, Mich. Enlisted October 20, 1861, at Holly. Aged 23 years. Farmer.

*Wm. Westbrook,* born in Saginaw county, Mich. Enlisted September 26, 1861, at —, Isabella county. Aged 22 years. Farmer.

*Ebenezer Williams,* born in Porter, N. Y. Enlisted October 30, 1861, at Roxand. Aged 44 years. Transferred to Company E April 21, 1862.

*A. E. Wisner,* born in Lake county, Ohio. Enlisted Nov. 8, 1861, at Flint. Aged 18 years. Farmer.

*Ebenezer Williams, Jr.,* born in Washtenaw county, Mich. Enlisted January 9, 1862, at Roxand. Aged 20 years. Farmer.

*Lewis C. Whiteman,* born in Madison county, N. Y. Enlisted February 17, 1862, at Portland. Aged 24 years. Farmer. Discharged July 16, 1862, at Detroit, Michigan.

## COMPANY C.

B. B. Redfield, of Oakland county, received permission from the Governor the 1st of September, 1861, to raise a company, but, failing to fill his company, he joined with Miron Bunnell, of Genessee county, who together received written authority of the Governor to raise a company to be assigned to some one of the regiments then forming. This authority was received September 24, 1861. B. B. Redfield took what men he had raised to Goodrich, Genesee county, and the drill in which they had already become well versed at Orion, Oakland county, was continued, and new recruits were brought in until the company numbered a minimum, which was about the first of November, 1861, when they were ordered to join the 10th Michigan Infantry, then forming at Flint. November 11th the company went into camp at Flint with eighty-six men, and was mustered into the United States service

February 6, 1862, with a maximum company. It was first known as the Orion Union Guards, and recruited principally in Oakland and Genesee counties.

*Capt. Myron Bunnell* was born in Oswego county, New York, in the year 1825. He moved to Michigan with his father when quite young. When about 18 years of age he went to California by the overland route, taking a train of twelve pairs of horses and five wagons. He was gone two years and returned to Michigan and engaged in teaching school, and also in the mercantile business. He was married in Genesee county, Michigan, in the year 1857. Received commission as Captain from October 1, 1861. He was troubled with his lungs, and suffered otherwise from ill health, after arriving in the field, until July, when he went home, and, after partially recovering, rejoined his regiment, but was obliged to resign November 18, 1862.

*1st Lieut. Benjamin B. Redfield* was born in Bainbridge, Chenango county, New York, February 11, 1813. Married Emily Smith, of Onondaga county, New York, March 17, 1833. He moved to Michigan in 1844. He led a farmer's life quite successfully until entering the military service—teaching school some twenty-five winters. Was considerable prominent in political circles, taking an active part in many of the political strifes of the day. After the defeat of our arms at Bull's Run, he felt a desire to engage in the great strife, which is still pending, and accordingly joined the service of the United States and received commission as 1st Lieutenant from October 1, 1861. Upon arriving in the field the change of climate was so great as to seriously affect his health, and he was obliged to resign, which he did June 2, 1862.

*2d Lieut. Alva A. Collins* was born September 14, 1823, in the village of Wyoming, Wyoming county, New York. At the age of five years he moved with his father to Rochester, New York, and at ten years of age to Attica, N Y., where he lived eleven years. He then left the parental roof and spent several years in Warsaw, Leroy and Byron, New York, at farming and other occupations. At Byron he began the profession of teaching primary schools, which he continued to follow most of the time until entering the military service. He was teaching at the breaking out of the rebellion and quit his school and enrolled himself as a soldier when Lieut. Redfield started to raise a company, and upon an election held to appoint officers, he was elected 2d Lieutenant unanimously, and received commission as such from October 1, 1861. He was promoted to 1st Lieutenant June 2, 1862, *vice* Redfield, resigned. Had command of his company most of the time after entering the field until April, 1863, on account of ill health of his superior officers. He is a thorough temperance officer.

### NON-COMMISSIONED OFFICERS.
#### *Sergeants.*

1*st. Harrison H. Wheeler* was born in Lapeer county, Michigan, March 22, 1839. He was married in Tuscola county, Michigan, January 29, 1859. Occupation before entering the military service was farming. He enlisted November 1, 1861, at Farmer's Creek, Michigan, and by vote of the company was made 1st Sergeant February 1, 1862, and appointed to rank as such from date of enlistment. Promoted to 2d Lieutenant, *vice* Collins promoted, June 2, 1862; and on March 31, 1863, promoted to 1st Lieutenant of Company 1, *vice* Titus promoted, and shortly after transferred to Company E, *vice* Vanderburg, deceased.

2d. *Fletcher W. Hewes*, born in Leroy, Genesee county, N.Y. Enlisted September 16, 1861, at Orion. Aged 23 years. School teacher. Appointed to rank as Sergeant from date of enlistment. Detailed as Ordnance Sergeant for the regiment January 12, 1863, where he still remains.

3d. *Mark H. Ridley*, born in Sussex, England. Enlisted September 14, 1861, at Orion. Aged 33 years. Shoemaker. Appointed to rank as Sergeant from date of enlistment.

4th. *Esli R. Redfield*, born in Onondaga county, N.Y. Enlisted September 14, 1861, at Orion. Aged 27 years. Painter.

Appointed to rank as Sergeant from date of enlistment. Promoted to 1st Sergeant September 1, 1862.

5th. *John S. Coryell*, born in Livingston county, N. Y. Enlisted October 2, 1861, at Orion. Aged 25 years. School teacher. Discharged September 8, 1862, at Columbus, Ohio.

### *Corporals.*

1st. *James R. Kipp*, born in Erie county, N. Y. Enlisted October 22, 1861, at Atlas. Aged 23 years.. Farmer. Appointed to rank as Corporal from date of enlistment. Promoted to Sergeant September 1, 1862.

2d. *Edmond O'Neil*, born in Ireland. Enlisted September 14, 1861, at Orion. Aged 20 years. Farmer. Appointed to rank as Corporal from date of enlistment.

3d. *Samuel J. W. Gibbs*, born in Genesee county, N. Y. Enlisted September 21, 1861, at Orion. Aged 29 years. Farmer. Appointed to rank as Corporal from date of enlistment.

4th. *John E. Beach*, born in Genesee county, N.Y. Enlisted October 5, 1861, at Goodrich. Aged 28 years Farmer. Appointed to rank as Corporal from date of enlistment. Died July 23, 1862, at General Hospital, near Farmington, Mississippi, of fever.

5th. *Milo Swears*, born in Genesee county, Mich. Enlisted October 22, 1861, at Atlas. Aged 23 years. Farmer. Appointed to rank as Corporal from date of enlistment. Promoted to Sergeant October 1, 1862.

6th. *Frederick Casamer*, born in Oakland county, Mich. Enlisted September 14, 1861, at Orion. Aged 22 years. Farmer. Appointed to rank as Corporal from date of enlistment.

7th. *Jasper Ingleheart*, born in Lyons, N. Y. Enlisted October 15, 1861, at Waterford. Aged 31 years. Farmer. Appointed to rank as Corporal from date of enlistment.

8th. *Geo. R. Collins*, born in Wyoming, N. Y. Enlisted September 14, 1861, at Orion. Aged 25 years. School teacher. Appointed to rank as Corporal from date of enlistment.

*James Lacy, Drummer,* born in Westchester, N. Y. Enlisted November 18, 1861, at Flint. Aged 64 years. Laborer.

*Ira Rogers, Fifer,* born in Oakland county, Mich. Enlisted October 2, 1861, at Orion. Aged 27 years. Farmer.

### PRIVATES.

*Elihu Orman,* born in N. Y. Enlisted November 2, 1861, at Flint. Aged 29 years. Farmer.

*Abel.Beckwith,* born in Addison, Vt. Enlisted October 28, 1861, at Watertown. Aged 29 years. Farmer. Transferred to Company H, April 30, 1862.

*Gilbert Beckwith,* born in Essex, N. Y. Enlisted October 28, 1861, at Goodrich. Aged 18 years. Farmer. Died on hospital boat, on the Tennessee River, of chronic diarrhœa, May 15, 1862.

*Lorson Beckwith,* born in Essex, N. Y. Enlisted October 25, 1861, at Marathon. Aged 15 years. Farmer. Discharged November 29, 1862, at Columbus, Ohio.

*Geo. W. Bidwell,* born in Wayne, N. Y. Enlisted October 17, 1861, at Forest. Aged 35 years. Farmer. Discharged September 12, 1862, at Columbus, Ohio.

*Henry S. Bidwell,* born in Portage, Ohio. Enlisted October 7, 1861, at Goodrich. Aged 29 years. Farmer. Appointed Corporal February 16, 1863.

*Daniel Burton,* born in Oswego county, N. Y. Enlisted October 14, 1861, at Orion. Aged 19 years. Farmer. Died January 26, 1862, at Flint, Michigan, of fever.

*Marvin Barney,* born in Genesee county, Mich. Enlisted October 2, 1861, at Goodrich. Aged 18 years. Mechanic. Appointed Corporal February 16, 1861.

*Geo. Bush,* born in Lapeer county, Mich. Enlisted October 5, 1861, at Goodrich. Aged 19 years. Farmer.

*Jno. Bush,* born in Lapeer county, Mich. Enlisted November 4, 1861, at Flint. Aged 21 years. Farmer.

*Geo. Beckett*, born in Lincolnshire, England. Enlisted January 3, 1862, at Flint. Aged 18 years. Farmer. Appointed Corporal October 1, 1862.

*Wm. Bartlett*, born in Oxfordshire, England. Enlisted February 12, 1862, at Flint. Aged 40 years. Farmer. Died January 5, 1863, at General Hospital No. 2, Nashville, Tenn. Buried in Nashville—soldiers' cemetery.

*Freeman Chapman*, born in Oakland county, Mich. Enlisted September 21, 1861, at Orion. Aged 30 years. Farmer.

*Nelson Confer*, born in Erie county, N. Y. Enlisted October 22, 1861, at Atlas. Aged 23 years. Farmer.

*Theodore Casamer*, born in Oakland county, Mich. Enlisted September 14, 1861, at Orion. Aged 18 years. Farmer.

*Frank Crittenden*, born in Calhoun county, Mich. Enlisted October 22, 1861, at Forest. Aged 24 years. Farmer.

*Martin Chaffee*, born in Genesee county, N. Y. Enlisted October 7, 1861, at Goodrich. Aged 30 years. Farmer. Appointed Corporal October 1, 1861. Discharged January 28, 1863, at Nashville, Tennessee.

*Wm. Clink*, born in Holton, Canada. Enlisted October 4, 1861, at Millington. Aged 21 years. Farmer. Transferred to 4th Regiment Cavalry December 11, 1862.

*John W. Currier*, born in Lorain, Ohio. Enlisted October 7, 1861, at Caledonia. Aged 24 years. Farmer. Transferred to Company I April 30, 1862.

*Stephen F. Commings*, born in Erie county, N. Y. Enlisted October 4, 1861, at Goodrich. Aged 35 years. Farmer.

*Oscar Cummings*, born in Genesee county, Mich. Enlisted October 4, 1861, at Goodrich. Aged 21 years. Farmer.

*John Chadburn*, born in Missisque, C. E. Enlisted October 18, 1861, at Richfield. Aged 52 years. Farmer. Transferred to Company I April 30, 1862.

*James H. Cornish*, born in Wayne county, N. Y. Enlisted October 24, 1861, at Orion. Aged 17 years. Farmer.

*Joel P. Colvin*, born in Lapeer county, Mich. Enlisted October 24, 1861, at Dryden. Aged 17 years. Farmer.

*Cyrus Cobb*, born in Ohio. Enlisted October 4, 1861, at

Goodrich. Aged 25 years. Farmer. Died February 15, 1862, at Burton, Genesee county, Michigan, of fever.

*Richard Carter*, born in Yorkshire, England. Enlisted September 25, 1861, at Flint. Aged 24 years. Farmer.

*Erastus Corwin*, born in Wayne county, Mich. Enlisted October 31, 1861, at Richfield. Aged 33 years. Farmer.

*Wm. Clark*, born in Lincolnshire, England. Enlisted Nov. 30, 1861, at Goodrich. Aged 32 years. Farmer.

*John Clark*, born in Lincolnshire, England. Enlisted January 8, 1862, at Flint. Aged 30 years. Farmer.

*Francis Crampton*, born in Lapeer county, Mich. Enlisted December 10, 1861, at Flint. Aged 20 years. Farmer. Transferred to 4th Regiment Cavalry December 15, 1862.

*Lewis Cheney*, born in Macomb county, Mich. Enlisted October 7, 1861, at Orion. Aged 17 years. Farmer.

*David Centre*, born in Wayne county, N. Y. Enlisted November 24, 1861, at Oakwood. Aged 32 years. Farmer. Transferred from Company I February 6, 1862. Discharged April —, 1862, at Flint.

*Thomas Downer*, born in Bennington, Vt. Enlisted November 2, 1861, at Goodrich. Aged 44 years. Farmer. Discharged July 24, 1862, at Columbus, Ohio. Died August 2, 1862, at Camp Dennison, Ohio, of chronic diarrhœa.

*Elijah B. Evans*, born in Genesee county, N. Y. Enlisted November 15, 1861, at Flint. Aged 38 years. Farmer. Discharged December 9, 1862, at Cincinnati, Ohio.

*Benjamin Frick*, born in Erie county, N. Y. Enlisted October 28, 1861, at Goodrich. Aged 25 years. Farmer.

*Ira C. Ford*, born in Canada. Enlisted October 30, 1861, at Goodrich. Aged 18 years. Farmer.

*Joseph Fifield*, born in Oakland, Mich. Enlisted November 18, 1861, at Goodrich. Aged 22 years. Farmer.

*Edgar E. Grilley*, born in Shiawassee, Mich. Enlisted October 18, 1861, at St. Charles. Aged 18 years. Farmer.

*James M. Gillett*, born in Genesee, Mich. Enlisted October 18, 1861, at St. Charles. Aged 18 years. Farmer. Died at Smith's Ferry, Tennessee, December 2, 1863.

*Nathaniel Green*, nativity unknown. Enlisted December 10, 1861, at Flint. Aged 18 years. Farmer. Taken from regiment by parents, before muster.

*Harrison Glynn*, born in Clarence county, N. Y. Enlisted January 27, 1862, at Willington. Aged 20 years. Farmer. Transferred to 4th Regiment Cavalry December 11, 1862.

*Edgar I. Hewes*, born in Genesee county, N. Y. Enlisted October 24, 1861, at Orion. Aged 17 years. Farmer.

*Allen Hunt*, born in Monroe county, N. Y. Enlisted October 10, 1861, at —, Lapeer county. Aged 43 years. Farmer. Discharged September 8, 1862, at Columbus, Ohio.

*Stephen J. Husted*, born in Oakland county, Mich. Enlisted October 22, 1861, at Atlas. Aged 25 years. Farmer.

*Daniel Hopler*, born in Oakland county, Mich. Enlisted October 2, 1861, at Oakland. Aged 23 years. Farmer. Discharged October 16, 1862, at Jefferson Barracks, Missouri.

*Hearker Hibbard*, born in Genesee county, N. Y. Enlisted November 13, 1861, at Flint. Aged 33 years. Farmer. Appointed Wagon Master November 21, 1862.

*Seely S. Hedglen*, born in Mercer county, Penn. Enlisted December 22, 1861, at Flint. Aged 29 years. Farmer.

*Edward E. Hedglen*, born in Ohio. Enlisted December 25, 1861, at Flint. Aged 18 years.

*Sylvester Haynes*, born in Sussex, N. J. Enlisted December 6, 1861, at Flint. Aged 25 years. Farmer.

*Harrison Haynes*, born in Sussex, N. J. Enlisted July 20, 1861, at Flint, in 8th Infantry. Transferred to 10th December 25, 1861. Aged 23 years. Farmer. Discharged November 5, 1862, at Camp Dennison, Ohio.

*Printis G. Harris*, born in Oakland, Mich. Enlisted January 13, 1862, at Pontiac. Aged 18 years. Farmer.

*Geo. Ingleheart*, born in Oakland county, Mich. Enlisted October 15, 1861, at Pontiac. Aged 18 years. Farmer.

*Oziel Inman*, born in Chenango county, N. Y. Enlisted November 21, 1861, at Tuscola. Aged 38 years. Farmer. Transferred to Company K February 6, 1862.

*Charles Johnson,* born in Lapeer, Mich. Enlisted November 10, 1861, at Hadley. Aged 22 years. Farmer. Appointed Corporal November 25, 1862. Died Dec. 24, 1862, at Nashville, Tennnessee, of typhoid fever.

*David Kittle,* born in Delaware, N. Y. Enlisted November 6, 1861, at 'Groveland. Aged 28 years. Farmer.

*Volentine Kittle,* born in Delaware, N. Y. Enlisted October 5, 1861, at Flint. Aged 21 years. Farmer. Died June 28, 1862, at Camp Big Springs, Mississippi.

*Wm. H. Lake,* born in Macomb county, Mich. Enlisted October 17, 1861, at Orion. Aged 19 years. Farmer. Transferred to Company I February 6, 1862.

*James C. Landon,* born in Wayne, N. Y. Enlisted October 10, 1861, at Lapeer. Aged 27 years. Farmer.

*Daniel Lynch,* born in Ireland. Enlisted November —, 1861, at —, Lapeer county. Aged 16 years. Farmer. Discharged at Flint, Mich. (Under age.)

*Henry Lincoln,* born in Oswego, N. Y. Enlisted November 1, 1861, at St. Charles. Aged 34 years. Farmer. Transferred to Company H April 30, 1862.

*Frank Munger,* born in N. Y. Enlisted October 2, 1861, at —, Shiawassee county. Aged 19 years. Farmer. Died in General Hospital, near Farmington, Mississippi, July 9, 1862 Rupture and chronic diarrhœa.

*Joseph Marston,* born in Oakland, Mich. Enlisted November 3, 1861, at Hadley. Aged 19 years. Farmer. Discharged December 25, 1862, at Nashville, Tennessee.

*John D. McIntire,* born in Monroe county, N. Y. Enlisted October 5, 1861, at Ortonville. Aged 22 years. Farmer. Discharged at Flint, Michigan.

*Ransom Myers,* born in Wayne, Mich. Enlisted November 15, 1861, at Watertown. Aged 21 years. Farmer. Discharged September 30, 1862, at St. Louis, Missouri.

*Thomas J. Merritt,* born in Crawford, Penn. Enlisted December 6, 1861, at Farmer's Creek. Aged 22 years. Farmer.

*Geo. Marvin,* born in Oakland, Mich. Enlisted September 14, 1861, at Orion. Aged 19 years. Farmer.

*Gary A. Newcombe,* born in Genesee, N. Y. Enlisted Nov. 21, 1861, at Richfield. Aged 25 years. Farmer. Transferred to Company H April 30, 1862.

*Henry Ostrander,* born in Monroe county, N. Y. Enlisted October 12, 1861, at Shiawassee. Aged 18 years. Farmer. Died August 22, 1862, at Tuscumbia, Alabama.

*Levi Ovitt,* born in Niagara, N. Y. Enlisted March 1, 1862, at Flint. Aged 19 years. Mechanic. Transferred to Company H April 30, 1862.

*Benjamin Overhalser,* born in Erie, N. Y. Enlisted October 7, 1861, at Richfield. Aged 25 years. Farmer. Discharged December 15, 1862, at Cincinnati, Ohio.

*Calvin Olmstead,* nativity unknown. Enlisted December 14, 1861, at Hadley. Age and occupation unknown. Never left Michigan. (Under age.)

*Lewis Parish,* born in N. Y. Enlisted November 14, 1861, at Goodrich. Aged 19 years. Farmer. Transferred to Company H April 30, 1862.

*Henry Punnell,* born in Wayne, N. Y. Enlisted October 28, 1861, at Goodrich. Aged 25 years. Mechanic. Drowned accidentally. Date unknown.

*Omer Pratt,* born in Clarence county, N. Y. Enlisted October 14, 1861, at Goodrich. Aged 17 years. Farmer. Died June 10, 1862, at Evansville, Indiana.

*John Potter,* born in Lapeer county, Mich. Enlisted September 14, 1861, at Oakland. Aged 22 years. Farmer.

*Martin B. Payne,* born in Orange county, Vt. Enlisted November 21, 1862, at Watertown. Aged 29 years. Farmer.

*Geo. W. Richmond,* born in Monroe county, N. Y. Enlisted November 17, 1861, at Goodrich. Aged 27 years. Farmer. Appointed Corporal October 1, 1862.

*Geo. S. Richmond,* born in Oakland county, Mich. Enlisted November 4, 1861, at Groveland. Aged 18 years. Farmer.

*Geo. Rutherford,* born in Addison, Vt. Enilsted September

23, 1861, at —, Lapeer county, Mich. Aged 29 years. Farmer.

*Alva Reinmgton*, born in Niagara county, N. Y. Enlisted October 3, 1861, at —, Shiawassee county, Mich. Aged 27 years. Farmer.

*Freeling H. Rich*, born in Livingston county, N. Y. Enlisted November 28, 1861, at Ortonville. Aged 17 years. Mechanic.

*Charles H. Ramlow*, born in Prussia. Enlisted December 6, 1861, at Flint. Aged 18 years. Farmer.

*Charles Rogers*, born in Stuben county, N. Y. Enlisted January 2, 1862, at Orion. Aged 40 years. Farmer. Discharged September 13, 1862, at St. Louis, Missouri.

*Geo. N. Shillinger*, born in N. Y. Enlisted October 2, 1861, at Goodrich. Aged 20 years. Mechanic.

*James Smith*, born in Cayuga county, N. Y. Enlisted November 8, 1861, at Marathon. Aged 26 years. Farmer. Died February 23, 1862, at Marathon, Michigan, of lung fever.

*John W. Saunders*, born in Kent, Eng. Enlisted November 8, 1861, at Goodrich. Aged 17 years. Farmer.

*Nelson Swears*, born in Genesee county, Mich. Enlisted November 25, 1861, at Atlas. Aged 19 years. Farmer.

*Danil Spear*, born in Orange county, Vt. Enlisted October 5, 1861, at Shiawassee. Aged 36 years. Farmer. Discharged September 5, 1862, at Detroit, Michigan.

*Geo. Stowe*, born in Roland county, Vt. Enlisted November 15, 1861, at Flint. Aged 37 years. Mechanic.

*Wm. E. Sprague*, born in Broome county, N. Y. Enlisted February 6, 1862, at Troy. Aged 18 years. Farmer.

*Job Trumball*, born in Clinton, Vt. Enlisted October 25, 1861, at Marathon. Aged 45 years. Farmer.

*Frank Thornley*, born in Oakland county, Mich. Enlisted September 23, 1861, at Orion. Aged 18 years. Farmer. Died March 16, 1863, at Nashville, Tennessee, of typhoid fever.

*Wm. Tuttle*, born in Sussex, N. J. Enlisted October 22, 1861, at Waterford. Aged 18 years. Mechanic.

*Henry E. Thomas*, born in Susquehanna, Penn. Enlisted October 5, 1861, at Ortonville. Aged 22 years. Farmer.

Died September 28, 1862, at General Hospital, Jackson, Tenn., of consumption.

*Asa Volentine*, born in Lapeer county, Mich. Enlisted October 25, 1861, at —, Lapeer county. Aged 17 years. Farmer.

*Daniel Vanburen*, born in Lapeer county, Mich. Enlisted October 18, 1861, at Flint. Aged 22 years. Farmer. Died July 26, 1862, at General Hospital, Keokuk, Iowa.

*Alonso Voluntine*, born in Lapeer county, Mich. Enlisted October 22, 1861, at —, Lapeer county. Aged 22 years. Farmer.

*James Vansickles*, born in Ontario county, N. Y. Enlisted December 31, 1861, at Elgen. Aged 38 years. Farmer. Discharged September 26, 1862, at St. Louis, Missouri.

*Augustus Welch*, born in Onondaga county, N. Y. Enlisted October 25, 1861, at Goodrich. Aged 31 years. Mechanic. Discharged at Flint, Michigan.

*Adin West*, born in Niagara county, N. Y. Enlisted October 24, 1861, at Goodrich. Aged 18 years. Farmer.

*Ira Wood*, born in Genesee county, N. Y. Enlisted November 18, 1861, at Hadley. Aged 20 years. Farmer.


## COMPANY D.

Company D was recruited principally in Sanilac county, by Israes Huckins, of Lexington, Sanilac county, under an order from the Governor of the State, to J. J. Scarritt, to raise five companies of men to join some of the regiments which were to be raised under the call for three years volunteers. Capt. Huckins began recruiting men October 21, 1862, and in one month entered camp of instruction at Flint, Michigan, having recruited fifty-five men and two Lieutenants. This company was filled to a minimum December 15, 1861, and mustered February 6, 1862, with an aggregate of ninety-five men. It was first known as Sanilac Pioneers, and was made up of hardy, industrious, intelligent men. It has always been a large company, owing partly to the hardiness of its men.

COMMISSIONED OFFICERS.

*Capt. Israel Huckins* was born in Westminster, Province of Canada, July 11, 1822. Moved to Lexington, Sanilac county, Michigan, in May, 1839. He was married September 12, 1843, at 21 years of age. He has successfully followed the occupation of farming, with the exception of four years which he served as County Treasurer, which office he filled satisfactorily. He is a man of firm principles and seldom if ever speaks or thinks unadvisedly. He is one of the few who have found that a military man can serve his country without the use of intoxicating drinks. (We are sure his brother officers will acknowledge that these remarks are but justly due Capt. Huckins.) He was commissioned as Captain from October 1, 1861. He was in command of his company most of the time after arriving in the field, as he had been with the regiment all of the time and sick but little, until September 12, 1863, when he was detailed on a Board of Claims, at Nashville, where he still serves.

*1st. Lieut. Hannibal H. Nims* was born in Richmond, Chittenden county, Vermont, August 23, 1834. He moved to Lexington, Sanilac county, Michigan, in May, 1854, and was married at that place January 28, 1863. His occupation before entering the military service was clerking. He enlisted in the fall of 1861, and received his commission as 1st Lieutenant from October 1, 1862. In July, 1861, he was, by an order for recruiting to fill up old regiments, sent to Michigan to recruit men for our regiment. Was promoted to Captain of Company K, July 5, 1863, *vice* Judd, resigned. He returned to his regiment and took command of his company April 12, 1863.

*2d. Lieut. Geo. W. Jenks* was born at Crown Point, N. Y., May 6, 1838. Moved to Lexington, Sanilac county, Michigan, in the fall of 1854. He was employed as a clerk in Lexington at the time of entering the military service. Joined the Sanilac Pioneers at their first organization, and received his commission as 2d Lieutenant October 1, 1861. Promoted to 1st Lieutenant July 5, 1862, *vice* Nims, promoted. Was taken sick at Nashville, Tennessee, and went home on a furlough to try to regain his health, but failing to do so, returned to the regiment and resigned, his resignation being accepted February 4, 1863.

*Sergeants.*

1st. *Richard Teal* was born April 29, 1823, at Westmoreland, Oneida county, N. Y. From his seventh until his eleventh year he was employed in a cotton factory at York Mills, near Utica, New York, then moved with his father to Harrison county, Ohio, and worked in a woolen factory until seventeen years of age. He then began the carpenter's and joiner's trade, at which he worked until 1845, when he enlisted on the 8th day of May, in Company C, 4th United States Infantry. He was with his regiment at Corpus Christi, in Gen. Taylor's three first battles, and at the siege of Vera Cruz, under Gen. Worth, in Gen. Scott's command. He served in Worth's Division during the remainder of the campaign, and was in all the battles fought by Gen. Scott's command except Contreras. At the close of the war he went with his regiment to Vera Cruz, thence to Pascagoula, Missippi, and to New Orleans, Louisiana, thence sailed to New York. From there they went to Detroit, Michigan, where he was discharged May 8, 1850. May 13, 1850, was married and was employed by the Michigan Central Railroad as car builder, at which he labored until October, 1854, when he commenced farming on new land. Enlisted October 29, 1861, and appointed to rank as 1st Sergeant from date of enlistment. March 31, 1863 was promoted to 2d Lieutenant, *vice* Beach, promoted.

2d. *Rudolph Papst* was born December 25, 1838, at York, York county, Canada West. He was trained according to the principles of the Episcopal Church. Moved to Michigan October 31, 1858, in the 20th year of his age. Is unmarried. His occupations have been various, having at different times shaved shingles, drove stage and farmed it considerable. At the time of his entering the military service he was employed as a clerk. Enlisted at Sand Beach, October 25, 1861, and appointed to rank as Sergeant from date of enlistment. Promoted to Sergeant Major May 28, 1862, *vice* Stewart, promoted. March 31, 1863, he was promoted to 2d Lieutenant Company E, *vice* McDonald, promoted.

3d. *Cyrene R. Bunker* was born in Duchess county, N. Y. Enlisted October 28, 1861, at Lexington. Aged 32 years. Lumberman. Appointed to rank as Sergeant from date of enlistment.

4th. *Watson Beach* was born in Litchfield county, Conn., January 3, 1840, and with his father moved to Michigan in the spring of 1843, his father taking up his residence in Port Huron, St. Clair county. After pursuing a proper course of study for a lawyer, he was admitted to practice in 1861, at the April term of the Circuit Court of Sanilac county, Michigan, Judge Sanford M. Green, presiding. He enlisted December 5, 1861, at Lexington, Sanilac county, Michigan, and was appointed to rank as Sergeant from date of enlistment. Promoted to 2d Lieutent July 5, 1862, *vice* Jenks, promoted, and March 31, 1863 promoted to 1st Lieutenant, *vice* Jenks, resigned.

5th. *Henry Wideman*, born in York county, C. W. Enlisted December 4, 1861, at Lexington. Aged 42 years. Farmer. Appointed to rank as Sergeant from date of enlistment. Promoted to 1st Sergeant April 3, 1863.

### Corporals.

1st. *Watson F. Bisbee*, born in London, C. W. Enlisted October 28, 1861, at Lexington. Aged 21 years. Farmer. Appointed to rank as Corporal from date of enlistment. Discharged at Nashville, Tennessee, February 12, 1863.

2d. *Robert F. Lewis*, born in London, C. W. Enlisted Oct. 23, 1862, at Lexington. Aged 21 years. Carpenter. Appointed to rank as Corporal from date of enlistment. Promoted to Sergeant August 1, 1862. Discharged November 10, 1863, at Murfreesboro, Tennessee.

3d. *Charles M. Cross*, born in Oneida, N. Y. Enlisted October 22, 1861, at Lexington. Aged 32 years. Laborer. Appointed to rank as Corporal from date of enlistment. Promoted to Sergeant July 1, 1862.

4th. *Theron J. Springstein*, born in Wentworth, C. W. Enlisted October 28, 1861, at Lexington. Aged 30 years. Carpenter. Appointed to rank as Corporal from date of enlistment. Promoted to Sergeant April 3, 1863. Promoted to 1st Lieut. 17th United States Infantry, colored troops, November 9, 1863.

5th. *Lemuel House*, born in Deerham, C. W. Enlisted Nov. 15, 1861, at Lexington. Aged 20 years. Laborer. Appointed Corporal January 27, 1862.

6th. *Stephen R. Moore*, born in Cayuga county, N. Y. Enlisted in regular service in 1856, and served five years on the frontier in the Indian Territory, Missouri and Kansas. Enlisted in the 10th Michigan Infantry December 28, 1861, at Lexington. Aged 23 years. Sailor. Appointed Corporal January 27, 1862. Promoted to Sergeant April 3, 1863.

7th. *Hugh McCaffry*, born in Ireland. Enlisted October 14, 1861, at Huron. Aged 42 years. Waiter. Appointed Corporal January 28, 1862. Promoted to Sergeant October 1, 1862.

*Joseph Clukey*, born in LeCole county, C. E. Enlisted November 18, 1861, at Lexington. Aged 27 years. Farmer. Appointed Corporal February 24, 1862.

MUSICIANS.

*Ira Miles, Drummer*, born in Madoc, Canada. Enlisted October 26, 1861, at Rubicon. Aged 19 years. Lumberman.

*John Jackson, Fifer*, born in Scotland. Enlisted January 15, 1862, at Lexington. Aged 39 years. Laborer. Reported as a deserter and dropped January 30, 1864.

PRIVATES.

*Jacob Amon*, born in Wittlesburg, Switzerland. Enlisted November 28, 1861, at Lexington. Aged 28 years. Farmer.

*John Aiken*, born in Oxford, Canada. Enlisted August 11, 1862, at Lexington. Aged 28 years. Farmer. Discharged January 3, 1860, at Nashville, Tennessee.

*Abram Brooks*, born in Lake county, Ohio. Enlisted October 29, 1861, at Huron. Aged 28 years. Farmer.

*Geo. Brimley*, born in Devonshire, England. Enlisted November 6, 1861, at Austin. Aged 30 years. Laborer.

*Charles N. Briggs*, born in Ontario county, Canada. Enlisted November 15, 1861, at Lexington. Aged 33 years. Farmer.

*Stephen Belknap*, born in Hulton county, Canada. Enlisted November 30, 1861, at North Sanilac. Aged 18 years. Laborer.

*Thomas Bell*, born in Canada. Enlisted November 27, 1861, at Lexington. Aged 31 years. Sailor. Died at Chattanooga, Tennessee, September 29, 1863.

*Harvey Baker*, born in Lancaster, C. W. Enlisted January 15, 1862, at Lexington. Aged 24 years. Farmer.

*Frederick C. Byam*, born in Black Rock, N. Y. Enlisted November 7, 1861, at Lexington. Aged 26 years. Laborer.

*Richard Butterfield*, born in London, Canada. Enlisted July 24, 1862, at Lexington. Aged 21 years. Farmer. Transferred to regular service December 19, 1862.

*James Campbell*, born in Huron county, Canada. Enlisted October 29, 1861, at Lexington. Aged 25 years. Laborer.

*James Close*, born in Oakland county, Mich. Enlisted November 7, 1861, at Lexington. Aged 20 years. Laborer.

*Joseph Cherboneau*, born in Lexington, Mich. Enlisted August 22, 1862, at Lexington. Aged 18 years. Laborer. Discharged at Nashville, Tennessee, August 9, 1863.

*Charles Dease*, born in Norfolk county, C. W. Enlisted December 13, 1861, at Lexington. Aged 20 years. Laborer. Discharged August 22, 1862, at Evansville, Indiana.

*Amos Ellsworth*, born in Canada West. Enlisted December 7, 1861, at Orion. Aged 31 years. Farmer. Appointed Corporal April 3, 1863.

*James Eaton*, born in Tompkins county, N. Y. Enlisted December 30, 1861, at Lexington. Aged 21 years. Farmer. Appointed Corporal October 1, 1862.

*George Edwards*, born in N. Y. Enlisted January 15, 1861, at Lexington. Aged 30 years. Farmer.

*Henry Edwards*, born in Middlesex county, C. W. Enlisted Jan. 23, 1862, at Lexington. Aged 21 years. Farmer. Deserted April 19, 1862, from Flint.

*Wm. S. Foster*, born in Sanilac county, Mich. Enlisted October 18, 1861, at Lexington. Aged 18 years. Farmer.

*Geo. Frazier*, born in Penobscot county, Me. Enlisted December 7, 1861, at Lexington. Aged 44 years. Farmer. Discharged August 30, 1862, at Detroit, Michigan.

*Freeman Frazier*, born in Penobscot county, Me. Enlisted December 7, 1861, at Lexington. Aged 22 years. Farmer. Died at Louisville, Kentucky, November 18, 1862.

*Lewis Facer*, born in Detroit, Mich. Enlisted January 22 1862, at Lexington. Aged 43 years. Lumberman. Transferred to Invalid Corps September 16, 1863.

*Charles A. Ford*, born in Oneida county, N. Y. Enlisted October 28, 1861, at Forest. Aged 24 years. Farmer.

*Gilbert Fox*, born in Yates county, N. Y. Enlisted August 9, 1862, at Lexington. Aged 22 years. Farmer.

*Daniel Fredrick*, born in Prince Edward, Canada. Enlisted July 21, 1862, at Lexington. Aged 39 years. Shoemaker. Discharged May 20, 1863, at Nashville. Tennessee.

*Marshal U. Gage*, born in Oneida county, N. Y. Enlisted October 28, 1861, at Lexington. Aged 24 years. Farmer. Discharged February 26, 1863, a New Albany, Indiana.

*Chester H. Grant*, born in Berlin, Vt. Enlisted November 4, 1861, at White Rock. Aged 42 years. Painter.

*John W. Gordon*, born in Oswego county, N. Y. Enlisted December 21, 1861, at Lexington. Aged 25 years. Laborer.

*Zeb Goodrich*, born in St. Luke, Canada. Enlisted December 30, 1861, at Lexington. Aged 25 years.. Teamster.

*Geo. Gardner*, born in Germany. Enlisted January 11, 1862, at Lexington. Aged 28 years. Farmer.

*Hignatus Horn*, born in Wurtemburg, Germany. Enlisted August 4, 1862, at Florence, Alabama. Aged 47 years. Shoemaker.

*Geo. Hedrick,* born in New York. Enlisted November 5, 1861, at Worth. Aged 34 years. Farmer. Discharged September 6, 1862, at St. Louis, Missouri.

*Geo. Henry,* born in Lancaster, Canada. Enlisted November 7, 1861, at Lexington. Aged 19 years. Laborer. Appointed Corporal April 3, 1863.

*John Henry,* born in Canada. Enlisted January 22, 1862, at Lexington. Aged 24 years. Farmer.

*John Harp,* born in Canada. Enlisted January 15, 1862, at Lexington. Aged 26 years. Farmer. Died July 8, 1862, in a wagon, at Farmington, Mississippi, while on the way to General Hospital.

*Harvey P. Hosley,* born in Shiawassee county, N. Y. Enlisted Dec. 5, 1861, at Lexington. Aged 18 years. Painter. Died at Farmington, Mississippi, July 8, 1862.

*Wm. Hale,* born in Gloucestershire, England. Enlisted November 27, 1861, at Lexington. Aged 31 years. Laborer.

*Wm. Henderson,* born in Tyrone, Ireland. Enlisted October 25, 1861, at Lexington. Aged 29 years. Painter.

*John L. House,* born in S. C. Enlisted August 23, 1862 at Florence, Alabama. Aged 42 years. Farmer. Died October —, 1862, at Nashville, Tennessee.

*Wm. J. Hoey,* born in Toronto, Canada. Enlisted July 20, 1862, at Lexington. Aged 25 years. Lumberman. Appointed Corporal April 3, 1863.*

*Samuel Hunter,* born in Canada. Enlisted February 12 1862, at Lexington, Mich. Aged 18 years. Fisherman. Deserted August 28, 1863.

*Harrison Jones,* born in Oswego county, N. Y. Enlisted January 23, 1862, at Lexington. Aged 21 years. Laborer. Deserted April —, 1862, from Canton, Michigan.

*Charles Kniling,* born in Ottenberg, Germany. Enlisted November 18, 1861, at Alpena. Aged 34 years. Cooper.

*Heman Keeler,* born in Oneida county, N. Y. Enlisted November 18, 1861, at Lexington. Aged 21 years. Laborer.

*John Kelly,* born in Scotland. Enlisted October 28, 1861, at Lexington. Aged 19 years. Student.

*Phillip Knapp*, born in Chicago, Ill. Enlisted March 5, 1862, at Lexington. Aged 18 years. Farmer. Appointed Corporal April 31, 1863.

*Daniel A. Larkin*, born in N. Y. Enlisted February 12, 1862, at Lexington. Aged 18 years. Farmer.

*Alonzo Louks*, born in Franklin county, Vt. Enlisted Nov. 2, 1861, at Rubicon. Aged 23 years. Farmer.

*Paul Laviolet*, born in Canada. Enlisted January 6, 1862, at Lexington. Aged 35 years. Laborer.

*James Lewis*, born in Canada. Enlisted February 10, 1862, at Lexington. Aged 18 years. Farmer. Died June 3, 1862, at Farmington, Mississippi, of inflammation of lungs.

*Socrates Lewis*, born in Wayne county, N. Y. Enlisted April 21, 1862, at Lexington. Aged 39 years. Carpenter.

*James Mascall*, born in Canada Enlisted October 25, 1861, at Lexington. Aged 27 years. Farmer.

*Robert ‖Merrick*, born in Kilmamock, Scotland. Enlisted November 6, 1861, at Lexington. Aged 38 years. Farmer.

*Jno. Merrick*, born in Kingston, Canada. Enlisted November 6, 1861, at Lexington. Aged 18 years. Farmer. Died on hospital boat going to Keokuck, Iowa.

*Wm. Miles*, born in Kingston, Canada. Enlisted October 26, 1861, at Huron. Aged 21 years. Laborer.

*Freeman Moore*, born in Penobscot county, Maine. Enlisted November 19, 1861, at Worth. Aged 21 years. Farmer.

*John D. McKenzie*, born in Dover, C. W. Enlisted December 18, 1861, at Lexington. Aged 37 years. Farmer.

*John McViger*, born in Antrim, Ireland. Enlisted November 5, 1861, at Lexington. Aged 44 years. Laborer.

*Berry B. Miller*, born in Oakland, Mich. Enlisted July 20, 1862, at Lexington. Aged 24 years. Lumberman.

*Thomas Oldfield*, born in Lancolnshire, England. Enlisted November 29, 1861, at Lexington. Aged 30 years. Sailor. Appointed Corporal July 1, 1862.

*Ralph Potts*, born in N. Y. Enlisted November 14, 1861, at Lexington. Aged 42 years. Farmer. Discharged at Nashville, Tennessee.

*Myron Potts*, born in Sanilac county, Mich. Enlisted Nov. 15, 1861, at Lexington. Aged 18 years. Farmer. Transferred to regular service December 19, 1862.

*Wm. Boachert*, born in Prussia. Enlisted October 26, 1861, at Huron. Aged 18 years. Laborer. Transferred to regular service December 19, 1862.

*John Patterson*, born in White Church, Canada. Enlisted November 14, 1861, at Lexington. Aged 21 years. Farmer.

*Thomas Parkiss*, born in Essex, England. Enlisted Nov. 23, 1861, at Lexington. Aged 18 years. Sailor.

*Charles Randall*, born in Brantford, Canada. Enlisted October 28, 1861, at —, Sanilac county. Aged 25 years. Carpenter.

*Nelson F. Ross*, born in Franklin, Vt. Enlisted November 4, 1861, at Marion. Aged 31 years. Farmer.

*Ananias Rockwood*, born in Crosby, Canada. Enlisted January 11, 1862, at Lexington. Aged 24 years. Farmer.

*Wm. Robinson*, born in Scotland. Enlisted August 25, 1862, at Lexington. Aged 27 years. Sawyer.

*Levi Smith*, born in Canada East. Enlisted November 12, 1861, at Rubicon. Aged 18 years. Farmer.

*Walter Seymour*, born in Dundas, Canada East. Enlisted January 3, 1862, at Lexington. Aged 31 years. Farmer.

*Archibald H. Springstein*, born in Wentworth, Canada. Enlisted October 25, 1861, at Lexington. Aged 24 years. Minister of the Gospel. Discharged November 19, 1863, at Nashville, Tennessee.

*Grover Scollay*, born in Macklain county, Canada. Enlisted November 9, 1861, at Lexington. Aged 23 years. Laborer.

*Augustus Sherman*, born in Erie county, Penn. Enlisted October 22, 1861, at Delaware. Aged 26 years. Farmer.

*Richard Sherman*, born in Summerset county, England. Enlisted November 19, 1861, at Worth. Aged 28 years. Farmer.

*Geo. W. Sample*, born in Montgomery county, N. Y. Enlisted November 18, 1861, at Lexington. Aged 30 years. Farmer.

*Homer Stiles*, born in Southampton, Mass. Enlisted Dec. 5, 1861, at Forestville. Aged 28 years. Laborer. Died at Farmington, Mississippi, June 26, 1862, of fever.

*Webster Stevens*, born in Brock, C. W. Enlisted November 26, 1861, at Lexington. Aged 28 years. Farmer. Died May 6, 1863, at Nashville, Tennessee, of inflammation of bowels.

*Cornelius See*, born in Jefferson county, N. Y. Enlisted August 22, 1861, at Forestville. Aged 21 years. Laborer.

*Charles Sissman*, born in Prussia. Enlisted March 3, 1862, at Forestville. Aged 18 years. Fisherman.

*Alexander Stacy*, born in Quebec, Canada. Enlisted February 10, 1862, at Lexington. Aged 37 years. Farmer.

*Horace Shaver*, born in Canada. Enlisted February 12, 1862, at Forestville. Aged 25 years. Farmer.

*Orson T. Taylor*, born in Hampshire county, Mass. Enlisted August 23, 1862, at Forestville. Aged 37 years. Fisherman.

*Samuel Utley*, born in Canada. Enlisted October 25, 1861, at Lexington. Aged 19 years. Farmer.

*Alexander Vanbrocklen*, born in Long Point, Canada. Enlisted July 21, 1862, at Lexington. Aged 26 years. Farmer.

*Albion S. Vincent*, born in Rich, Canada. Enlisted August 13, 1862, at Lexington. Aged 24 years. Farmer.

*Joseph Vancamp*, born in Matilda, C. W. Enlisted November 5, 1861, at Worth. Aged 43 years. Farmer. Died in Hospital at Keokuck, Iowa, August 22, 1862, of chronic diarrhœa.

*Samuel Vancamp*, born in Dorlington, C. W. Enlisted November 5, 1861, at Worth. Aged 25 years. Farmer.

*Lemuel Wixon*, born in Toronto, C. E. Enlisted December 28, 1861, at Lexington. Aged 30 years. Farmer. Died July 15, 1862, in General Hospital, near Farmington, Mississippi, of fever.

*John Wixon*, born in Pinckney, Canada. Enlisted October 25, 1861, at Lexington. Aged 21 years. Farmer. Discharged at Nashville, Tennessee, February 12, 1863.

*Daniel Wixon*, born in Sanilac county, Mich. Enlisted October 28, 1861, at Lexington. Aged 18 years. Farmer.

*Lyman Ward*, born in Ontario county, Canada. Enlisted November 2, 1861, at Worth. Aged 25 years. Farmer.

*Charles Whaley*, born in Baden, Germany. Enlisted Nov. 4, 1861, at Lexington. Aged 24 years. Sailor.

*George Wilson*, born in Rophine, Scot. Enlisted October 28, 1861, at Lexington. Aged 28 years. Laborer.

*Edward Wilkes*, born in Maine. Enlisted October 21, 1861, at Lexington. Aged 23 years. Laborer.

*Wm. Webster*, born in Otsego county, N. Y. Enlisted Nov. 25, 1861, at Forestville. Aged 47 years. Farmer.

*Peter Wyckman*, born in Brock, Canada. Enlisted November 26, 1861, at Forestville. Aged 23 years. Laborer. Discharged January 3, 1863, at St. Louis, Missouri.

*Richard Welch*, born in Canada. Enlisted January 23, 1862, at Lexington. Aged 18 years. Farmer. Discharged July 13, 1862, at Detroit, Michigan.

*Benjamin F. Youngs*, born in Royal Oak, Mich. Enlisted November 12, 1861, at Huron. Aged 25 years. Fisherman. Died at Louisville, Kentucky.

*Peter G. Zoll*, born in Dantzic, Prussia. Enlisted November 5, 1861, at Lexington. Aged 35 years.. Farmer. Discharged November 21, 1862, at Evansville, Indiana.


## COMPANY E.

Company E was recruited by Wm. Hartsuff, of Port Huron, St. Clair county, Michigan, who received authority to raise a company from Gov. Blair. He began recruiting men October 18, 1861, and entered camp November 30th with 30 men. Daniel D. Leach, of China, St. Clair county, entered camp about the same time with a number of men, and these two parts of companies were drilled together and finally consolidated—Wm. Hartsuff as Captain, and D. Leach as 1st Lieutenant. The company was full to the minimum January 3,

1862, and mustered February 6th, with an aggregate of ninety-seven men. It was raised principally in St. Clair county, and was known at its first organization as Scarritt Guards.

COMMISSIONED OFFICERS.

*Capt. Wm. Hartsuff* was born in Seneca county, New York, in the year 1835. He was married at Port Huron, St. Clair county, Michigan. At the time of entering the military service he was engaged in the mercantile business. He received his commission as Captain from October 1, 1861, and was transferred to Brig. Gen. Hartsuff's Staff September 10, 1862. His brother, Gen. Hartsuff, was subsequently promoted to Major General, and Capt. Hartsuff was made Assistant Inspector General, with rank and pay of Lieutenant Colonel.

*1st Lieut. Daniel D. Leach* was born in Oneida county, New York, in the year 1810. He had served sixteen years in the regular service previous to volunteering in this regiment. He received commission as 1st Lieutenant from October 1, 1861. He died at Camp Big Springs, Mississippi, July 7, 1862, of cholera morbus. His death was sudden. On the morning of the day he died he was stirring about camp and apparently well. During the day was taken sick and at night had an attack of cholera morbus, which proved fatal.

*2d Lieut. Edward F. Bunce* was born in Windsor, Vermont, June 23, 1822. While quite young he moved with his parents to Michigan. They settled on the bank of St. Clair River, about four miles from where Port Huron now stands—then marked only by a wilderness through which the Indian made his narrow trail—where he passed his chilhood. At the age of 8 years moved with his parents to Jefferson county, N. Y., where in 1842 he was married, and resided until 1846, when he went with his brother to Michigan and purchased a tract of land and engaged in the lumbering business. He remained in this business until entering the regiment. Received his commission as 2d Lieutenant October 1, 1861. After arriving at the seat òf war, during the campaign before Corinth, his health failed and he was obliged to resign. His resignation was accepted June 20, 1862.

NON-COMMISSIONED OFFICERS.

### Sergeants.

1st. *F. M. Vanderburg* was born in the city of New York, August 27, 1838. Moved to Port Huron, Michigan, in the fall of 1854. Previous to entering the military service he had been employed for some time in a banking house in Port Huron, as book-keeper. He enlisted at Port Huron, November 15, 1861. Appointed to rank as 1st Sergeant from date of enlistment. He was promoted to 2d Lieutenant June 20, 1862, *vice* Bunce resigned, and promoted to 1st Lieutenant August 1, 1862, *vice* Leach, deceased. Lieut. Vanderberg died April 18, 1863, of wounds received April 10th, on the Nashville and Chattanooga Railroad, when in charge of a guard on a passenger train returning from Murfreesboro. They were fired upon by guerrillas, and Lieut. Vanderburg rallied his men, and it was not until he received the third wound that he fell. His father arriving from Michigan before his death, took the remains home to his afflicted relatives and friends.

2d. *Wm. McDonald,* born in Amsterdam, Montgomery county, New York, October 13, 1826. Moved to Michigan in May, 1854, and was married at Lockport July 18, 1858. He was employed in the lumbering and mercantile business previous to entering the army. At the time of joining Captain Hartsuff's company he was offered the position of 2d Lieutenant, and accordingly left his occupation and engaged in enlisting men. After having enlisted some thirty-three men it was found that the company could not be filled in time for the 10th, and a consolidation was ordered, and upon a consultation of the officers, McDonald withdrew his claims and took the position of 2d Sergeant. He was appointed to rank as Sergeant from date of enlistment. Promoted to 1st Sergeant June 20, 1862, and Aug. 1, 1862, was promoted to 2d Lieutenant, *vice*

Vanderburg, promoted, and March 31, 1863, was promoted to 1st Lieutenant Company F, *vice* Hart, promoted.

3d. *Wm. E. Westbrook*, born in Columbus, Mich. Enlisted November 10, 1861, at China. Aged 20 years. Clerk. Appointed to rank as Sergeant from date of enlistment. Transferred to the 24th Michigan Volunteer Infantry, by promotion, July 28, 1862.

4th. *Owen C. Corbett*, born in Montreal, Canada. Enlisted January 21, 1862, at Detroit. Aged 24 years. Clerk. Appointed to rank as Sergeant from date of enlistment.

5th. *Danforth P. Goss*, born in Bunfield, Mass. Enlisted November 20, 1861, at Kenokee. Aged 44 years. Laborer. Appointed to rank as Sergeant from date of enlistment. Discharged January 13, 1863, at Evansville, Indiana.

*Corporals.*

1st. *Wm. Whitby*, born in Yorkshire, England. Enlisted November 30, 1861, at Lakeport. Aged 44 years. Farmer. Appointed to rank as Corporal from date of enllstment. Deserted April 23, 1862, from Detroit, Michigan.

2d. *Orange F. Linsday*, born in Egypt, Mich. Enlisted November 11, 1831, at China. Aged 18 years. Farmer. Appointed to rank as Corporal from date of enlistment.

3d. *James G. Brown*, born in Scotland. Enlisted October 31, 1861, at Kenokee. Aged 44 years. Farmer. Appointed to rank as Corporal from date of enlistment.

4th. *James Farrell*, born in Canada. Enlisted Dec. 2, 1861, at Port Huron. Aged 22 years. Potter. Appointed to rank as Corporal from date of enlistment.

5th. *Eugene K. Chase*, born in Jefferson county, N. Y. Enlisted October 15, 1861, at Kenokee. Aged 21 years. Farmer. Appointed to rank as Corporal from the date of enlistment.

6th. *Joseph Moore*, born in Brant county, Canada. Enlisted December 2, 1861, at Port Huron. Aged 23 years. Laborer. Appointed to rank as Corporal from date of enlistment. Promoted to Sergeant April 3, 1863.

7th. *Edmond Shirts*, born in Wayne county, N. Y. Enlisted January 3, 1862, at Capac. Aged 20 years. Farmer. Appointed to rank as Corporal from date of enlistment. Died June 21, 1862, in General Hospital near Farmington, Mississippi, of consumption.

8th. *Edward Phillips*, born in London, England. Enlisted October 31, 1861, at Kenokee. Aged 32 years. Farmer. Appointed to rank as Corporal from date of enlistment. Discharged October 9, 1862, at St. Louis, Missouri.

### Musicians.

*John Pomroy*, *Drummer*, born in Macomb county, Mich. Enlisted January 3, 1862, at Capac. Aged 18 years. Sash maker.

### Privates.

*Elihue Ackerman*, born in Jefferson county, N. Y. Enlisted November 28, 1861, at Clyde. Aged 33 years. Farmer. Discharged July 24, 1863, at Detroit, Michigan.

*Silas Ackerman*, born in Jefferson county, N. Y. Enlisted November 26, 1861, at Clyde. Aged 21 years. Farmer.

*Adna Allen*, born in Genesee county, N. Y. Enlisted October 12, 1861, at China. Aged 29 years. Farmer. Appointed Corporal September 16, 1862.

*Luther Allen*, born in Jefferson county, N. Y. Enlisted December 19, 1861, at Clyde. Aged 18 years. Laborer.

*Philander Allen*, born in Oneida county, N. Y. Enlisted November 30, 1861, at Casco. Aged 36 years. Farmer.

*Wm. Ayres*, born in Huntingdon, England. Enlisted Dec. 9, 1861, at —, St. Clair county. Aged 41 years. Laborer.

*John Bennett*, born in Canada. Enlisted November 22, 1861, at Lakeport. Aged 19 years. Farmer. Appointed Corporal September 16, 1862.

*John M. Bartlett*, born in Livingston county, Mass. Enlisted December 18, 1861, at Flint. Aged 44 years. Farmer. Discharged July 10, 1863, at Detroit, Michigan.

*Geo. W Bartlett*, born in Livingston county, N. Y. Enlisted

December 18, 1861, at Flint. Aged 18 years. Farmer. Killed in action April 10, 1863, at Antioch, Tennessee.

*James Beele,* born in Livingston county, N. Y. Enlisted November 4, 1861, at —, St. Clair county. Aged 44 years. Farmer. Transferred to Invalid Corps September 16, 1863.

*Geo. Banfill,* born in Mich. Enlisted January 3, 1862, at Capac. Aged 18 years. Mechanic.

*Artemus Briggs,* born in Vt. Enlisted January 10, 1862, at —, St. Clair county. Aged 28 years. Mechanic.

*James Chapman,* born in Whitby, Canada. Enlisted Nov. 21, 1861, at Casco. Aged 24 years. Farmer. Appointed Corporal July 1, 1862. Promoted to Sergeant Sept. 1, 1862. Died of wounds April 14, 1863, at Antioch, Tennessee.

*J. M. Carrington,* born in Port Huron, Mich. Enlisted Feb. 7, 1862, at Port Huron. Aged 20 years. Clerk. Appointed Corporal March 20, 1862. Promoted to Sergeant July 1, 1862. Promoted to 1st Sergeant Aug. 1, 1862. Discharged January 1, 1864, at camp near Rossville, Georgia.

*Samuel Conley,* born in Belfast, Ireland. Enlisted November 21, 1861, at Lakeport. Aged 32 years. Laborer. Died November 15, 1862, at Lakeport, Michigan.

*Henry A. Cope,* born in Canada. Enlisted October 31, 1861, at Emmet. Aged 22 years. Farmer. Discharged October 9, 1862, at St. Louis, Missouri.

*John Carle,* born in Canada. Enlisted December 26, 1861, at Lakeport. Aged 45 years. Farmer.

*Joel Cross,* born in N. Y. Enlisted August 20, 1862, at Lexington. Aged 34 years. Farmer.

*S. S. E. Cartwright,* born in Schenectady, N. Y. Enlisted October 8, 1861, at Roxand. Aged 24 years. Laborer. Transferred from Company B April 21, 1862.

*Wm. Dunn,* born in Genesee county, N. Y. Enlisted Nov. 21, 1861, at Brockway. Aged 44 years. Laborer. Discharged January 27, 1862, at Cincinnati, Ohio.

*Benjamin Duchene,* born in China, Mich. Enlisted October 27, 1861, at China. Aged 22 years. Laborer.

*James Derr*, nativity unknown. Enlisted March 1, 1862, at
—, St. Clair county. Aged 18 years. Farmer.

*Jeremiah Dorsey*, nativity unknown. Enlisted December 12,
1861, at Clyde. Aged 19 years. Lumberman. Deserted
March 10, 1862, at Flint.

*Wm. Delhooke*, born in Ireland. Enlisted January 13, 1862,
at Lakeport. Aged 33 years. Physician. Discharged January 20, 1863, at Cincinnati, Ohio.

*James Dewar*, born in Scotland. Enlisted January 3, 1862,
at Capac. Aged 29 years. Farmer.

*Wm. Dukee*, born in Devonshire, England. Enlisted Aug.
17, 1863, at Detroit, Michigan. Aged 50 years. Sawyer.

*Benedict Elmer*, born in Otsego county, N. Y. Enlisted
December 18, 1861, at —, St. Clair county. Aged 44 years.
Printer. Discharged April 30, 1862, at St. Louis, Missouri.

*Orange F. Ellsworth*, born in Oakland county, Mich. Enlisted November 22, 1861, at —, St. Clair county. Aged
18 years. Farmer. Died January 2, 1862, at Flint, Michigan,
of inflammation on lungs.

*Michael Flinn*, born in Galway, Ireland. Enlisted December 2, 1861, at Port Huron. Aged 21 years. Laborer.

*Lewis Fecht*, born in Wayne county, Mich. Enlisted Nov.
29, 1861, at Clyde. Aged 20 years. Blacksmith.

*S. A. Flannegan*, born in Clyde, Mich. Enlisted November
29, 1861, at Port Huron. Aged 18 years. Farmer.

*Geo. L. Fairfield*, born in Springfield, Mass. Enlisted November 6, 1861, at China. Aged 20 years. Farmer. Died
July 8, 1862, at General Hospital, near Farmington, Miss., of
fever.

*Edward Fry*, born in St. Clair county, Mich. Enlisted
November 28, 1861, at Kenokee, Michigan. Aged 18 years.
Teamster.

*Isaac D. Frazur*, born in Canada. Enlisted November 16,
1861, at Casco. Aged 22 years. Farmer. Died July 17, 1862,
at Hamburg, Tennessee.

*James Forbes*, born in Canada. Enlisted January 13, 1862,
at China. Aged 35 years. Laborer.

*John W. Garner*, born in Canada. Enlisted December 20, 1861, at Lakeport. Aged 25 years. Laborer.

*Henry Graham*, born in Frontenac, Canada. Enlisted January 10, 1862, at Lakeport. Aged 31 years. Blacksmith.

*John Henries*, born in Germany. Enlisted December 3, 1861, at —, St. Clair county. Aged 26 years. Laborer. Appointed Corporal April 3, 1863.

*Nathan Hull*, born in Canada. Enlisted January 28, 1862, at Port Huron. Aged 28 years.. Farmer. Deserted March 7, 1862, from Flint, Michigan.

*Charles Hull*, born in Canada. Enlisted January 28, 1862, at Port Huron. Aged 20 years. Farmer. Deserted March 7, 1862, at Flint, Michigan.

*John Johnson*, born in Glasgow, Scotland. Enlisted Dec. 11, 1861, at Port Huron. Aged 32 years. Laborer.

*Kirk Johnson*, born in Wayne county, N. Y. Enlisted March 10, 1862, at Whales. Aged 21 years. Farmer.

*James Johnston*, born in Birmingham, England. Enlisted November 1, 1861, at —, St. Clair County. Aged 28 years. Farmer. Appointed Sergeant July 1, 1862.

*Henry W. Johnson*, born in Mass. Enlisted at Lakeport, December 18, 1861. Aged 24 years. Sailor.

*Elias Jones*, born in China, Mich. Enlisted November 11, 1861, at China. Aged 18 years. Laborer. Discharged Feb. 29, 1863, at St. Louis, Missouri.

*Joanathn Jones*, born in China, Mich. Enlisted November 1,1, 1861, at China. Aged 20 years. Laborer.

*Wm. Jones*, born in London, Eng. Enlisted January 6, 1862, at Clyde. Aged 24 years. Joiner. Killed in action, at Antioch, Tennessee, April 10, 1863.

*Merrill Jones*, born in Canada. Enlisted December 16, 1861, at Lakeport. Aged 23 years. Laborer. Deserted January —, 1862, from Flint, Michigan.

*John W. Jennings*, born in England. Enlisted October 9, 1862, at Nashville, Tenn. Aged 14 years. Laborer.

*John C. Kelly*, born in Bellville, Canada. Enlisted August

22, 1862, at Lexington. Aged 23 years. Farmer. Died at Chattanooga, Tenn., January 13, 1864.

*Wm. Knospe*, born in Germany. Enlisted January 9, 1862, at Port Huron. Aged 40 years. Laborer. Deserted March 13, 1862, from Flint.

*James Lowe*, born in China, St. Clair county, Mich. Enlisted November 11, 1861, at China. Aged 20 years. Farmer.

*Theophilus Leverre*, nativity unknown. Enlisted December 19, 1861, at Lakeport. Aged 26 years. Occupation unknown.

*Patrick Lane*, born in Ireland. Enlisted November 30, 1861, at Lakeport. Aged 37 years. Laborer.

*James Linen*, born in New York. Enlisted December 30, 1861, at Detroit. Aged 22 years. Farmer.

*Henry H. Lamphier*, born in Pennsylvania. Enlisted January 9, 1862, at —, St. Clair county. Aged 18 years. Farmer.

*Frank H. Morse*, born in St. Clair county, Mich. Enlisted October 29, 1861, at —, St. Clair county. Aged 23 years. Farmer.

*O. F. Morse*, born in New Hampshire. Enlisted November 6, 1861, at —, St. Clair county, Mich. Aged 20 years. Printer. Discharged at Flint, Mich.

*James Murphy*, born in New York. Enlisted November 30, 1861, at Port Huron. Aged 19 years. Laborer. Died April 12, 1863, at Antioch, Tenn., of wounds.

*Sanford Monroe*, born in Windham county, Vt. Enlisted November 13, 1861, at Lakeport. Aged 43 years. Laborer. Died July 10, 1862, at Cincinnati, O., of dysentery.

*Theodore Meyer*, born in Prussia. Enlisted December 6, 1861, at Port Huron. Aged 39 years. Baker. Disappeared from boat on Mississippi River, April 25, 1862.

*Alexander McKay*, born in Southerland county, Scotland. Enlisted January 9, 1862, at Port Huron. Aged 40 years. Printer. Deserted April 22, 1862, from Flint, Mich.

*Julius Milika*, born in Prussia. Enlisted January 9, 1862, at St. Clair. Aged 30 years. Butcher. Deserted September 12, 1862, from Nashville, Tenn. Executed May 15, 1863.

*Lemuel O'Comb*, born in Sanilac county, Mich. Enlisted August 22, 1862, at Lexington. Aged 33 years. Sawyer.

*Wm. H. Parsons*, born in China, Mich. Enlisted November 9, 1861, at China. Aged 19 years. A farmer. Appointed Corporal July 1, 1862.

*John Porter*, born in Canada. Enlisted February 25, 1862, at Flint. Aged 32 years. Sailor. Deserted February 26, 1862, from Flint, Mich.

*John Phillips*, born in Canada. Enlisted December 24, 1861, at Lakeport. Aged 43 years. Laborer.

*Robert Peake*, born in Canada West. Enlisted February 17, 1862, at Port Huron. Aged 18 years. Farmer. Transferred to Invalid Corps December 6, 1863.

*Urias Peake*, born in Canada. Enlisted August 30, 1862, at Lexington. Aged 34 years. Fisherman. Discharged July 24, 1863, at Louisville, Ky.

*Henry J. Palmer*, born in London, England. Enlisted December 25, 1861, at Lakeport, Mich. Aged 25 years. Joiner.

*Albert Papst*, born in York county, C. W. Enlisted April 7, 1863, at Lexington, Mich. Aged 21 years. Farmer.

*John H. Robinson*, born in Medcalf, C. W. Enlisted November 1, 1861, at St. Clair. Aged 18 years. Farmer. Died April 13, 1862, at Nashville, Tenn., of typhoid fever.

*Wm. H. Robinson*, born in Medcalf, C. W. Enlisted November 1, 1861, at Abbottsford. Aged 21 years. Farmer.

*Valentine Rewhle*, born in Baden, Germany. Enlisted November 22, 1861, at St. Clair. Aged 19 years. Farmer.

*Peter Smith*, born in Canada. Enlisted November 25, 1861, at Port Huron. Aged 18 years. Laborer.

*Samuel Smith*, nativity unknown. Enlisted January 3, 1862, at Capac. Aged 36 years. Laborer.

*Wm. H. Smith*, born in Canada. Enlisted December 21, 1861, at Whales. Aged 26 years. Mason. Died November 6, 1862, at St. Louis, Mo., of phthisis pulmonalis.

*Henry Smith*, born in New York. Enlisted February 5, 1862, at Port Huron. Aged 19 years. Laborer.

*Thomas Strickland*, born in Detroit, Mich. Enlisted November 21, 1861, at Lakeport. Aged 29 years. Engineer.

*Robert Settle*, born in Canada. Enlisted November 27, 1861, at Lakeport. Aged 21 years. Farmer. Appointed Corporal April 3, 1863.

*Henry Shelden*, born in Vermont. Enlisted December 3, 1861, at St. Clair. Aged 18 years. Mechanic.

*John Stokes*, born in Canada. Enlisted December 5, 1861, at Lakeport. Aged 30 years. Laborer. Transferred to 4th Reg. Cavalry, December 18, 1862.

*James Simpson*, born in Canada. Enlisted January 6, 1862, at Port Huron. Aged 18 years. Laborer.

*Simon Shirts*, born in Wayne county, N. Y. Enlisted January 3, 1862, at Capac. Aged 22 years. Farmer. Discharged December 5, 1862, at Keokuk, Iowa.

*Robert Stevens*, born in Canada. Enlisted December 16, 1861, at Lakeport. Aged 23 years. Farmer.

*Geo. Spranklin*, born in New York. Enlisted January 20, 1862, at Port Huron. Aged 24 years. Peddlar. Deserted March 21, 1862, from Flint, Mich.

*Abram Savage*, born in Cayuga county, N. Y. Enlisted November 18, 1861, at Roxand. Aged 45 years. Mechanic. Transferred from Company B, April 21, 1862. Discharged July 16, 1862, at Detroit, Mich.

*Francis Thomas*, born in Wayne county, Mich. Enlisted November 25, 1861, at St. Clair. Aged 37 years. Mason. Appointed Corporal February 10, 1863.

*Frank Tacy*, born in St. Lawrence county, N. Y. Enlisted January 10, 1862, at Lakeport. Aged 30 years. Farmer. Killed in action April 10, 1863, at Antioch, Tenn.

*John D. Tippan*, born in Ireland. Enlisted February 5, 1862, at Port Huron. Aged 35 years. Sailor. Discharged December 29, 1862, at Cincinnati, O.

*Ezekiel Townsend*, born in Canada. Enlisted November 21, 1861, at Clyde. Aged 39 years. Farmer. Died January 26, 1862, at Flint, Mich.

*Perry Tracy*, born in Cork, Ireland. Enlisted August 17, 1863, at Detroit, Mich. Agéd 25 years. Laborer.

*Michael Williams*, born in Lockport, N. Y. Enlisted December 18, 1861, at Lakeport. Agod 20 years. Teamster.

*Henry Woodcock*, born in Lenox county, Canada. Enlisted November 30, 1861, at Lakeport. Aged 37 years. Farmer. Discharged August 13, 1861, at Detroit, Mich.

*Mathew Wasey*, born in England. Enlisted December 6, 1861, at St. Clair. Aged 37 years. Farmer.

*Peter Welch*, born in Ireland. Enlisted December 20, 1861, at Port Huron. Aged 35 years. Laborer. Discharged February 6, 1863, at Evansville, Ind.

*Geo. Watkins*, born in England. Enlisted January 13, 1862, at Lakeport. Aged 40 years. Laborer. Appointed Corporal July 1, 1862.

*Charles H. Westbrook*, born in Pennsylvania. Enlisted December 26, 1861, at Port Huron. Aged 26 years.. Carpenter.

*Ebenezer Williams*, born in New York. Enlisted October 30, 1861, at Roxand. Aged 24 years. Farmer. Transferred from Company B, April 21, 1862. Discharged July 17, 1862, at Detroit, Mich.

*George Wood*, born in Ireland. Enlisted August 22, 1862, at Lexington. Aged 26 years. Farmer.

*Edward Young*, born in Franklin, N. Y. Enlisted November 26, 1861, at Lakeport. Aged 33 years. Laborer. Discharged October 4, 1862, at St. Louis, Mo.

*Freeman Young*, born in Franklin, N. Y. Enlisted November 26, 1861, at Lakeport. Aged 35 years. Farmer.

*Alexander Young*, born in Franklin, N. Y. Enlisted January 10, 1862, at Lakeport. Aged 31 years. Farmer.

*Levi Young*, born in New York. Enlisted November 26, 1861, at Lakeport. Aged 18 years. Laborer. Deserted January 20, 1862, from Flint, Mich.

## COMPANY F.

The authority to raise this Company was received by Walter P. Beach, October 23, 1861, from Gov. Blair. Mr. Beach lived in Almont, Lapeer county, Mich., and in that county most of the company was recruited. The company entered the camp of instruction at Flint, December 4, 1861, with sixty-two men. It was full to a minimum, January 10, 1862, and mustered into United States service February 6, 1862. It was known under its primary organization as the Holt Guards.

### COMMISSIONED OFFICERS.

*Capt. Walter P. Beach,* was born in Hartford, Conn., in the year 1823, and moved to Michigan and settled in Lapeer county in 1840. He was married in Boston, Mass., in 1848. Previous to entering the military service he was engaged in mercantile business. He received a commission as Captain from October 1st, 1861. He resigned June 26, 1862, on account of ill health.

*1st Lieut. Noah H. Hart,* was born in the town of Cromwell, Litchfield county, Conn., October 30, 1813. He was one of the pioneers of the State of Michigan, having moved there with his father's family as early as 1832. Having pursued his law studies under the supervision of E. H. Thomson, he was admitted to the bar in 1841, and the following year was married in Attica, Wyoming county, N. Y. For many years he held the various offices of County Clerk, Prosecuting Attorney, Postmaster and Justice of the Peace in Lapeer, Mich. In 1850 he was Delegate to the State Constitutional Convention, and the following year was elected member of the State Legislature. He entered the military service at the time of the first enlistments in the "Holt Guards," and received a commission as 1st Lieutenant from October 1, 1861. He was promoted to Captain, March 31, 1861, *vice* Lyon, resigned.

*2d Lieut. Calvin M. Hall,* was born in Erie county, N. Y.,

January 10, 1830. Moved to Michigan in June, 1832, with his parents, who took up their residence in Washington, Macomb county. His father died July 13, 1839. After the death of his father he left home and worked upon a farm summers and attended school winters, until he was twenty-two years of age. The succeeding summer he was engaged with a party of surveyers in the north part of Michigan, in subdividing townships into sections. Since that time he had been most of the time engaged in exploring or surveying in the north part of Michigan until entering the military service. He was married in Almont, Lapeer county, Mich., in November, 1860. He received a commission as 2d Lieutenant from October 1st, 1861. On account of ill health he resigned June 2, 1862.

NON-COMMISSIONED OFFICERS.
*Sergeants.*

1st. *Wm. H. Corkett,* was born in Otsego county, N. Y., September 8, 1827. He was married November 9, 1845, in Onondaga county, N. Y., and moved to Lapeer, Lapeer county, Mich., April 5, 1854. His occupation before entering the army was painting. He entered the military service October 25, 1861, and was subsequently, by an unanimous vote of the company, elected 1st Sergeant, and was appointed to rank as such from date of enlistment. He was promoted to 2d Lieutenant June 2, 1862, *vice* Hall, resigned. He was, by an order for recruiting, sent to Michigan on that service in July, 1862, and returned to the regiment April 12, 1863. Resigned June 18, 1863, on account of ill health.

2d. *John S. Fletcher,* was born in Windsor, Vt.; enlisted November 2, 1861, at Waterford. Aged 36 years. Peddlar. Appointed to rank as Sergeant from date of enlistment. Promoted to 1st Sergeant June 2, 1862. Promoted to 2d Lieutenant, *vice* Corkett, resigned, July 15th, 1863.

3d. *Samuel Starmers,* born in Clark, C. W. Enlisted November 21, 1861, at Dryden, Mich. Aged 25 years. Farmer. Appointed to rank as Sergeant from date of enlistment. Promoted to 1st Sergeant July 15, 1863.

4th. *Peter Jackson*, nativity unknown. Enlisted November 4, 1861, at Groveland, Mich. Aged 25 years. Farmer. Appointed to rank as Sergeant from date of enlistment. Discharged July 16, 1862, at Detroit.

5th. *Smith C. P. Williams*, born in Genesee, Mich. Enlisted November 14, 1861, at Hadley. Aged 19 years. Blacksmith. Appointed to rank as Sergeant from date of enlistment. Taken prisoner September 30, 1863, at Wicklow's Ferry, on Tennessee River, near Bridgeport, Ala.

### Corporals.

1st. *Andrew Currey*, born in Genesee, N. Y. Enlisted October 29, at Almont. Aged 19 years Farmer. Appointed to rank as Corporal from the date of enlistment.

2d. *Andrew W. Bradley*, born in Oxford, C. W. Enlisted December 20, 1861, at Almont. Aged 34 years.. Carpenter. Appointed to rank as Corporal from date of enlistment. Promoted to Sergeant, November 1, 1862.

3d. *Lewis B. Wells*, born in Crawford, Penn. Enlisted December 26, 1861, at Grand Blanc. Aged 24 years. Harness maker. Appointed to rank as Corporal from date of enlistment. Promoted to Sergeant September 1, 1862.

4th. *Benjamin Cummings*, born in Oxford, Canada. Enlisted December 23, 1861, at Almont. Aged 24 years. Farmer. Appointed to rank as Corporal from date of enlistment. Died August 1, 1862, at Evansville, Ind., of consumption.

5th. *Isaac Abbott*, born in Onondaga, N. Y. Enlisted December 18, 1861, at Arcada, Mich. Aged 24 years. Mason. Appointed to rank as Corporal from date of enlistment.

6th. *Luther M. Ellison*, born in Macomb county, Mich. Enlisted December 13, 1861, at Hadley. Aged 26 years. Mason. Appointed to rank as Corporal from date of enlistment. Discharged July 1, 1862, at Evansville, Ind.

7th. *Wm. A. France*, born in Warren, N. J. Enlisted November 8, 1861, at Independence. Aged 22 years. Farmer. Appointed to rank as Corporal from date of enlistment.

8th. *Morgan D. Mercer*, born in Oakland, Mich. Enlisted November 12th, 1861, at Oregon. Aged 24 years. Farmer. Appointed to rank as Corporal from date of enlistment.

## Musicians.

1st. *Ezra B. Madison, drummer*, born in New York. Enlisted January 10, 1862, at Hadley. Aged 26 years. Farmer. Appointed principal musician January 12, 1862.

2d. *Corridon E. Foote, drummer*, born in Genesee county, Mich. Enlisted January 9, 1862, at Flint. Aged 13 years. School-boy.

## Privates.

*Wm. Armstrong*, born in Erie, N. Y. Enlisted November 2, 1861, at Almont. Aged 20 years. Farmer. Discharged January 17, 1863, at Detroit, Mich.

*Geo. Alger*, born in Lapeer, Mich. Enlisted November 18, 1861, at Berlin. Aged 17 years. Farmer.

*John G. Alport*, born in Seneca, N. Y. Enlisted December 31, 1861, at Flint. Aged 22 years. Clerk.

*James W. Armstrong*, born in Erie, N. Y. Enlisted April 21, 1862, at Flint, Mich. Aged 45 years. Mechanic. Appointed Commissary Sergeant July 10, 1862.

*Samuel H. Burton*, born in Oswego, N. Y. Enlisted November 2, 1861, at Dryden. Aged 28 years. Farmer. Discharged July 23, 1862, at St. Louis, Mo.

*Wm. A. Blair*, born in Canada West. Enlisted October 29, 1861, at Almont. Aged 22 years. Farmer. Dropped as a deserter May 1, 1863, by order of Lieut. Col. Dickerson.

*Ruben Bradshaw*, born in Macomb county, Mich. Enlisted December 30, 1861, at Oregon. Aged 21 years. Farmer.

*Norman Burton*, born in Oswego, N. Y. Enlisted November 30, 1861, at Almont. Aged 18 years. Farmer.

*Joseph Brooks*, born in Lapeer, Mich. Enlisted at Flint, February 7, 1862. Aged 20 years. Farmer.

*Lawrence D. Bourk*, born in Tipperary, Ireland. Enlisted

November 30, 1861, at Almont. Aged 19 years. Farmer. Discharged January 20, 1863, at St. Louis, Mo.

*Colvin O. Bently*, born in Macomb, Mich. Enlisted January 10, 1862, at Oregon. Aged 18 years. Farmer. Appointed Corporal September 1, 1862.

*Richard R. Boyle*, born in Perth, Canada. Enlisted February 3, 1862, at North Branch. Aged 32 years Tailor. Appointed Corporal September 1, 1862. Killed at Nashville, Tenn., July 13, 1863.

*Wm. R. Bacon*, born in Portage, Ohio. Enlisted February 18, 1862, at Flint. Aged 44 years. Farmer. Discharged May 4, 1863, at Evansville, Ind.

*John E. Becraft*, born in Byron, Canada. Enlisted February 16, 1862, at Almont. Aged 39 years. Farmer. Discharged June 15, 1863, at Detroit, Mich.

*John Benham*, nativity unknown, and no description of him was ever placed upon record. He died January 17, 1862, at Flint, of congestion on the lungs.

*John Cady*, born in Chemung, N. Y. Enlisted November 18, 1861, at Independence. Aged 23 years. Well-digger Died June 14, 1862, at St. Louis, Mo., of fever.

*Geo. Crankshaw*, born in Onondaga, N. Y. Enlisted November 16, 1861, at Elba. Aged 19 years. Farmer.

*Jacob Crankshaw*, born in Onondaga, N. Y. Enlisted November 16, 1861, at Elba. Aged 21 years. Blacksmith.

*Daniel Comton*, born in New York. Enlisted January 10, 1862, at Oregon. Aged 20 years. Farmer. Deserted before muster, February 6, 1862, and has not been heard of since.

*Geo. Clark*, born in Hampton, Mass. Enlisted January 10, 1862, at Elba. Aged 28 years. Farmer.

*John Chase*, born in Elgin, C. W. Enlisted December 10, 1861, at North Branch. Aged 44 years. Farmer.

*Alfred Chase*, born in Elgin, C. W. Enilsted December 10, 1861, at North Branch. Aged 17 years. Farmer.

*Franklin L. Carpenter*, born in Lapeer, Mich. Enlisted March 21, 1862, at Almont. Aged 21 years. Farmer. Discharged September 8, 1862, at Evansville, Ind.

*James E. Calkins,* born in Erie, N. Y. Enlisted June 2, 1863, at Detroit, Mich. Aged 40 years. Farmer.

*James Davis,* born in Macomb, Mich. Enlisted February 7, 1862, at —, Macomb county, Mich. Aged 22 years. Blacksmith.

*Franklin Evans,* born in Middleburg, Mass. Enlisted November 1, 1861, at Lapeer. Aged 50 years. Farmer.

*John Edwards,* born in New London, Canada. Enlisted December 8, 1861, at Independence. Aged 30 years. Wagonmaker.

*Edward Evans,* born in Onondaga, N. Y. Enlisted November 25, 1861, at —, Lapeer county, Mich. Aged 31 years. Farmer.

*Aaron Furgerson,* born in Macomb, Mich. Enlisted November 25, 1861, at Almont. Aged 19 years. Farmer.

*Warren Fisher,* born in Wooster, Mass. Enlisted January 5, 1862, at Almont. Aged 39 years. Farmer.

*Linas G. Fisher,* born in Lapeer, Mich. Enlisted January 5, 1862, at Almont. Aged 26 years. Farmer.

*Samuel J. Gibbs,* born in Vermont. Enlisted January 21, 1862, at Almont. Aged 18 years. Farmer. Discharged September 8, 1862, at Camp Chase, Ohio.

*Aaron Gummerson,* born in Macomb, Mich. Enlisted December 18, 1861, at Lapeer. Aged 30 years. Blacksmith.

*Daniel W. Gregory,* born in Oakland county, Mich. Enlisted January 21, 1862, at Rochester. Aged 17 years. Laborer.

*Wm. Glover,* born in Burlington, Vt. Enlisted November 2, 1862, at Almont. Aged 38 years. Farmer.

*Nathaniel Greenman,* born in Macomb, Mich. Enlisted February 15, 1862, at Almont. Aged 22 years. Farmer. Died October 22, 1862, at Nashville, Tenn., of congestion of brain.

*James Greenwood,* born in Ireland. Enlisted May 26, 1863, at Newport, Mich. Aged 40 years. Shoemaker.

*M. M. Hedges,* born in Washington, Vt. Enlisted December 22, 1861, at North Branch. Aged 31 years. Joiner. Appointed Sergeant May 12, 1862.

11

*Amos Hurd*, born in Lapeer, Mich. Enlisted November 19, 1861, at Lapeer. Aged 24 years. Farmer.

*Horace F. Horton*, born in Monroe, N. Y. Enlisted November 22, 1861, at Metamora. Aged 20 years. Farmer.

*Martin Heenan*, born in Tipperary, Ireland. Enlisted November 2, 1861, at Almont. Aged 33 years. Farmer.

*Cornelius Howard*, born in Lapeer, Mich. Enlisted December 13, 1861, at Dryden. Aged 20 years. Farmer.

*Edward Huston*, born in Oakland county, Mich. Enlisted December 15, 1861, at White Lake. Aged 17 years. Farmer.

*Edward A. Hough*, born in Lapeer, Mich. Enlisted December 14, 1861, at Almont. Aged 24 years. Farmer.

*Elizier J. Hathaway*, born in Canada West. Enlisted October 27, 1861, at Almont. Aged 17 years. Farmer. Discharged July 23, 1862, at Camp Dennison, Ohio.

*Elger S. Hathaway*, born in New York. Enlisted November 18, 1861, at Almont. Aged 56 years. Farmer. Died August 9, 1862, at Tuscumbia, Ala., of fever.

*Peter Hannan*, born in Kings, Ireland. Enlisted November 25, 1861, at Almont. Aged 44 years. Farmer.

*David Hill*, born in Livingston, N. Y. Enlisted November 18, 1861, at Almont. Aged 48 years. Farmer.

*Abram Horning*, born in Wentworth, C. W. Enlisted February 20, 1862, at Lapeer. Aged 44 years. Farmer. Discharged July 10, 1862, at Detroit, Mich.

*James O. Hodgson*, born in Onondaga, N. Y. Enlisted November 30, 1861, at —, Lapeer county. Aged 23 years. Farmer.

*Albert Hascall*, born in Lapeer, Mich. Enlisted December 13, 1861, at Arcadia. Aged 24 years. Farmer.

*Thomas Langworthy*, born in Columbia, N. Y. Enlisted October 29, 1861, at —, Lapeer county. Aged 30 years. Farmer. Appointed Corporal February 6, 1862.

*John Lathrope*, born in Onondaga, N. Y. Enlisted November 30, 1861, at Almont, Mich. Aged 44 years. Farmer.

*Wm. Lucas*, born in Oxford, England. Enlisted December 10, 1861, at North Branch. Aged 41 years. Farmer.

*Cornelius McMonegal*, born in Dunnegal, Ireland. Enlisted November 2, 1861, at Almont. Aged 39 years. Farmer. Appointed Corporal November 1, 1862.

*Edward Morgan*, born in Lapeer, Mich. Enlisted November 26, 1861, at Almont. Aged 18 years. Farmer. Died February 5, 1863, at Nashville, Tenn., of typhoid fever.

*Albert Middleditch*, born in Lapeer, Mich. Enlisted November 26, 1861, at Almont. Aged 18 years.. Farmer.

*James E. Mundy*, born in Oakland, Mich. Enlisted December 8, 1861, at Waterford. Aged 19 years. Farmer.

*Wm. Mulkin*, born in Chateny, N. Y. Enlisted December 13, 1861, at Lapeer. Aged 31 years. Mason. Died July 14, 1862, at general Hospital near Farmington, Miss., of fever.

*Robert J. McConkey*, born in Kent, N. Y. Enlisted December 28, 1861, at Almont. Aged 25 years. School-teacher. Deserted July 31, 1862, from Tuscumbia, Ala.

*George Morrison*, born in Almont, Mich. Enlisted January 21, 1862, at Almont. Aged 17 years. Farmer.

*Clinton Miller*, born in Macomb, Mich. Enlisted February 22, 1862, at —, Macomb county, Mich. Aged 19 years. Farmer.

*Oscar Moore*, born in Canada West. Enlisted November 21, 1861, at Elba. Aged 19 years. Laborer. Deserted before muster. Dropped from rolls May 1, 1863, as a deserter, by order of Lieut. Col. C. J. Dickerson.

*James Manery*, born in Down, Ireland. Enlisted August 13, 1862, at Detroit. Aged 40 years. Farmer.

*John A. Miller*, born in Jolliett, Ill. Enlisted June 2, 1863, at Detroit, Mich. Aged 26 years. Farmer.

*Owen Nolan*, born in Hungerford, C. W. Enlisted January 22, 1862, at Almont. Aged 22 years. Laborer.

*John Nesbit*, born in East Lothin, Scotland. Enlisted December 23, 1862, at Almont. Aged 36 years. Farmer. Appointnd Corporal September 1, 1862. Discharged January 9, 1863, at Camp Chase, O.

*Talmon C. Owen*, born in Lapeer, Mich. Enlisted February 7, 1862, at Almont. Aged 20 years. Farmer.

*John W. Osborne,* born in Stuben county, N. Y. Enlisted December 13, 1861, at —, Lapeer county. Aged 36 years. Farmer. Died May 14, 1862, at Hamburg, Tenn., of diarrhœa.

*David Poss,* born in Canada. Enlisted November 1, 1861, at —, Lapeer county. Aged 38 years. Farmer.

*James Petterson,* born in Perth, Scotland. Enlisted January 3, 1862, at Almont. Aged 32 years. Farmer.

*John F. Patterson,* born in Lapeer county, Mich. No date of enlistment. Aged 25 years. Sadler. Deserted from Flint, Mich., before muster.

*Wm. J. Pendleton,* born in Franklin, Vt. Enlisted December 13, 1861, at Arcadia. Aged 32 years. Farmer. Died July 11, 1862, at general hospital near Farmington, Miss., of fever.

*Andrew Patrick,* born in Westminster, C. W. Enlisted December 3, 1861, at —, Lapeer county. Aged 21 years. Farmer.

*Samuel Reeser,* born in Erie county, N. Y. Enlisted November 13, 1861, at Elba. Aged 33 years. Farmer. Died June 14, at general hospital near Farmington, Miss., of fever.

*Lafayette M. Reed,* born in Monroe, N. Y. Enlisted November 18, 1861, at Almont. Aged 29 years. Farmer. Appointed Corporal April 3, 1863.

*Darwin Reed,* born in Lapeer, Mich. Enlisted November 25, 1861, at Almont. Aged 22 years. Farmer.

*Wm. A. Reed,* born in Monroe, N. Y. Enlisted November 13, 1861, at Almont. Aged 31 years. Farmer. Discharged June 5, 1863, at Camp Dennison, O.

*Ami M. Roberts,* born in Erie, N. Y. Enlisted December 25, 1861, at Almont. Aged 25 years. Musician. Appointed Quartermaster Sergeant, April 1, 1863.

*Wm. H. Reemer,* born in Oregon, Mich. Enlisted January 10, 1862, at —, Lapeer county. Aged 20 years. Farmer.

*James Robinson,* born in Tioga, N. Y. Enlisted December 18, 1861, at Lapeer. Aged 21 years. Farmer. Appointed Corporal September 1, 1862.

*Leander L. Skinner,* born in New York. Enlisted January

25, 1862, at —, Lapeer county. Aged 17 years. Farmer. Discharged September 8, 1862, at Camp Chase, O.

*Samuel Stevens*, born in Ontario, C. W. Enlisted January 27, 1862, at Dryden. Aged 26 years. Joiner.

*Wheeler A. Stone*, born in Monroe county, N. Y. Enlisted February 28, 1862, at Almont. Aged 24 years. Farmer.

*Forest W. Sutphen*, born in Washtenaw, Mich. Enlisted February 7, 1862, at Almont. Aged 20 years. Farmer.

*Shelden Thomas*, born in Chataeny, N. Y. Enlisted February 8, 1862, at —, Lapeer county. Aged 30 years. Mason.

*Dwight Vanpatten*, born in Livingston county, N. Y. Enlisted December 10, 1861, at Almont. Aged 16 years. Farmer. Died June 25, 1862, at Camp Big Springs, Miss., of diptheria.

*Simon R. Warren*, born in Genesee county, N. Y. Enlisted November 12, 1861, at Lapeer. Aged 38 years. Huntsman.

*Myron C. Watson*, born in Lapeer, Mich. Enlisted November 25, 1861, at Elba. Aged 17 years. Farmer.

*Peter E. White*, born in St. Clair county, Mich. Enlisted November 12, 1861, at —, Lapeer county. Aged 16 years. Farmer. Assassinated by a planter in Alabama, August 1, 1862.

*Geo. Watkins*, born in Monmouth, England. Enlisted November 11, 1861, at Oregon. ' Aged 37 years. Farmer.

*Michael Welch*, born in Nova Scotia. Enlisted November 18, 1861, at Elba. Aged 35 years. Farmer.

*Joseph Woodrow*, born in Canada. Date of enlistment unknown. Enlisted at Attica. Aged 19 years. Farmer.

*Warren Woodward*, born in Onondaga county, N. Y. Enlisted November 8, 1861, at —, Lapeer county. Aged 30 years. Farmer.

*Wm. H. Watson*, born in Oneida county, N. Y. Enlisted February 30, 1862, at Almont. Aged 18 years. Laborer.

*Reuben Waite*, born in Pery Posa, Canada. Enlisted August 18, 1862, at Detroit. Aged 27 years. Farmer.

This company is one made up of two parts of companies, and consolidated in Camp Thomson. Authority to raise a company was given to E. Newcomer, of Memphis, St. Clair county, September, 1861. He began recruiting immediately, and entered camp at Flint, November 7, with forty-seven men. L. L. Deming, of Jackson, Jackson county, received authority to raise a company, October 24, 1861, and he entered camp at Flint, December 24, with twenty-four men. A consolidation was made about February 1, 1862, which made a minimum company, Daniel Deming taking the place of Captain, and E. Newcomer returning home. The company was mustered with an aggregate of eighty-five men, February 6, 1862. It was raised principally in Jackson, Lapeer, St. Clair and Sanilac counties, and was at first known as "Lum Guards."

### COMMISSIONED OFFICERS.

*Capt. Lafayette L. Deming,* was born in Barrington, Mass., in the year 1826. At the time of entering the military service he was residing in Jackson, Jackson county, Mich. He received commission as Captain October 1, 1861. His health failing after entering the field, he resigned. His resignation was accepted November 12, 1862. His wife accompanied him into the field, and was with the regiment until a short time after the evacuation of Corinth.

*1st Lieut. Wm. H. Dunphy,* was born December 20, 1835, in Boston, Mass. At the age of twelve years he went to sea with his father, who was Captain of a vessel. He remainted at sea four years, and then went to Erie county, N. Y. After remaining there two years he went to Canada, and was employed on the Great Western Railway for one year. He then spent two years in traveling through the Eastern and Western States. In the fall of 1856 he moved to Michigan, and after spending some time in the western counties, he engaged in the lumbering business. In 1858 he was employed on the Detroit and Milwaukee Railroad. He remained there until the spring of 1859, when he was employed on the Grand Trunk Railroad, then building. He was married, October 28, 1860, and still remained in the employ of the Grand Trunk Railroad Company at the time of entering the army. He was commissioned as 1st Lieutenant from October 1, 1861, and was promoted to Captain March 31, 1863, vice Deming, resigned. His wife accompanied him to the seat of war, and remained until the march from Tuscumbia to Nashville. ·

2d Lieut. Hiram B. Pierson, was born in Burlington, Vt., in 1834. At the time of his entering the service he was living in Jackson, Jackson county, Mich., engaged in business as a leather merchant. He was married November 15, 1861. His commission as 2d Lieutenant dated from October 1, 1861. After arriving in the field his health failed, and he tendered his resignation, which was accepted, to take effect November 7, 1862.

NON-COMMISSIONED OFFICERS.

*Sergeants.*

1. *Dewitt C. Welling*, 1st *Sergeant*, was born January 25, 1840, in Jackson, Jackson county, Mich. At the time of the breaking out of the war he was employed as a clerk, and was a member of the "Jackson Grays," an independent company of militia then organized in Jackson. When the call for 75,000 men was made, Capt. Wm. H. Whittington commanding the company, after calling a special meeting of the "Grays," with his men offered their services to the country and were accepted. The company was immediately enlisted, and Mr. Welling was appointed 4th Corporal, and served as such during the campaign of the three months troops. He was with the regiment at Bull Run, and all through its service, and returned with it to Detroit. To use his own words: "After remaining at home a long three months," he enlisted in the "10th," November 4, 1861, at Jackson, and was appointed 1st Sergeant, to rank as such from date of enlistment. He was sent home on recruiting

service in July, 1862, and returned to the regiment April 12, 1863. He was promoted to 2d Lieutenant, Company C, November 10, 1862, and July 15th promoted to 1st Lieutenant, Company A.

2. *Joseph A. Gleason*, born in Crawford, Randolph county, Penn. Enlisted October 6, 1861, at Memphis. Aged 21 years. Farmer. Appointed to rank as Sergeant from date of enlistment. Promoted to 1st Sergeant April 3, 1863.

3. *Henry W. Shipman*, born in Genesee county, N. Y. Enlisted October 31, 1861, at Jackson. Aged 30 years. Farmer. Appointed to rank as Sergeant from date of enlistment.

4. *Cyrus Lawrence*, born in Grimsby, Canada. Enlisted September 5, 1861, at Memphis. Aged 34 years. Farmer. Appointed to rank as Sergeant from date of enlistment. Discharged February 11, 1863, at Detroit, Mich.

5. *Henry Conklin*, born in Herkimer county, N. Y. Enlisted October 15, 1861, at Dryden. Aged 22 years. Shoemaker. Appointed to rank as Sergeant from date of enlistment. Discharged at Evansville, Ind.; date unknown.

### Corporals.

1. *Charles Cook*, born in Maumee, O. Enlisted September 12, 1861, at Memphis. Aged 38 years. Farmer. Appointed to rank as Corporal from date of enlistment. Promoted to Sergeant April 3, 1863.

2. *Wm. Keene*, born in London, England. Enlisted November 14, 1861, at Jackson. Aged 18 years. Gentleman. Appointed to rank as Corporal from date of enlistment. Promoted to Sergeant August 15, 1862.

3. *Thomas Weaver*, born in Ohio. Enlisted October 23, 1861, at Almont. Aged 22 years. Farmer.. Appointed to rank as Corporal from date of enlistment.

4. *Standish Maxfield*, born in Columbia, N. Y. Enlisted October 12, 1861, at Memphis. Aged 44 years. Farmer. Appointed to rank as Corporal from date of onlistment.

5. *Charles Bennett*, born in Wayne, N. Y. Enlisted Octo-

ber 20, 1861, at Putnam. Aged 29 years. Laborer. Appointed to rank as Corporal from date of enlistment. Promoted to Sergeant August 15, 1862.

6. *Thomas Porter*, born in Trent, Canada. Enlisted October 8, 1861, at Berlin. Aged 28 years. Farmer. Appointed to rank as Corporal from date of enlistment. Died July 2, 1862, in general hospital near Farmington, Miss., of diptheria.

7. *Jason Clark*, born in Claredon county, Vt. Enlisted October 7, 1861, at Memphis. Aged 21 years. Farmer. Appointed to rank as Corporal from date of enlistment.

8. *Gordon Rudd*, born in Queen's county, Ireland. Enlisted October 22, 1861, at Dryden. Aged 20 years. ' Farmer. Appointed to rank as Corporal from date of enlistment.

### Musicians.

1. *Phillip Goodin, bugler*, born in Berlin, Prussia. Enlisted January 14, 1862, at Shiawassee. Aged 36 years. Miller. Discharged March 4, 1863, at Keokuk, Iowa.

2. *Joseph Cudworth, drummer*, born in New York. Enlisted September 20, 1861, at Memphis. Aged 23 years. Farmer·

### Privates.

*James B. Ackerman*, born in Staten Island, N. Y. Enlisted November 1, 1861, at Jackson. Aged 20 years. Engraver. Deserted from Stevenson, Ala., Sept. —, 1863.

*Jacob Anglemeyer*, born in New York. Enlisted November 18, 1861, at Jackson. Aged 40 years. Cabinet-maker. Discharged November 30, 1862, at Louisville, Ky.

*Wm. Applyn*, born in Grimsby, Canada. Enlisted October 15, 1861, at Wales. Aged 22 years. Laborer.

*Charles Ashley*, born in Franklin county, N. Y. Enlisted September 26, 1861, at Memphis. Aged 27 years. Laborer.

*Noah Arnold*, born in Brownsville, Canada. Enlisted October 29, 1861, at Memphis. Aged 18 years. Farmer.

*Joseph Barber*, born in Ann Arbor, Mich. Enlisted January 1, 1862, at Jackson. Aged 23 years. Farmer. Appointed Corporal August 15, 1862.

*Wm. Bunker,* born in New York. Enlisted January 6, 1862, at Jackson. Aged 28 years. Farmer.

*Geo. Bennett,* born in Chicago, Ill. Enlisted January 22, 1862, at Flint. Aged 22 years. Laborer. Died July 14, 1862, of fever, at Farmington, Miss.

*Wm. H. Bailey,* born in Benham, Canada. Enlisted October 26, 1861, at Wales. Aged 18 years. Farmer.

*Hiram E. Barritt,* born in Stuben county, N. Y. Enlisted December 28, 1861, at Lenox. Aged 38 years. Farmer. Died July 3, 1862, at Farmington, Miss., of fever.

*Cyrus Carpenter,* born in Ohio. Enlisted December 18, 1861, at Memphis. Aged 26 years. Farmer.

*James Caughell,* born in Yarmouth, Canada. Enlisted October 21, 1862, at Memphis. Aged 33 years. Farmer.

*David Campeau,* born in Marquette, Mich. Enlisted December 3, 1861, at Memphis. Aged 19 years. Sailor.

*Charles P. Conant,* born in Masten, N. Y. Enlisted November 13, 1862, at Flint. Aged 18 years. Farmer. Discharged November 14, 1862, at Cincinnati, O.

*John Carr,* born in C. W. Enlisted February 1, 1863, at Detroit. Aged 18 years. Peddler. Deserted from Stevenson, Ala., September —, 1863.

*Enos Delong,* born in Monroe county, Mich. Enlisted January 15, 1862, at Jackson. Aged 18 years. Farmer.

*Wm. H. Derby,* born in Erie, Penn. Enlisted October 22, 1861, at Dryden. Aged 21 years. Farmer.

*John Derby,* born in Macomb county, Mich. Enlisted January —, 1862, at Mt. Clemens. Aged 22 years. Sailor. Died August 28, 1862, at Farmington, Miss. of general debility.

*James Drown,* born in Caledonia, Vt. Enlisted August 20, 1862, at Lexington. Aged 33 years. Farmer. Discharged June 1, 1863, at Camp Dennison, O.

*Charles Ellsworth,* born in Burford, C. W. Enlisted December 17, 1861, at Almont. Aged 21 years.. Farmer.

*John Edwards,* born in Lenawee county Mich Enlisted November 28, 1861, at Jackson. Aged 20 years. Laborer.

171

*Wm. H. Edwards*, nativity unknown. Enlisted November 28, 1861, at Jackson. Aged 18 years. Deserted January 16, 1862, at Flint, Mich.

*Lawrence Freeman*, born in Perth, Canada. Enlisted September 12, 1861, at Almont. Aged 25 years. Farmer. Discharged September 25, 1862, at Jackson, Miss.

*Yates Furgeson*, born in Lapeer county, Mich. Enlisted November 20, 1861, at —, Lapeer county. Aged 19 years. Farmer.

*Albert Gordinier*, born in Oakland county, Mich. Enlisted October 22, 1861, at Dryden. Aged 24 years. Farmer.

*Asa Gordinier*, born in Macomb county, Mich. Enlisted October 22, 1861, at Dryden. Aged 19 years. Farmer.

*Jay Gordinier*, born in Macomb county, Mich. Enlisted February 25, 1862, at Flint. Aged 18 years. Farmer.

*Martin Gordinier*, born in Macomb county, Mich. Enlisted February 25, 1862, at Flint. Aged 17 years. Farmer.

*Leland Gregory*, born in New York. Enlisted September 12, 1861, at Flint. Aged 40 years. Farmer. Discharged January 20, 1863, at Louisville, Ky.

*Joel Glover*, born in Canada West. Enlisted October 29, 1861, at Memphis. Aged 18 years. Farmer.

*Marvin M. Grow*, born in Orleans county, N. Y. Enlisted August 20, 1861, at Lexington. Aged 33 years. Mechanic.

*Silas K. Hanse*, born in Livingston county, Mich. Enlisted October 20, 1861, at Putnam. Aged 24 years. Farmer.

*Benjamin F. Hands*, born on the Atlantic Ocean. Enlisted November 26, 1861, at Jackson. Aged 38 years. Nurseryman.

*Daniel Haveland*, born in Rose, N. Y. Enlisted October 12, 1861, at Memphis. Aged 30 years. Mason. Died August 23, 1863, at Nashville, Tenn.

*Mortimer Huntly*, born in Lapeer county, Mich. Enlisted October 13, 1861, at Dryden. Aged 19 years. Farmer.

*Geo. A. Haynes*, born in Bruce, Mich. Enlisted October 23, 1861, at Dryden. Aged 21 years. Farmer.

*Wallace Huntley*, born in Lapeer county, Mich. Enlisted October 22, 1861, at Dryden. Aged 18 years. Farmer.

*Miron Howard*, born in Lapeer county, Mich. Enlisted November 14, 1861, at Dryden. Aged 19 years. Farmer.

*Geo. H. Howard*, born in Warwick, Canada. Enlisted November 19, 1861, at Dryden. Aged 18 years. Farmer. Discharged January 13, 1863, at Nashville, Tenn.

*Justice Hedges*, born in Rice Lake, Canada West. Enlisted December 12, 1861, at —, Lapeer county. Aged 18 years· Farmer.

*Charles C. Hunt*, born in New Canaan, Conn. Enlisted January 2, 1862, at Columbus. Aged 55 years. Farmer. Discharged August 2, 1862, at St. Louis, Mo.

*Wm. H. Hanna*, born in St. Joseph, Mich. Enlisted February 3, 1862, at Jackson. Aged 21 years. Farmer. Promoted to Hospital Steward, September 6, 1863.

*Horace Hanse*, born in Livingston county, Mich. Enlisted January 31, 1862, at Putnam. Aged 19 years. Farmer. Discharged September 11, 1862, at St. Louis, Mo.

*Dallas Hogle*, born in Ionia, Mich. Enlisted January 13, 1862, at Jackson. Aged 18 years. Farmer. Died July 11, 1862, at Farmington, Miss., of chronic diarrhœa.

*Samuel A. Hooper*, born in Lenawee county, Mich. Enlisted January 28, 1862, at Clarence. Aged 18 years. Gentleman.

*Jacob E. Johnston*, born in Burlington county, N. J. Enlisted November 22, 1861, at Dryden. Aged 37 years. Farmer. Appointed Corporal August 15, 1862.

*Wm. Kennedy*, born in Brighton, Mich. Enlisted October 21, 1861, at Putnam. Aged 21 years. Farmer. Discharged May 6, 1863.

*Franklin Knapp*, born in Waukegon, Ill. Enlisted August 20, 1862, at Lexington. Aged 22 years. Farmer. Died November 13, 1862, at Nashville, Tenn.

*Geo. Kitchen*, born in Ancaster, Canada. Enlisted October 7, 1861, at Memphis. Aged 20 years. Farmer.

*Jackson A. Kimball*, born in Toledo, O. Enlisted December 27, 1861, at Toledo, Ohio. Aged 23 years. Laborer.

*Geo. R. Knapp,* born in Shiawassee county, Mich. Enlisted February —, 1862, at Flint. Aged 18 years. Farmer.

*Marvin Lenox,* born in Clark, Canada. Enlisted October 15, 1861, at Lapeer. Aged 21 years. Carpenter.

*Raselouse Lawrence,* born in Smithville, Canada. Enlisted October 5, 1861, at Memphis. Aged 18 years. Farmer.

*Alfred Louden,* born in Ireland. Enlisted November 21, 1861, at Jackson. Aged 34 years. Laborer. Deserted January 16, 1862, from Flint.

*Ira Mitchell,* born in Lyons, N. Y. Enlisted November 21, 1861, at Jackson. Aged 26 years. Laborer.

*Cephas C. Miller,* born in Wayne, Mich. Enlisted August 20, 1862, at Lexington. Aged 20 years. Farmer.

*John McGary,* born in Toronto, Canada. Enlisted October 16, 1861, at Memphis. Aged 24 years. Carriage-maker.

*Christopher Mattoon,* born in Lapeer county, Mich. Enlisted October 22, 1861, at —, Lapeer county. Aged 26 years. Farmer. Appointed Corporal August 15, 1862.

*Bradley Mattoon,* born in Greenfield, N. Y. Enilsted October 15, 1861, at Almont. Aged 24 years. Farmer. Appointed Corporal April 3, 1863.

*Peter McCoy,* born in Lockport, N. Y. Enlisted November 5, 1861, at Memphis. Aged 20 years. Farmer.

*Kenneth McKoy,* born in Prince Edward Island. Enlisted February 10, 1861, at Memphis. Aged 30 years. Farmer.

*Wm. McCoy,* born in Rutland county, Vt. Enlisted February 20, 1862, at Flint. Aged 45 years. Farmer. Died July 6, 1862, at Covington, Ky., of chronic diarrhœa.

*Edward McConnell,* born in Macomb county, Mich. Enlisted February 27, 1862, at Memphis. Aged 18 years. Blacksmith.

*Russel Newberry,* born in Erie county, N. Y. Enlisted December 20, 1861, at —, Lapeer county. Aged 44 years. Cooper. Discharged April 13, 1863, at Nashville, Tenn.

*Geo. B. Nestill,* born in Canada West. Enlisted October 23, 1861, at Wales. Aged 27 years. Farmer.

*Eugene Norton,* born in Memphis, St. Clair county, Mich.

Enlisted February 27, 1862, at Memphis. Aged 16 years. Farmer.

*Wm. H. Newton*, born in Canada West. Enlisted February 27, 1862, at Flint. Aged 30 years. Farmer. Deserted February —, 1862, from Flint.

*Hiram Osgood*, born in Jackson, Mich. Enlisted September 12, 1862, at Jackson. Aged 19 years. Carpenter.

*Walter Popple*, born in Chemung county, N. Y. Enlisted January 10, 1862, at Jackson. Aged 85 years. Farmer. Discharged April 13, 1863, at Nashville, Tenn.

*Hubert Phelps*, born in Washtenaw county, Mich. Enlisted November 23, 1861, at Jackson. Aged 18 years. Farmer.

*Eli Parish*, born in Jackson, Mich. Enlisted October 21, 1861, at Jackson. Aged 21 years. Farmer.

*Charles Phillips*, born in Jackson, Mich. Enlisted November 13, 1861, at Jackson. Aged 18 years. Farmer.

*Edwin Postle*, born in Canada. Enlisted February 22, 1862, at —, Lapeer county, Mich. Aged 18 years. Clerk.

*Thomas Proctor*, born in Ireland. Enlisted January 1, 1862, at Armeda. Aged 26 years Farmer.

*Daniel Parshal*, born in Jackson county, Mich. Enlisted November 10, 1861, place unknown. Aged 18 years. Farmer. Discharged February 5, 1862, at Flint, Mich.

*Charles Quigley*, born in Leoni, Mich. Enlisted November 12, 1861, at Jackson. Aged 21 years. Laborer. Discharged December 6, 1862, at Keokuk, Iowa.

*John J. Robertstone*, born in C. W. Enlisted October 22, 1861, at Dryden. Aged 19 years. Farmer.

*Miles O. Rugg*, born in Wyoming county, N. Y. Enlisted October 12, 1861, at Memphis. Aged 25 years. Farmer. Died October 29, 1862, at Mound City, Ill., of chronic diarrhœa.

*Geo. M. Richards*, nativity unknown. Enlisted September 26, 1861, at Beebe's Corners. Aged 42 years. Joiner. Deserted April 2, 1862, from Flint.

*David W. Reed*—no record is found upon the books, save that he deserted in January, 1862, from Flint.

*Henry Spencer*, born in Macomb county, Mich. Enlisted October 15, 1861, at Dryden. Aged 18 years. Farmer.

*Franklin Sweet*, born in Danby, Vt. Enlisted December 20, 1861, at Memphis. Aged 25 years. Farmer. Deserted April 22, 1862, from Flint.

*Wm. II. Sergeant*, born in Wyandotte county, O. Enlisted February 10, 1862, at Jackson. Aged 27 years. Farmer. Discharged October 25, 1862, at Cincinnati, O.

*Wm. Seely*, born in Canada West. Enlisted October 8, 1861, at Memphis. Aged 24 years. Farmer. Deserted February —, 1862, from Flint.

*Wm. Smith*, born in Canada West. Enlisted December 31, 1861, at Memphis. Aged 24 years. Farmer. Deserted May —, 1862, from Hamburg, Tenn.

*Leander A. Sperry*, born in New York. Enlisted October 7, 1861, at Memphis. Aged 21 years. Farmer. Appointed Corporal August 15, 1862. Deserted from Northern Hospital.

*James St. John*, born in Cleveland, O. Enlisted February 18, 1862, at Flint. Aged 20 years. Laborer.

*Vincent Teeter*, born in Lansing, N. Y. Enlisted October 28, 1861, at Jackson, Mich. Aged 33 years. Joiner.

*Samuel True*, born in Macomb county, Mich. Enlisted December 20, 1861, at Mt. Clemens. Aged 18 years. Stavecutter.

*Frederick Volker*, born in Germany. Enlisted December 27, 1861, at Baltimore. Aged 18 years. Farmer.

*Alexander Vanbrocklin*, born in Long Point, Canada. Enlisted July 21, 1862, at Lexington. Aged 28 years. Farmer.

*Putnam Welling*, born in Jackson, Mich. Enlisted November 27, 1861, at Jackson. Aged 18 years. Gentleman.

*Andrew Walworth*, born in Jackson, Mich. Enlisted November 29, 1861, at Jackson. Aged 18 years. Farmer.

*Albert Wildey*, born in Spring Arbor, Mich. Enlisted December 29, 1861, at Jackson. Aged 19 years. Farmer.

*Wm. W. Webster*, born in Armada, Mich. Enlisted November 20, 1861, at Berk's Corners. Aged 21 years. Farmer:

*Samuel C. Waite*, born in Westfield, N. Y. Enlisted January 1, 1862, at Jackson. Aged 19 years. Clerk. Died July 7, 1862, at General Hospital near Farmington, Miss., of diarrhœa.

*Geo. Wilson,* nativity unknown. Enlisted January 15, 1862, at Jackson. Aged 20 years. Farmer. Deserted February 8, 1862, from Flint, Mich.

*Simon Wright,* nativity unknown. Enlisted December 2, 1861, at Jackson. Aged 32 years. Deserted November —, 1861, from Flint.

*Jeffries Walters,* born in Oakland, Mich. Enlisted March 8, 1862, at Flint. Aged 23 years. Cooper.

## COMPANY H.

Authority to raise this Company was received by John Pierson, of Pontiac, Oakland county, October 4, 1861, from Gov. Blair. • The minimum number was recruited, and the company entered into camp November 22, 1861. They went into camp that day with forty-four men. The recruiting was continued until the company was full. It was mustered February 6, 1862. The men constituting this company were recruited in Oakland, Lapeer, Tuscola, St. Clair and Sanilac counties, at a time when citizens thought men enough had been raised to put down the rebellion; consequently but little interest was manifest to assist in recruiting, and it was attended with a great amount of labor and expense. Company H was known under its first organization as "McClellan Guards."

### COMMISSIONED OFFICERS.

*Capt. John Pierson,* was born in Schoharie county, State of New York, February 13, 1813. He moved to Michigan in August, 1834. Was married in Hartwick, Otsego county, N. Y., in May, 1836. For several years previous to the breaking out of the war, he was engaged in the mercantile business and in the manufacture of lumber. At the time of entering the military service he was residing in Pontiac, Oakland county, Mich. He received a commission as Captain from October 1, 1861.

1st *Lieut. Sylvan Ter Bush,* was born in Kingston, N. Y., July 30, 1836. Moved to Michigan the autumn of 1838, and had been employed as salesman for several years previous to entering the army. He entered the service September 4, 1861, and received commission as 1st Lieutenant from October 1, 1861.

2d *Lieut. Nathan Levy,* was born February 4, 1839, in Shwersen, Poland. He emigrated to America with his parents in 1852. Embarking at Hamburg, he sailed to Hull, England. Re-embarking at Liverpool he sailed for New York, where he arrived after a long and disastrous voyage, during which the ship was nearly destroyed by fire, May 2, 1852. From New York he sailed to New Orleans, *via* Cuba; thence to Mobile, Ala., and was employed in his brother's clothing store as a clerk. In the fall of 1852 he sailed to New York, and finally settled in Rochester, N. Y., and engaged in the clothing business, (in which he was employed until joining the army,) in many of the principal cities. At the breaking out of the war he owned a clothing store in Grand Rapids, Mich. Received a commission as 2d Lieutenant October 1, 1862. Promoted to 1st Lieutenant, Company I, July 15, 1863, *vice* Titus, promoted. Resigned January 12, 1864.

NON-COMMISSIONED OFFICERS.

*Sergeants.*

1. *John W. Griffin,* 1st *Sergeant,* born in Troy, Oakland county, Mich. Enlisted October 8, 1861, at Farmer's Creek. Aged 26 years. Book-keeper. Appointed to rank as 1st Sergeant from date of enlistment. Discharged August16, 1862, at Keokuk, Iowa.

2. *Wm. C. Clark,* born in Orion, Oakland county, Mich. Enlisted November 16, 1861, at Orion. Aged 23 years. Merchant. Appointed to rank as Sergeant from date of enlistment.

12

3. *Warren G. Nelson,* born in Pontiac, Oakland county, Mich. Enlisted November 5, 1861, at Pontiac. Aged 18 years. Student. Appointed to rank as Sergeant from date of enlistment. Promoted to 1st Sergeant April 3, 1863.

4. *Cornelius L. Smith,* born in Wayne county, N. Y. Enlisted November 23, 1861, at Deerfield. Aged 29 years. Farmer. Appointed to rank as Sergeant from date of enlistment.

5. *John Knox,* born in Edinburg, Scotland, April 17, 1821. He left Scotland in July, 1841, to fulfill a three year's engagement as harness-maker in Demerara. He returned to Scotland in December, 1854, and emigrated to Canada in 1856. Moved to Dayton, Tuscola county, Mich., May, 1860. Enlisted at Marathon, November 23, 1861. He was, at the time of his entering the service, engaged in clearing a new farm. He was appointed to rank as Sergeant from date of enlistment. Promoted to 1st Sergeant August 27, 1862, and to 2d Lieutenant, Company K, March 31, 1863, *vice* Smith, promoted.

### Corporals.

1. *Albert W. Simmons,* born in Huntington, C. W. Enlisted October 8, 1861, at Lexington. Aged 20 years. Farmer. Appointed to rank as Corporal from date of enlistment.

2. *John Hargar,* born in Alleghany county, Penn. Enlisted October 16, 1861, at Lapeer. Aged 45 years. Farmer. Appointed to rank as Corporal from date of enlistment. Discharged August 20, 1862, at Keokuk, Iowa.

3. *Roland H. Hicks,* born in Chila, Monroe county, N. Y. Enlisted December 9, 1861, at Lenox. Aged 29 years. Farmer. Appointed to rank as Corporal from date of enlistment. Discharged September 1, 1862, at Detroit, Mich.

4. *John Chamberlin,* born in Toronto, C. W. Enlisted November 18, 1861, at Pontiac. Aged 25 years. Farmer. Appointed to rank as Corporal from date of enlistment. Promoted to Sergeant August 27, 1862.

5. *Nathan Wheeler,* born in Sackett's Harbor, N. Y. En-

listed November 4, 1861, at Greenwood.   Aged 25 years.
Farmer.   Appointed to rank as Corporal from date of enlistment.

6. *Ruben Right*, born in Pickering, C. W.   Enlisted October 29, 1861, at Lexington.   Aged 22 years.   Farmer.   Appointed to rank as Corporal from date of enlistment.   Promoted to Sergeant, August 27, 1862.

7. *Wm. R. Lawrence*, born in Oakland county, Mich.   Enlisted January 29, 1862, at Flint.   Aged 26 years.   Farmer.
Appointed to rank as Corporal from date of enlistment.

8. *John Clayton*, born in New Brunswick.   Enlisted November 8, 1861, at —, St. Clair county.   Aged 35 years.
Farmer.   Appointed to rank as Corporal from February 1st,
1862.   Discharged October 12, 1862, at St. Louis, Mo.

## Musicians.

1. *John N. Harris*, *drummer*, born in Delaware, C. W.
Enlisted October 8, 1861, at Lexington.   Aged 16 years.
Farmer.   Died October 14, 1862, at Farmington, Miss., of
typhoid fever.

2. *Frederick Kipp*, *bugler*, born in Baden, Germany.   Enlisted October 8, 1861, at Lexington.   Aged 26 years.
Farmer.

## Privates.

*Ethan Burgher*, nativity unknown.   Enlisted November 23,
1861, at Deerfield.   Aged 23 years.   Farmer.

*Lawrence Butler*, born in Erie county, N. Y.   Enlisted
November 7, 1861, at Greenwood.   Aged 18 years.   Farmer.

*Nathan M. Berry*, born in Niagara county, N. Y.   Enlisted
November 23, 1861, at Watertown.   Aged 40 years.   Farmer.
Discharged August 29, 1862, at Cairo, Ill.

4. *John Butler*, born in Erie county, N. Y.   Enlisted December 9, 1861, at Greenwood.   Aged 21 years.   Farmer.

*Hiram Beach*, born in Wayne county, N. Y.   Enlisted December 16, 1861, at Highland. Aged 19 years. Farmer. Appointed Corporal August 27, 1862.

*John Baird*, born in Huntington, Penn. Enlisted January 2, 1862, at Port Huron. Aged 19 years. Farmer. Died July 5, 1862, at Henderson, Ky., of typhoid fever.

*Jacob B.sler*, born in Arrow, Switzerland. Enlisted October 21, 1861, at Port Sanilac. Aged 31 years. Farmer.

*Robert J. Ballard*, born in New York. Enlisted February 3, 1862, at Flint. Aged 18 years. Farmer. Discharged February 22, 1862, at Flint, Mich.

*Ira Blowers*, born in Murray, N. Y. Enlisted December 30, 1861, at Highland. Aged 31 years. Farmer. Transferred to Company K, February 6, 1862.

*Hiram E. Belcher*, born in Jefferson county, N. Y. Enlisted February 16, 1862, at Port Huron. Aged 36 years. Farmer. Appointed Corporal May 20, 1862. Promoted to Sergeant April 3, 1863, and designated to carry the colors of the regiment by the Colonel.

*Samuel Basler*, born in Germany. Enlisted October 21, 1861, at Port Sanilac. Aged 35 years. Laborer.

*Wm. Belcher*, born in Jefferson county, N. Y. Enlisted March 15, 1862, at Port Huron. Aged 23 years. Farmer.

*Abel Beckwith*, born in Addison, Vt. Enlisted October 28, 1861, at Watertown. Aged 29 years. Farmer. Transferred from Company C, April 30, 1862.

*Frank Champagne*, born in Montreal, C. E. Enlisted October 12, 1862, at Port Sanilac. Aged 21 years. Farmer.

*Peter Counter*, born in Montreal, C. E. Enlisted October 12, 1861, at Port Sanilac. Aged 25 years. Farmer.

*Billy J. Cleveland*, born in Albany, N. Y. Enlisted October 28, 1861, at Forestville. Aged 35 years. Farmer. Discharged October 20, 1862, at Camp Dennison, O.

*Geo. W. Credit*, born in Chenango county, N. Y. Enlisted October 16, 1861, at —, Lapeer county. Aged 18 years. Farmer.

*Christian Cline*, born in Wirtemburg, Germany, Enlisted

November 19, 1861, at Port Huron. Aged 36 years. Cooper. Discharged November 21, 1862, at Evansville, Ind.

*Joseph Crawford*, born in Middlesex, C. W. Enlisted November 23, 1861, at Deerfield. Aged 43 years. Farmer. Discharged March 25, 1863, at Cincinnati, O.

*Levant Carter*, born in Lapeer county, Mich. Enlisted December 3, 1861, at Metamora. Aged 18 years. Farmer.

*James Cawkins*, born in Deerland, C. W. Enlisted December 9, 1861, at North Branch. Aged 18 years. Farmer.

*Francis Carman*, born in New York. Enlisted December 6, 1861, at Worth. Aged 29 years. Farmer.

*Robert Cidd*, born in Clarkston, Monroe county, N. Y. Enlisted January 3, 1862, at Detroit. Aged 37 years. Farmer. Discharged at Nashville, Tenn., September 15, 1863,

*Benj. Clark*, born in Sandusky, O. Enlisted October 7, 1861, at Lexington. Aged 21 years. Farmer.

*John Crothers*, born in Toronto, C. W. Enlisted October 10, 1861, at Lexington. Aged 21 years. Farmer.

*John Derrick*, born in Pearn, Switzerland. Enlisted October 8, 1861, at Lexington. Aged 31 years. Farmer.

*John Decker*, born in Wayne county, New York. Enlisted January 25, 1862, at Flint. Aged 22 years. Farmer. Discharged December 20, 1862, at Quincy, Ill.

*Samuel Evans*, born in Walworth county, N. Y. Enlisted November 15, 1861, at —, Lapeer county. Aged 27 years. Farmer.

*James J. Ezbert*, born in Warren county, N. Y. Enlisted October 8, 1861, at Pontiac. Aged 45 years. Farmer. Discharged July 17, 1862, at Detroit, Mich.

*Edward Frank*, born in Germany. Enlisted October 21, 1861, at Port Sanilac. Aged 19 years. Farmer. Discharged August 25, 1862, at Keokuk, Iowa.

*Phillip Greene*, born in Canada West. Enlisted November 23, 1861, at Arcadia. Aged 21 years. Artist. Discharged January 22, 1863, at Bowling Green, Ky.

*Gustavus Goff*, born in Oakland county, Mich. Enlisted March 29, 1862, at Flint. Aged 19 years. Farmer. Died

July 8, 1862, at General Hospital near Farmington, Miss., of fever.

*Wm. G. Harris,* born in Delaware, C. W. Enlisted October 8, 1861, at Lexington. Aged 19 years. Farmer.

*Murny N. Heath,* born in Ticonderoga, C. W. Enlisted December 9, 1861, at Greenwood. Aged 18 years. Farmer.

*Elijah Hinckley,* born in Lenawee county, Mich. Enlisted January 14, 1862, at Highland. Aged 22 years. Farmer. Reported as a deserter and dropped from rolls, December 31, 1863.

*Mishuel Hull,* born in New Jersey. Enlisted December 30, 1861, at Highland. Aged 28 years. Carpenter. Transferred to Company K, February 6, 1862.

*A. W. Hurlburt,* nativity unknown. Enlisted December 9, 1861, at Pontiac. Aged 18 years.

*Mercier M. Hungerford,* born in Niagara county, N. Y. Enlisted February 10, 1862, at Linden. Aged 18 years. Farmer.

*Edwin F. Holmes,* born in Orleans county, N. Y. Enlisted February 10, 1862, at Flint. Aged 18 years. Farmer. Appointed Corporal August 27, 1862.

*Joseph Heister,* born in Chemung county, N. Y. Enlisted February 25, 1862, at Flint. Aged 30 years. Farmer. Discharged March 25, 1862, at Flint.

*Hiram Howland,* born in Ontario, N. Y. Enlisted February 27, 1862, at Flint. Aged 32 years. Farmer. Died of wounds accidentally received, November 14, 1863.

*Abram Harris,* born in London, C. W. Enlisted March 20, 1862, at Lexington. Aged 22 years. Farmer.

*John H. Hope,* born in Brandon, Mich. Enlisted March 1, 1862, at Flint. Aged 20 years. Clerk.

*David Henry,* born in Lancaster, C. W. Enlisted August 11, 1862, at —, Sanilac county. Aged 18 years. Farmer. Discharged July 10, 1863, at Nashville, Tenn.

*John C. A. Heule,* born in Baden, Germany. Enlisted August 28, 1862, at Lexington. Aged 35 years. Miller.

*Albert Hill,* born in Canada West. Enlisted August 22,

1861, at Lexington. Aged 29 years. Farmer. Discharged September 3, 1863, at Murfreesboro, Tenn.

*Andrew P. Hughes*, born in Smith county, Tenn. Enlisted December 24, 1862, at Nashville, Tenn. Aged 29 years. Farmer. Deserted August 28, 1863.

*Oziel Inman*, born in Wyoming county, N. Y. Enlisted November 21, 1861, at Watertown. Aged 38 years. Farmer. Transferred from Company K, May 20, 1862. Died June 22, · 1862, at General Hospital near Farmington, Miss., of typhoid fever.

*David D. Ingles*, born in Dumfries, Canada. Enlisted April 4, 1862, at Flint. Aged 18 years. Teamster.

*Welcome L. Inman*, born in Wyoming county, N. Y. En-listed November 30, 1861, at Watertown. Aged 23 years. Farmer. Died June 15, 1862, at General Hospital near Farm-ington, Miss., of fever.

*Albert E. Kelly*, born in Oakland county, Mich. Enlisted February 17, 1862, at Flint. Aged 23 years. Farmer. Dis-charged December 4, 1862, at Evansville, Ind.

*James H. Lawrence*, born in Summersetshire, England. En-listed October 14, 1861, at Pontiac. Aged 18 years. Farmer. Died July 10, 1862, at General Hospital near Farmington, Miss., of heart disease.

*Levi Lawrence*, born in . Oakland county, Mich. Enlisted November 25, 1861, at Marathon. Aged 29 years. Farmer.

*Nathan E. Lewis*, born in Middlesex county, Conn. En-listed October 26, 1861, at Metamora. Aged 45 years. Farmer.

*Henry Lincoln*, born in Oswego, N. Y. Enlisted November 1, 1861, at St. Charles. Aged 34 years. Farmer. Transferred from Company C, April 30, 1862. Discharged July 25, 1863, at Detroit, Mich.

*John Lashbrook*, born in Buckingham, England. Enlisted August 29, 1862, at Lexington. Aged 21 years. Farmer. ·

*James McCarthy*, born in Manie, Ireland. Enlisted October 14, 1861, at Pontiac. Aged 28 years. Farmer.

*Constantine Miller*, born in Baden, Germany. Enlisted October 21, 1861, at Port Sanilac. Aged 22 years. Farmer. Appointed Corporal August 27, 1862.

*Archibald Madison*, born in Rhone, Canada. Enlisted November 4, 1861, at Greenwood. Aged 18 years. Farmer.

*Frank Masey*, born in Yorkshire, England. Enlisted November 23, 1861, at Flint. Aged 18 years. Farmer.

*John Moffit*, born in Ireland. Enlisted November 28, 1861, at Flint. Aged 33 years. Farmer. Deserted from steamer Gladiator, on the Mississippi River, April 25, 1862.

*Hendri Mein*, born in Sternburg, Germany. Enlisted December 9, 1861, at Port Huron. Aged 24 years. Farmer.

*John McKenzie*, born in Canada. Enlisted December 9, 1861, at Greenwood. Aged 25 years. Farmer. Discharged January 20, 1863, at St. Louis, Mo.

*Harrison C. Madison*, born in Trenton, Genesee county, Mich. Enlisted December 12, 1861, at Fentonville. Aged 18 years. Farmer.

*Wilder Maine*, nativity unknown. Enlisted December 26, 1861, at Metamora. Aged 22 years. Discharged February 6, 1862, at Flint, Mich.

*Lewis Meaker*, born in Fenton, Genesee county, Mich. Enlisted December 23, 1861, at Fentonville. Aged 18 years. Farmer.

*James Newton*, born in Oakland county, Mich. Enlisted October 14, 1861, at Greenwood. Aged 18 years. Farmer.

*Gary A. Newcombe*, born in Genesee, N. Y. Enlisted November 21, 1861, at Richfield. Aged 25 years. Farmer. Transferred from Company C, April 30, 1862.

*Richard Oldfield*, born in Glasgow, Scotland. Enlisted October 28, 1861, at Attica. Aged 45 years. Farmer. Discharged June 20, 1862, at Detroit.

*Levi Ovitt*, born in Niagara county, N. Y. Enlisted March 1, 1842, at Flint. Aged 19 years. Mechanic. Transferred from Company C, April 30, 1862.

*Watson J. Peasley*, nativity unknown. Enlisted December 9, 1862, at Detroit. Aged 18 years.

*Josiah Powell*, born in New York. Enlisted December

185

9, 1861, at Flint. Aged 28 years. Farmer. Died May 30, 1862, at Farmington, Miss., of typhoid fever.

*Wm. Porter*, born in N. Y. Enlisted Dec. 9, 1861, at Port Huron. Aged 19 years. Farmer.

*Porter Palmer*, born in Erie county, N. Y. Enlisted Dec. 16, 1861, at Highland. Aged 29 years. Carpenter.

*Russel L. Post*, born in Cateraugus county, N. Y. Enlisted Dec. 19, 1861, at Flint. Aged 29 years. Farmer.

*Geo. F. Phipps*, born in Oakland county, Mich. Enlisted Feb. 5, 1862, at Flint. Aged 18 years. Farmer. Died July 5, 1862, at General Hospital, near Farmington, Miss., of fever.

*Lewis Parish*, born in New York. Enlisted November 4, 1861, at Goodrich. Aged 19 years. Farmer. Transferred from Co., C, April 30, 1861. Discharged July 19, 1862, at Detroit, Mich.

*Robert Reynolds*, born in Jersey City, N. J. Enlisted Oct. 26, 1861, at Metamora. Aged 18 years. Carpenter.

*Samuel Rogers*, born in Lapeer county, Mich. Enilsted Dec. 19, 1861, at Flint. Aged 18 years. Farmer.

*Silas J. Sloat*, born in London, C. W. Enlisted Dec. 8, 1861, at Lexington. Aged 19 years. Farmer.

*Danforth Starks*, born in Wayne county, N. Y. Enlisted Oct. 22, 1861, at Metamora. Aged 22 years. Farmer.

*Martin O. Stiles*, born in Lapeer county, Mich. Enlisted Oct. 16, 1861, at Lapeer. Aged 25 years. Farmer. Discharged April 16, 1863, at Nashville, Tenn.

*Eli B. Smith*, nativity unknown. Enlisted November 23, 1861, at Deerfield. Aged 26 years. Deserted from Flint, Mich., Dec. —, 1861.

*Alfred Shaw*, born in Nottingham, England. Enlisted Dec. 17, 1861, at Flint. Aged 18 years. Farmer. Appointed Corporal August 1, 1862.

*Abram J. Sloat*, born in London, C. W. Enlisted Oct. 8, 1861, at Flint. Aged 22 years. Farmer.

*Hiram Slocum*, born in N. Y. Enlisted Feb. 24, 1862, at Flint. Aged 19 years. Farmer. Discharged Oct. 11, 1862, at Camp Dennison, O.

*Miles Simmons*, born in Huntington, C. W. Enlisted Dec. 6, 1861, at Lexington. Aged 22 years. Farmer. Appointed Corporal August 27, 1862.

*James S. Sharp*, born in Dorchester, C. W. Enlisted Aug. 13, 1862, at Lexington. Aged 19 years. Farmer.

*Charles Semler*, born in Hamburgh, Germany. Enlisted August 13, 1863, at Detroit, Mich. Aged 24 years Laborer.

*Wallace Tuttle*, born in Erie county, O. Enlisted Oct. 28, 1861, at Dryden. Aged 29 years. Shoemaker. Died July 23, 1862, at Camp Big Springs, Miss., of typhoid fever.

*Daniel Thomas*, born in Woodstock, C. W. Enlisted Oct. 9, 1861, at Port Sanilac. Aged 19 years. Farmer. Discharged October 4, 1862, at St. Louis, Mo.

*Geo. W. Thomas*, born in Woodstock, C. W. Enlisted Oct. 9, 1861, at Port Sanilac. Aged 21 years. Farmer.

*Henry Thompson*, born in Wayne county, N. Y. Enlisted September 16, 1861, at Highland. Aged 18 years. Farmer. Discharged August 5, 1862, at Jefferson Barracks, Mo.

*Joseph H. Thomas*, born in Marrillatown, N. Y. Enlisted March 19, 1862, at Flint. Aged 28 years. Carpenter. Discharged September 12, 1862, at Camp Dennison O.

*Simmons Thomas*, born in Marrillatown, N. Y. Enlisted March 19, 1862, at Flint. Aged 24 years. Carpenter.

*Lorenzo F. Taylor*, born in Waterford, Conn. Enlisted September 16, 1861, at —, Midland county, Mich. Aged 43 years. Farmer. Transferred from Company B, February 5, 1862. Discharged June 20, 1862, at Detroit, Mich.

*Jessie Vancamp*, born in London, C. W. Enlisted October 18, 1861, at Lexington. Aged 18 years. Farmer.

*Amos Witter*, born in Ontario county, N. Y. Enlisted December 19, 1861, at Highland. Aged 44 years. Hotel keeper. Died September 16, 1862, at Camp Dennison, O.

*Jerome B. Worden*, born in Oakland county, Mich. Enlisted November 2, 1861, at Pontiac. Aged 18 years. Laborer.

*Benjamin Wallace*, born in Lapeer county, Mich. Enlisted February 17, 1862, at Flint. Aged 18 years. Farmer. Killed April 10, 1863, at Antioch, Tenn., by Gurillas.

*Isaac Wright*, born in Pickering, C. W. Enlisted August 11, 1862, at Lexington. Aged 26 years. Farmer. Discharged April 16, 1863, at Nashville, Tenn..

*Archie Willis*, born in South Rochester, C. W. Enlisted August 12, 1862, at Lexington. Aged 22 years. Farmer.

## COMPANY I.

This Company is composed of two parts of Companise, consolidated in Flint. Russell M. Barker, of Flint, Gennessee county, Michigan, was authorized by the Governor to raise a company, November 15, 1861, and immediately began recruiting. He entered camp of the 10th Michigan Volunteer Infantry, at Flint, December 14, 1861, with 31 men.

P. S. Titus, of Lapeer county, received authority to raise a Company, October 4, 1862, and entered camp of instruction with his men, November 20, 1861. Both companies failing to recruit as fast as was necessary, a consolidation was effected. The company was full to the minimum and mustered February 6, 1862, into the U. S. service.

This company was raised principally in Lapeer and Gennessee counties, and known at first, from the time of the consolidation to the assigning or numbering of the companies, as Gennessee Rangers.

COMMISSIONED OFFICERS.

*Capt. Russell M. Barker*, was born in Maddison county, New York, A. D. 1828. At the time of the call for volunteers he was living at Flint, Gennessee county, Michigan. He entered the service as 1st Lieutenant, company A, 8th Mich. Vol. Inf., and was promoted to Captain of said company in June, 1861, and on account of the failure of his health, he was obliged to resign, which we did September 21, 1861. But unwilling to give it up so he tried a second time, and received commission as Captain in the 10th, from October 1, 1861. But his health again failed him, and he resigned November 29, 1862. Before entering the army he was engaged in the blacksmithing business. He was married in Shiawassee county, Michigan, in 1855, and is now residing at Flint, Michigan.

1st *Lieut. P. S. Titus*, was born in Cayuga county, N. Y. in February, 1819, and came to Michigan in 1835, where he has resided most of the time since.

Previous to the Mexican war he had been a student in the University of Michigan, and at the commencement of the war he was studying law. After the close of that war he was engaged in farming most of the time until the breaking out of the rebellion. His military history or life was begun in the winter of 1837, at which time he served one month in the volunteer service, at Detroit, Michigan. He was twice a member of the Brady Guards, at Detroit; the last time in 1846. In March, 1847, he was appointed 2d Lieutenant 15th U. S. A., commanded by Col. Geo. W. Morgan, (now Br'g. Gen.) to serve during the war with Mexico. He enlisted 23 men for and joined his company and regiment about the 1st of May. He immediately marched with the regiment to New Orleans, thence to Verra Cruz, where it landed about the middle of June. He was with his regiment, under command of Major Gen. Pillow with 2500 men, in its march on Mexico. At Puebla they were placed in the advance. Lieut. Titus was in the following battles around and near Mexico,—the capitol: Contraras, August 18 and 19; Cherubusco, August 19; Molena Del Ray, September 8, and at the storming of Chepultapec, September 13, and was among the first to enter that stronghold, calling on his men to follow. The latter battle was conducted by Capt. (now Major Gen.) Joe Hooker, commanding army of Potomac, who was at that time Adj't Gen. to Gen. Pillow. After the treaty of peace Lieut. Titus returned to the U. S. with his regiment, and was mustered out of the service on the 10th day of August, 1848. In July, 1861, Lieut. Titus received notice that he was appointed Captain in the 18th regiment U. S. Infantry, and ordered to report to Headquarters at Columbus, Ohio, which he did promptly, but found that he had been displaced by some more fortunate political favorite. Returning again to Michigan, he enlisted a part of a company, and received commission as 1st Lieutenant 10th Michigan Infantry, from October 1, 1861. He entered the field in command of his company, and has been in command of it most of the time since. He was promoted to Captain March 31, 1863, vice Barker resigned.

*2d Lieut. John Algoe,* was born May 16, 1832, near St. Johns, New Brunswick. His parents emigrated from Scotland in the spring of 1820. He moved with his parents from New Brunswick to Michigan, in 1837, where they purchased a tract of land, and settled in Oakland county. Here Lieutenant Algoe was taught to "earn his bread by the sweat of his brow." In the spring of 1849 he engaged as a clerk and telegraph operator. He was employed as a clerk until 1854, when he entered into business for himself, and continued in the mercantile business six years, when he sold out to settle the estate of a deceased partner. He married Miss Emily, second daughter of Fitch R. and Charlotte Tracey, at Flint, June 3, 1858. In 1859 he went to Kansas, and while there assisted in building a school house in the Cotton wood valley, and taught the first school ever kept in that country. Returning to Michigan in the spring he was appointed Deputy Register of Deeds, for Gennessee county, and was thus engaged until entering the military service. He enlisted in Capt. Barker's company, and was elected 2d Lieutenant, and received commission as such from October 1, 1862. March 31, 1863 he was promoted to 1st Lieutenant company G, *vice* Dunphy promoted.

#### NON-COMMISSIONED OFFICERS.

#### · *Sergeants.*

1. *Harvey J. Clark,* 1st *Sergeant,* born in Independence, Michigan. Enlisted November 1, 1861, at Clarkston. Aged 22 years. School teacher. Appointed to rank as 1st Sergeant from date of enlistment. Discharged July 21, 1862, at Camp Dennison, O.

2. *Henry R. Chittenden,* born in Gennessee county, Mich. Enlisted October 16, 1861, at Flint. Aged 19 years. Farmer.

Appointed to rank as Sergeant from date of enlistment. Discharged February 4, 1863, at Gallatin, Tenn.

3. *Geo. AppLyn*, born in Gennessee county, Michigan. Enlisted October 23, 1861, at Flint. Aged 23 years. School teacher. Appointed to rank as Sergeant from date of enlistment.

4. *Joseph E. Tupper*, born in Gennessee county, Michigan. Enlisted December 29, 1861, at Flint. Aged 23 years. Jeweller. Appointed to rank as Sergeant from date of enlistment. Promoted to 1st Sergeant September 1, 1862. Promoted to Sergeant Major March 3, 1863. Promoted to 2d Lieutenant, company G, July 15, 1863. Promoted to Major 17th U. S. Infantry, Colored Troops, November 9, 1863.

5. *Thos. Branch*, born in Cornwall, England, in 1823. In the year 1831 emigrated with his parents to Quebec, Canada, where he resided nearly three years, making two visits to the old country. He then moved with his parents to Maine, thence to White Hall, N. Y. While living there his father died and he lived with his mother two years, and they both moved to Buffalo, N. Y. He was married about the time of the breaking out of the Mexican war. In 1847 he moved to Detroit, Mich., and in 1849 to Flint, Mich. At the breaking out of the "Patriot war" he volunteered in the British service, in he 8th Zouaves, and served 1 year and 9 months. By occupation he was a brick and stone mason before entering the service, but had worked at many other trades also. He enlisted November 20, 1861, at Flint, and was appointed to rank as Sergeant from date of enlistment. He was detailed as Regimental wagon master until November 21, 1862, and promoted to 2d Lieutenant, March 31, 1863, for " meritorious conduct."

*Corporals.*

1. *Wm. H. Davie*, born in N. Y. Enlisted November 4, 1861, at Flint. Aged 24 years. Blacksmith. Appointed to rank as Corporal from date of enlistment.

2. *Langdon B. Rice*, born in Gennessee county, N. Y. Enlisted November 28, 1861, at Hadley. Aged 31 years.

Shoemaker. Appointed to rank as Corporal from date of enlistment. Promoted to Sergeant September 1, 1862. Promoted to 1st Sergeant April 3, 1863.

3. *Arba Smith*, born in Lapeer county, Mich. Enlisted December 13, 1861, at Flint. Aged 19 years. Farmer. Appointed to rank as Corporal from date of enlistment.

4. *Albert Perry*, born in Oakland county, Mich. Enlisted December 17, 1861, at Oakwood. Aged 23 years. Farmer. Appointed to rank as Corporal from date of enlistment. Died August 6, 1862, in hospital at Keocuck, Iowa, of Consumption.

5. *Lyman E. Davie*, born in Wyoming county, N. Y. Enlisted November 4, 1861, at Flint. Aged 21 years. Farmer. Appointed to rank as Corporal from the date of enlistment. Promoted to Sergeant April 3, 1863. Promoted to 1st Lieutenant 17th U. S. Colored troops, November 9, 1863.

6. *Worthy E. Millard*, born in Mich. Enlisted December 12, 1861, at Clarkston. Aged 21 years. Cooper. Appointed to rank as Corporal from date of enlistment.

7. *Benjamin M. Bradshaw*, born in Oakland county, Mich. Enlisted December 13, 1861, at Flint. Aged 23 years. Cooper. Appointed to rank as Corporal from date of enlistment. Discharged March 13, 1863, at Flint, Mich.

8. *Moses Carr*, born in N. Y. Enlisted December 18, 1861, at Oakwood. Aged 33 years. Farmer. Appointed to rank as Corporal from date of enlistment.

*Musician.*

1. *Abram Houghton, Drummer*, born in Bennington county, Vt. Enlisted November 15, 1861, at Clarkston. Aged 18 years.

*Privates.*

*Jason L. Austin*, born in Conn. Enlisted December 10, 1861, at Flint. Aged 34 years. Farmer. Discharged October 23, 1862, at St. Louis, Mo.

*Theodore Armstrong*, born in Gennessee county, Mich. Enlisted November 24, 1861, at Flint. Aged 18 years. Farmer. Died June 3, 1862, at Farmington, Miss., of typhoid fever.

*John Arthur*, born in Sussex, N. J. Enlisted October 11, 1861, at Pontiac. Aged 40 years. Farmer.

*Mark Boice*, born in Oakland county, Michigan. Enlisted December 13, 1861, at Clarkston. Aged 21 years. Blacksmith. Discharged September 5, 1862, at Col. O.

*Wm. E. Bard*, born in Otsego county, N. Y. Enlisted January 3, 1862, at Oakwood. Aged 26 years. Farmer. Deserted September 4, 1862, from northern hospital.

*Terry Bird*, born in Ireland. Enlisted January 17, 1862, at Flint. Aged 30 years. Laborer. Deserted April 18, 1862, from Flint, Mich.

*Wm. H. Badgely*, born in N. Y. Enlisted January 2, 1862, at Flint. Aged 45 years. Farmer. Discharged April 19, 1862, at Flint, Mich.

*Charles W. Brewer*, born in Livingston county, N. Y. Enlisted November 2, 1861, at Flint. Aged 19 years. Painter. Died June 20, 1862, in Gen. Hospital, Cin. O., of debility.

*Richard Backenstose*, born in Seneca county, N. Y. Enlisted December 21, 1861, at Oakwood. Aged 48 years. Tailor. Discharged at Nashville, Tenn., March 11, 1863.

*John A. Baird*, born in Otsego county, N. Y. Enlisted December 12, 1861, at Oakwood. Aged 24 years Farmer.

*Josiah N. Berkley*, born in Ghetford Mich. Enlisted November 22, 1861, at Flint. Aged 22 years. Farmer. Discharged April 17, 1862, at Flint, Mich.

*Joseph Barton*, born in Cambridge, Vt. Enlisted November 30, 1861, at Flint. Aged 45 years. Farmer. Disharged July 18, 1861, at Flint, Mich.

*Thomas E. Brabson*, born in Gennessee county, Mich. Enlisted November 18, 1861, at Flint. Aged 18 years. Farmer.

*John Broadbeck*, born in Baden, Germany. Enlisted Aug. 16, 1862, at Fentonville. Aged 36 years. Farmer.

*John Brown*, born in Orleans, N. Y. Enlisted March 24, 1862, at Flint. Aged 18 years. Farmer. Discharged Sept. 20, 1862, at St. Louis, Mo.

*Geo. W. Cady*, born in Oakland county, Mich. Enlisted

October 7, 1861, at —, Lapeer county. Aged 18 years. Farmer. Discharged September 8, 1862, at Columbus, O.

*Charles B. Clark*, born in Lockport, N. Y. Enlisted Oct. 15, 1861, at Farmer's Creek. Aged 19 years. Preacher. Discharged December 6, 1862, at Cincinnati, O.

*Abram Chase*, born in Mich. Enlisted November 12, 1861, at Flint. Aged 18 years. Farmer. Discharged December 10, 1862, at Cairo, Ill.

*Patrick Coffee*, born in Clare county, Ireland. Enlisted November 21, 1861, at Flint. Aged 31 years. Farmer. Deserted April 18, 1862, from Flint.

*Edwin Crittenden*, born in Calhoun county, Mich. Enlisted November 19, 1861, at Flint. Aged 19 years. Farmer.

*W. H. Church*, born in Livingston county, Mich. Enlisted December 16, 1861, at Oakwood. Aged 22 years. Farmer. Discharged September 5, 1862, at Col., O.

*Lewis Church*, born in Oakland, Mich. Enlisted December 14, 1861, at Clarkston. Aged 17 years. Moulder.

*John Cook*, born in Tyrone, county, Ireland. Enlisted December 11, 1861, at Flint. Aged 19 years. Laborer. Deserted April 19, 1862, from Flint.

*David Centre*, born in N. Y. Enlisted November 24, 1861, at Oakwood. Aged 23 years. Farmer.

*David Campbell*, born in Sussex N. Y. Enlisted March 25, 1862, at Flint. Aged 18 years Saddler. Reported as a deserter December 30, 1863.

*John Chadburn*, born in Canada. Enlisted October 8, 1861, at Goodrich. Aged 52 years. Farmer. Transferred from Company C, April 30, 1862. Died August 1, 1862, at camp Dennison, O., of chronic diarrhœa.

*John W. Currier*, born in Lorane, O. Enlisted October 7, 1861, at Goodrich. Aged 24 years. Farmer. Transferred from Company C, April 30, 1862.

*Hiram G. Diamond*, born in Canada. Enlisted November 13, 1861, at Flint. Aged 33 years. Farmer. Discharged September 26, 1862, at St. Louis, Mo.

*Daniel P. Deming*, born in Mich. Enlisted December 18, 1861, at Oakwood. Aged 17 years. Farmer.

*Chester Darling*, born in Lapeer, Mich. Enlisted March 19, 1862, at Flint. Aged 18 years. Farmer.

*Samuel Evans*, born in N. Y. Enlisted November 18, 1861, at Flint. Aged 28 years. Farmer. Died July 7, 1862, at camp Big Springs, Miss., of cholera morbus.

*Delos Elsworth*, born in N. Y. Enlisted March 17, 1862, at Flint. Aged 17 years. Farmer. Deserted March 24, 1862, from Flint, Mich.

*Timothy Elsworth*, born in Orleans, N. Y. Enlisted March 13, 1862, at Flint. Aged 24 years. Farmer. Discharged January 31, 1863, at St. Louis, Mo.

*Horace Fleming*, born in Gennessee county, N. Y. Enlisted October 20, 1861, at Flint. Aged 28 years. Laborer. Deserted November 4, 1862, from hospital.

*Wm. Francis*, born in Ontario county, N. Y. Enlisted October 12, 1861, at Farmer's Creek. Aged 52 years. Farmer. Discharged June 26, 1862, at Detroit, Mich.

*Chester Farrar*, born in N. Y. Enlisted November 30, 1861, at Flint. Aged 19 years. Farmer. Discharged October 22, 1862, at Flint, Mich.

*Joseph Fifield*, born in Oakland, Mich. Enlisted November 18, 1861, at Goodrich. Aged 22 years. Farmer. Transferred from Company C, February 6, 1862. Died July 15, 1862, at Gen. Hospital, near Farmington, Miss., of chronic diarrhœa.

*Henry Griffin*, born in Ontario county, N. Y. Enlisted October 8, 1861, at —, Lapeer county. Aged 21 years. Farmer.

*Mortimer B. Gillman*, born in Genesee county, Mich. Enlisted November 19, 1862, at Flint. Aged 20 years. Hostler. Discharged September 26, 1862, at St. Louis, Mo.

*David W. Gillett*, born in Canada. Enlisted December 20, 1861, at Flint. Aged 23 years. Farmer.

*Wm. B. Gillett*, born in N. Y. Enlisted December 3, 1861, at Flint. Aged 25 years. Farmer. Discharged June 21, 1862, at Columbus, O.

*Oliver Gordon*, born in Canada. Enlisted February 10, 1862, at Flint. Aged 23 years. Farmer.

*George Gordon*, born in Canada. Enlisted February 10, 1862, at Flint. Aged 19 years. Farmer. Died June 23, 1862, at Paducah, Ky., of chronic diarrhœa.

*John Gordon*, born in Canada. Enlisted February 15, 1862, at Flint. Aged 48 years. Farmer. Died February 20, 1863, at Nashville, Tenn., of fever.

*Newton Hodge*, born in N. Y. Enlisted November 20, 1861, at Flint. Aged 18 years. Farmer. Appointed Corporal September 1, 1862. Promoted to Sergeant April 3, 1863.

*Abram C. Harrison*, born in Columbia, N. Y. Enlisted October 23, 1861, at Flint. Aged 34 years. Farmer. Discharged March 25, 1863, at Nashville, Tenn.

*Rufus Hathley*, born in East Oxford, Canada. Enlisted November 6, 1861, at Flint. Aged 19 years. Farmer.

*Byron Hunt*, born in N. Y. Enlisted November 14, 1861, at Pontiac. Aged 18 years. Farmer. Died June 10, 1862, at Gen. Hospital, near Farmington, Miss, of chronic diarrhœa.

*Frank D. Hopkins*, born in Erie county, N. Y. Enlisted November 16, 1861, at Flint. Aged 19 years. Farmer. Died June 29, 1862, at Gen. Hospital, near Farmington, Miss., of diarrhœa.

*Drake Hubbard*, born in Mich. Enlisted December 21, 1861, at Oakwood. Aged 19 years. Farmer. Died June 5, 1862, near Boonville, Miss., of typhoid fever.

*Geo. Husted*, born in Lower Phelps, N. Y. Enlisted December 9, 1861, at Oakwood. Aged 17 years. Farmer. Discharged April 21, 1862, at Flint Mich.

*David Houghton*, born in Bennington county, Vt. Enlisted November 15, 1861, at Clarkston. Aged 45 years. Farmer. Discharged September 8, 1862, at Cairo, Ill.

*Rolph Hollingsworth*, born in England. Enlisted November 15, 1861, at Flint. Aged 45 years. Farmer. Discharged April 2, 1862, at Flint. Mich.

*Hiram Howell*, born in N. Y. Enlisted December 4, 1861,

at Flint. Aged 22 years. Blacksmith. Appointed Corporal April 3, 1863.

*John Judd,* born in N. Y. Enlisted March 4, 1862, at Flint. Aged 27 years. Farmer.

*Collins Kelley,* born in N. Y. Enlisted October 16, 1861, at Pontiac. Aged 44 years. Joiner. Discharged January 8, 1864, at camp near Rossville, Ga.

*Prismins Klock,* born in N. Y. Enlisted December 13, 1861, at Tuscola county. Aged 25 years. Farmer.

*Sanders K. Kellogg,* nativity unknown. Enlisted December 20, 1861, at Pontiac, under age, and was taken by his parents before muster.

*Oscar Knowlton,* nativity unknown. Enlisted December 13, 1861, at Flint. Deserted January 1, 1862, from Flint.

*Edward Livermore,* born in Mich. Enlisted December 24, 1861, at Oakwood. Aged 22 years. Farmer.

*Wm. H. Lake,* born in Macomb county, Mich. Enlisted October 17, 1861, at Orion. Aged 19 years. Farmer. Transferred from Company C, February 6, 1862.

*Wilber Lamphried,* born in Boston county, Canada. Enlisted December 9, 1861, at Flint. Aged 18 years. Farmer.

*Wm. O. Morse,* born in N. Y. Enlisted November 20, 1861, at Flint. Aged 19 years. Sawyer. Appointed Corporal April 3, 1863.

*Isaac Measuroll,* born in Oakland, Mich. Enlisted December 12, 1861, at Clarkston. Aged 17 years. Farmer.

*Aaron Middaugh,* born in Canada. Enlisted January 22, 1862, at Flint. Age unknown. Sailor. Discharged October 29, 1862, at Louisville, Ky.

*Wm. McComb,* born in Canada. Enlisted February 19, 1862, at Flint. Aged 41 years. Farmer. Discharged November 28, 1862, at Louisville, Ky.

*George Marshall,* born in Huron county, O. Enlisted March 25, 1862, at Flint. Aged 21 years. Farmer. Appointed Corporal April 3, 1863.

*Thomas McCelhoney,* born in Donnegal county, Ireland. Enlisted February 28, 1862, at Flint. Aged 30 years. Farmer.

*Harvey McConnell*, born in Canada. Enlisted August 11, 1862, at Forestville. Aged 21 years. Farmer.

*Jacob Newkirk*, born in Orange county, N. Y. Enlisted December 19, 1861, at Clarkston. Aged 30 years. Farmer.

*Hezakiah Pearce*, born in Oneida, N. Y. Enlisted February 22, 1862, at Flint. Aged 45 years. Farmer.

*Gleason F. Perry*, born in N. Y. Enlisted December 17, 1861, at Oakwood. Aged 20 years Farmer. Appointed Corporal September 1, 1862.

*Simeon Perrigo*, born in N. Y. Enlisted January 13, 1862, at Flint. Aged 19 years. Farmer.

*James Phillips*, born in N. Y. Enlisted December 17, 1861, at Flint. Aged 41 years. Farmer. Died June 20, 1862, at Gen. Hospital, near Farmington, Miss., of quick consumption.

*Almon D. Quick*, nativity unknown. Enlisted December 13, 1861, place unknown. Aged 18 years. Deserted from Flint, December 27, 1861.

*Lewis Raisin*, born in Germany. Enlisted November 18, 1861, at Flint. Aged 18 years. Farmer.

*James E. Sherman*, born in Oakland, Mich., Enlisted October 15, 1861, at Farmer's Creek. Aged 21 years. Farmer.

*John Shatto*, born in Trumble county, O. Enlisted November 5, 1861, at Flint. Aged 45 years. Farmer. Died June 14, 1862, at St. Louis, Mo., of diarrhœa.

*Charles E. Stewart*, born in Mich. Enlisted December 17, 1861, at Oakwood. Aged 24 years. Farmer. Appointed Corporal April 18, 1861. Promoted to Sergeant April 3, 1863.

*Ameriah Sanborn*, born in N. Y. Enlisted January 20, 1862, at Flint. Aged 33 years. Farmer. Discharged September 12, 1862, at Columbus, O.

*Calvin Soper*, born in N. Y. Enlisted February 12, 1862, at Flint. Aged 17 years. Farmer.

*Simon Scamlon*, born in Munster, Ireland. Enlisted April 21, 1862, at Flint. Aged 17 years. Farmer. Died February 25, 1863, at Nashville, Tenn.

*Geo. Shoemaker*, born in Baden, Germany. Enlisted August 16, 1862, at Forestville. Aged 37 years. Farmer.

*Wm. Sweikheirt*, born in Baden, Germany. Enlisted August 14, 1862, at Forestville. Aged 21 years. Farmer.

*Orlando Smith*, born in Lapeer county, Mich. Enlisted January —, 1862, at Flint. Aged 18 years. Farmer. Discharged September 2, 1862, at Detroit, Mich.

*Elias Terry*, born in Oakland county, Mich. Enlisted October 14, 1861, at Pontiac. Aged 39 years. Farmer. Discharged February 4, 1863, at Nashville, Tenn.

*Nathaniel Taylor*, born in Cuyahoga, O. Enlisted October 26, 1861, at Flint. Aged 29 years. Joiner.

*Michael Veit*, born in Canada. Enlisted October 23, 1861, at Flint. Aged 24 years. Farmer.

*Henry Vantassel*, born in N. Y. Enlisted January 6, 1862, at Pontiac. Aged 45 years. Farmer.

*Wm. Wood*, nativity unknown. Enlisted November 21, 1861, place unknown. Aged 18 years. Taken home by parents before muster.

*John Winters*, born in Oswego county, N. Y. Enlisted December 14, 1861, at Clarkston. Aged 32 years. Farmer.

*Henry Whitney*, born in New York. Enlisted January 2, 1862, at Clarkston. Aged 22 years. Farmer.

*Aaron Walters*, born in Mich. Enlisted January 2, 1862, at Flint. Aged 18 years. Laborer.

*Augustus Welch*, born in Onondaga county, N. Y. Enlisted October 25, 1861, at Goodrich. Aged 31 years. Artist. Transferred from Company C, April 30, 1862.

*Henry C. Webster*, born in Macomb county, Mich. Enlisted April 7, 1862, at Flint. Aged 19 years. Farmer. Died June 29, 1862, at Henderson, Ky.

*Almer Warren*, born in Ontario county, N. Y. Enlisted March 27, 1862, at Flint. Aged 22 years. Farmer.


## COMPANY K.

The authority to raise Company K, was given to Ethel Judd, by Gov. Blair, November 20, 1861. He began recruiting his Company immediately. The Company entered camp at

Flint, December 26, 1861, with 32 enlisted men. Was full to minimum February 5, 1862, and mustered into the U. S. service February 6, 1862, with an aggregate of 85 men. This Company was mostly recruited in Hillsdale county, Mich. It was known at first as " Dickerson Guards."

*Capt. Ethel Judd*, was born in Herkimer county, N. Y. in the year 1807. At the time of entering the military service he was living in North Adams, Hillsdale county, Michigan, and engaged in farming. He received commission as Capt. from October 1, 1861, and finding that a soldier's life was too ardous for his strength and years, and his health having failed very much he was obliged to resign. His resignation was accepted July 5, 1862, while the regiment was resting and recruiting at Camp Big Springs, Miss.

*1st Lieut. John F. Storer*, came from Mass., and at the time of the breaking out of the war was pursuing a course of studies at Hillsdale, Hillsdale county, Michigan. He entered the "Dickerson" as 1st Lieutenant, and received commission as such from October 1st, 1861. His health failed soon after entering the service, and he was on this account obliged to resign; his resignation taking date from June 16, 1862. His illness proved fatal for he died a few weeks after arriving at his home.

*2d Lieut. John R. Thomson*, was born in Erie county, New York, in the year 1836. Spent several years in Flint, Michigan, living near his father's residence. At the breaking out of the war he was employed as a clerk, in Buffalo, New York, and when the 10th was formed took position as 2d Lieutenant, and received commission as such from October 1, 1861, and was promoted to 1st Lieutenant, *vice* Storer, resigned, June 23, 1862. He was dismissed the service November 22, 1862.

*Sergeants.*

1. *Warren Merritt*, 1st *Sergeant*, born in Wayne county, N Y. Enlisted December 5, 1861, at Cambria. Aged 26

years.   Farmer.   Appointed to rank as 1st Sergeant from
date of enlistment.  Discharged July 21, 1862, at Camp Dennison, Ohio.

2. *Avery Smith*, was born in Steuben county, Indiana, July
5, 1841.   In the spring of 1849 he moved with his parents to
Cambria, Hillsdale county, Michigan.   Here he resided, following the avocation of a farmer until joining the army.   He
enlisted December 7, 1861, at Cambria, and was subsequently
elected 2d Sergeant by members of the company, and received
Appointment to rank as such from date of enlistment.   He was
Promoted to 2d Lieutenant, *vice* Thomas promoted, June 23,
1862.   He was in command of his company a large share of
the time on account of absence, etc., of his superior officers.
March 31, 1863, he was promoted to 1st Lieutenant, *vice*
Thomson dismissed.

*Millard Lamb*, born in Lenawee county, Mich.   Enlisted
November 23, 1861, at Adams.   Aged 23 years.   Laborer.
Appointed to rank as Sergeant from date of enlistment.   Dis-
charged July 8, 1862, at Tuscumbia, Ala.                        .

4. *John Cronk*, born in Victor, N. Y.   Enlisted December
1, 1862, at —, Hillsdale county.   Aged 44 years.   Laborer.
Appointed to rank as Sergeant from date of enlistment.
Died June 3, 1862, at Farmington, Miss., of typhoid fever.

5. *Jasper G. McBuin*, born in Culey, N. Y.   Enlisted December 5, 1861, at Somerset.   Aged 44 years.   Farmer.
Appointed to rank as Sergeant from date of enlistment.   Discharged August 1, 1862, at Mound City, Ill.

*Corporals.*

1. *Frederick J. Baker*, born in Monroe county, N. Y.   En-
listed December 15 1861, at Woodbridge.   Aged 28 years.
Mechanic.   Appointed to rank as Corporal from date of
Enlistment.   Promoted to Sergeant June 23, 1862.

2. *Gideon H. Sherman*, born in Marion, N. Y.   Enlisted
December 15, 1861, at Woodbridge.   Aged 24 years.
Mechanic.   Appointed to rank as Corporal from date of enlist-
ment.   Promoted to Sergeant June 23, 1862.   Promoted to
Sergeant January 1, 1863.

3. *Abner B. Clark*, born in Seneca, county, N. Y. Enlisted January 12, 1862, at Grand Blanc. Aged 27 years. Farmer. Appointed to rank as Corporal from date of enlistment. Discharged August 14, 1862, at Cincinnati, O.

4. *Marshal I. Bartlett*, born in Clairmont, N. H. Enlisted December 25, 1861, at Adams. Aged 25 years. Laborer. Appointed to rank as Corporal from date of enlistment.

5. *Benjiah C. Baker*, born in Ranclier county, N. Y. Enlisted December 5, 1861, at Woodstock. Aged 37 years. Farmer. Appointed to rank as Corporal from date of Enlistment.

6. *Jasper Bryan*, born in Lenawee county, Mich. Enlisted December 18, 1861, at Woodbridge. Aged 21 years. Laborer. Appointed to rank as Corporal from date of enlistment.

7. *Henry G. Bacon*, born in Hartford, Conn. Enlisted December 16, 1861, at Adams. Aged 24 years. Laborer. Appointed to rank as Corporal from date of enlistment.

8. *John Gibson*, born in Alleghany, N. Y. Enlisted December 25, 1861, at Cambria. Aged 20 years. Farmer. Appointed to rank as Corporal from date of enlistment.

*Musicians.*

1. *Samuel Lamfrom, fifer,* born in Baden, Germany. Enlisted December 15, 1861, at Adams. Aged 23 years. Musician.

2. *Geo. Jay, drummer,* born in Birmingham, O. Enlisted November 19, 1861, at Lee. Aged 18 years. Laborer.

*Privates.*

*Noah Austin,* born in Gennessee county, N. Y. Enlisted August 14, 1862, at Lexington. Aged 31 years. Farmer.

*Ira Blowers,* born in Murry, N. Y. Enlisted January 6, 1861, at Highland. Aged 24 years. Farmer. Transferred from Company H, February 6, 1862. Died February 5, 1863, at Nashville, Tenn., of typhoid fever.

*Albert Bates,* born in Hillsdale, Mich. Enlisted December 7, 1861, at Amboy. Aged 18 years. Laborer.

*Geo. Bostick*, born in England. Enlisted December 12, 1861, at Marshall. Aged 44 years. Farmer. Discharged July —, 1862, at Camp Dennison, O.

*Wm. Bostick*, born in Marshall, Mich. Enlisted December 12, 1861, at Marshall. Aged 18 years. Laborer.

*Seymor C. Beach*, nativity unknown. Enlisted December 9, 1861, at —, Lenawee county. Aged 25 years. Artist. Died March 14, 1862, at Flint, Mich., of typhoid fever.

*Daniel Bates*, born in Onondaga county, N. Y. Enlisted February 14, 1862, at Woodbridge. Aged 24 years. Painter. Discharged December 5, 1862, at Quincy, Ill.

*Wm. H. Bassit*, born in Gennessee county, N. Y. Enlisted March 6, 1862, at Flint. Aged 27 years. Farmer. Discharged July 24, 1862, at Cin. O.

*Thos. J. Baker*, born in Lancaster, C. W. Enlisted August 13, 1862, at Lexington. Aged 18 years. Farmer.

*John P. Bingal*, born in Germany. Enlisted August 9, 1862, at Lexington. Aged 32 years. Laborer.

*Geo. Baker*, born in Amboy, Mich. Enlisted May 7, 1863, at Amboy. Aged 18 years. Farmer.

*John S. Corwin*, born in Cayuga county, N. Y. Enlisted December 1, 1861, at Woodstock. Aged 23 years. Shoemaker. Discharged November 17, 1862, at Cin. O.

*John Cleveland*, nativity unknon. Enlisted December 1, 1861, at Hillsdale. Aged 19 years. Deserted April 10, 1862, from Flint, Mich.

*Horace S. Crosby*, born in Lenawee county, Mich. Enlisted December 17, 1861, at Woodstock. Aged 20 years. Laborer. Died May 31, 1862, at Farmington, Miss., of cogestive chills.

*Lothario F. Chase*, born in Alleghany county, N. Y. Enlisted December 10, 1861, at Cambria, Aged 30 years. Farmer. Discharged July 1, 1862, at Detroit, Mich.

*Eugene Cronk*, born in Hillsdale county, Mich. Enlisted December 26, 1861, at Hillsdale. Aged 18 years. Laborer. Discharged —, 1862, at Cin. O.

*Sheldon W. Curtice*, born in Lock, N. Y. Enlisted November 20, 1862, at Adams. Aged 31 years. Laborer.

*Dennis Clarry*, born in King county, Ind. Enlisted August 22, 1862, at Forestville. Aged 28 years. Farmer.

*Geo. Doty*, nativity unknown. Enlisted February 3, 1862, at Albion. Aged 22 years. Deserted March —, 1862, from Flint, Mich.

*Wesley Doty*, born in Livingston, N. Y. Enlisted December 9, 1861, at Adams. Aged 20 years. Cooper. Discharged September 2, 1862, at Evansville, Ind.

*Thomas Dean*, born in Cork, Ireland. Enlisted December 1, 1861, at Jonesville. Aged 40 years. Laborer. Discharged July 15, 1862, at Camp Dennison, O.

*Norman Dolittle*, born in Monroe county, Mich. Enlisted December 19, 1861, at Wheatland. Aged 24 years. Laborer. Died July 12, 1862, at Camp Dennison, O., of fits.

*Theodore Dense*, born in Yates county, N. Y. Enlisted January 10, 1862, at Grand Blanc. Aged 30 years. Farmer.

*Wm. H. Dawson*, born in Caledon, C. W. Enlisted August 11, 1862, at Lexington. Aged 25 years. Farmer. Appointed Corporal April 2, 1863.

*Nathan W. Dawson*, born in Caledon, C. W. Enlisted August 11, 1862, at Lexington. Aged 19 years. Farmer.

*James Fuller*, born in Wayne county, N. Y. Enlisted Dec. 15, 1861, at Woodbridge. Aged 18 years. Laborer. Died at Camp Dennison, O., March 18, 1862, of fever.

*Samuel Fuller*, born in Washington, N. Y. Enlisted December 15, 1861, at Woodbridge. Aged 37 years. Carpenter. Died March 18, 1863, at Nashville, Tenn. of typhoid fever.

*Geo. Freedon*, born in Adrian, Mich. Enlisted December 1, 1861, at Adrian. Aged 25 years. Laborer.

*James H. Finn*, born in England. Enlisted March 1, 1862, at Fenton. Aged 43 years. Mechanic. Discharged August 11, 1862, at —.

*Thomas Faulkner*, born in Orange county, N. Y. Enlisted January 27, 1862, at Reading. Aged 37 years. Laborer. Appointed Sergeant June 1, 1862.

*James Fifield*, born in Onondaga county, N. Y. Enlisted January 1, 1862, at Woodbridge. Aged 27 years. Farmer. Discharged October 8, 1862, at Camp Dennison, O.

*Joseph Frink*, nativity unknown. Enlisted December 13, 1861, at Cambria. Aged 23 years. Farmer. Deserted Feb. 8, 1862, from Flint.

*Goo. H. Fishell*, born in Monroe county, N. Y. Enlisted February 18, 1862, at Flint. Aged 18 years. Laborer.

*Paul Fifield*, born in Plattsburg, N. Y. Enlisted January 1, 1862, at Woodbridge. Aged 34 years. Farmer. Discharged July 24, 1862, at Camp Dennison, O.

*Charles Goodrich*, born in O. Enlisted January 8, 1862, at Hillsdale. Aged 18 years. Laborer.

*Adriel Gibson*, born in Alleghany, N. Y. Enlisted Feb. 14, 1862, at Reading. Aged 18 years. Laborer.

*John Gallinger*, born in Glasgow, Scotland. Enlisted August 22, 1862, at Lexington. Aged 32 years. Farmer.

*Henry Haskins*, born in Seneca county, N. Y. Enilsted November 17, 1861, at Maringo. Aged 23 years. Laborer. Discharged July 24, 1862, at Cincinnati, O.

*Chase F. Houk*, born in Watertown, N. Y. Enlisted December 8, 1861, at Woodstock. Aged 24 years. Shoemaker.

*Christian Howald*, born in Switzerland. Enlisted December 5, 1861, at Amboy. Aged 19 years. Laborer.

*Samuel Hooper*, born in Lenawee county, Mich. Enlisted November 16, 1861, at Allison. Aged 18 years. Laborer.

*Nathan Hartwell*, born in Clinton county, N. Y. Enlisted November 5, 1861, at Maringo. Aged 25 years. Farmer. Died June 28, 1862, at Farmington, Miss., of typhoid fever.

*Hamilton Holloway*, born in Genesee county, Mich. Enlisted January 25, 1862, at Richmond. Aged 35 years. Mechanic. Died March 25, 1863, at Nashville, Tenn., of typhoid fever.

*Michael Hulle*, born in Sussex, N. J. Enlisted January 14, 1862, at Highland. Aged 38 years. Carpenter.

*Thos. Holton*, born in Buffalo, N. Y. Enlisted October 25, 1861, at Newton. Aged 20 years. Laborer.

*James R. Harpster*, born in Medina county, O. Enlisted November 5, 1861, at Albion. Aged 20 years. Laborer.

*Jeremiah Hardin,* born in Port Huron, Mich. Enlisted February 12, 1862, at Fentonville, Mich. Aged 21 years. Blacksmith.

*Oziel Inman,* born in Chenango, N. Y. Enlisted November 21, 1861, at Tuscola. Aged 38 years. Farmer. Transferred from Company C, February 6, 1862. Transferred to Company H, May 20, 1862.

*Wilson Judd,* born in Hillsdale county, Mich. Enlisted December 1, 1861, at Woodbridge. Aged 19 years. Laborer. Died November 4, 1862, at Keokuk, Iowa.

*Albert Jones,* born in Ontario, C. W. Enlisted August 22, 1862, at Lexington. Aged 33 years. Farmer.

*John Kaneman,* born in Olivia, France. Enlisted August 22, 1862, at Lexington. Aged 42 years. Farmer. Died March 14, 1863, at Louisville, Ky.

*Aaron Langdon,* nativity unknown. Enlisted December 18, 1861, at Woodstock. Aged 28 years. Deserted from Flint, February 18, 1862.

*Ebin M. Lewis,* born in Dover, O. Enlisted December 5, 1861, at Woodbridge. Aged 21 years. Laborer.

*Oscar D. Lason,* born in Genesee county, Mich. Enlisted December 17, 1861, at Grand Blanc. Aged 28 years. Farmer.

*Henry Livingston,* born in Genesee, N. Y. Enlisted July 19, 1862, at Lexington. Aged 24 years. Laborer.

*Henry Litchenburg,* born in Kingston, Russia. Enlisted August 22, 1862, at Lexington. Aged 39 years. Farmer.

*Thos. H. Levitte,* born in Quebec, Canada. Enlisted January, 15, 1863, at Nashville. Aged 28 years. Clerk. Deserted from Stevenson, Ala., September 21, 1863.

*Giles Meesick,* born in N. Y. Enlisted December 11, 1861, at Adams. Aged 24 years Laborer.

*John McGuiggan,* born in Ireland. Enlisted December 1, 1861, at Jonesville. Aged 20 years. Laborer. Died at Stevenson, Ala., October 6, 1863.

*Daniel S. Merrill,* born in Troy, N. Y. Enlisted December 12, 1861, at Marshall. Aged 38 years. Laborer.

*John Mudge,* born in London, C. W. Enlisted August 22,

1862, at Lexington. Aged 33 years. Farmer. Appointed Sergeant, September 22, 1862.

*Homer Northrup*, born in Berkshire, Mass. Enlisted January 10, 1862, at Woodbridge. Aged 39 years. Farmer. Died September —, 1862, at Keokuk, Iowa, of typhoid fever.

*Wm. Otto*, born in Sciota county, O. Enlisted December 11, 1861, at Adams. Aged 18 years. Laborer.

*Ampster Otto*, born in Wayne county, N. Y. Enlisted December 5, 1861, at Adams. Aged 43 years. Farmer. Discharged July 25, 1862, at Cin., O.

*John C. Olin*, born in Shermont, N. Y. Enlisted December 1, 1861, at Moscow. Aged 21 years. Laborer. Appointed Corporal January 1, 1863.

*Frank Potter*, born in Penn. Enlisted February 1, 1862, at Fentonville. Aged 18 years. Laborer.

*Ira E. Payson*, born in Genesee, Mich. Enlisted March 6, 1862, at Flint. Aged 18 years. Farmer.

*Volentine Riggs*, born in Wayne county, N. Y. Enlisted November 22, 1861, at Woodbridge. Aged 22 years. Laborer. Appointed Corporal June 23, 1862. Promoted to Sergeant April 3, 1863.

*Franklin Reeder*, born in N. Y. Enlisted March 17, 1862, at Detroit. Aged 20 years. Farmer.

*Thomas Russell*, born in Branch county, Mich. Enlisted January 15, 1862, at California. Aged 30 years. Laborer.

*Charles Roberts*, born in Courtland county, N. Y. Enlisted November 12, 1861, at Litchfield. Aged 26 years. Laborer. Died June 3, 1862, at Farmington, Miss., of typhoid fever.

*Wm. C. Russell*, born in Niagara county, N. Y. Enlisted January 20, 1862, at Camden. Aged 19 years. Farmer.

*Alexander Robb*, nativity unkown. Enlisted December 5, 1861, at Amboy. Aged 19 years. Died January 30, 1862, at Flint, Mich., of lung fever.

*Geo. Rose*, born in Greene county, O. Enlisted December 11, 1861, at Adams. Aged 19 years. Laborer.

*Sanford Robins*, born in Oakland county, Mich. Enlisted March 11, 1862, at Flint. Aged 18 years. Laborer.

*John Robinson*, born in Antrim, Ireland. Enlisted August 22, 1862, at Lexington. Aged 42 years. Farmer. Discharged August 18, 1863, at Nashville, Tenn.

*Phillip Spencer*, born in Richmond county, O. Enlisted December 1, 1861, at Hillsdale. Aged 19 years. Laborer.

*Adin Squires*, born in Senecca county, N. Y. Enlisted December 15, 1861, at —, Williams county, O. Aged 35 years. Farmer. Died July 12, 1862, at Mound City, Ill.

*Abram Stall*, born in O. Enlisted December 10, 1861, at Camden. Aged 44 years. Farmer.

*Jacob N. Squires*, born in Geneseo county, Mich. Enlisted December 1, 1861, at Amboy. Aged 31 years. Farmer.

*Chas. H. Spencer*, born in Richmond county, O. Enlisted December 25, 1861, at Hillsdale. Aged 21 years. Laborer Discharged September 20, 1862, at Evansville, Ind.

*Geo. Salmon*, born in England. Enlisted December 15, 1861, at Amboy. Aged 27 years. Farmer.

*Geo. G. Spencer*, born in Jackson county, Mich. Enlisted February 17, 1862, at Adams. Aged 24 years. Laborer.

*J. A. Sullivan*, born in London, Conn. Enlisted December 1, 1861, at Woodstock. Aged 40 years. Laborer. Discharged at Jefferson Barracks, Mo., date unknown.

*Lewis Sissman*, born in Bolivar, Prussia. Enlisted August 22, 1862, at Lexington. Aged 24 years. Mechanic.

*Richard W. Sherman*, born in Genesee, N. Y. Enlisted August 14, 1862, at Lexington. Aged 42 years. Farmer.

*Andrew S. Sherman*, born in Erie county, Pa. Enlisted August 18, 1862, at Lexington. Aged 37 years. Farmer.

*Wm. Stillwell*, born in C. W. Enlisted August 15, 1862, at Forestville. Aged 35 years. Laborer.

*Chas. H. Thornton*, born in Wayne county, N. Y. Enlisted January 10, 1862, at Albion. Aged 23 years. Mechanic.

*Seth Thomas*, nativity unknown. Enlisted October 26, 1861, at Albion. Aged 23 years.

*Oscar Tuttle*, born in N. Y. Enlisted November 4, 1861, at Sheridan. Aged 18 years. Laborer. Appointed Corporal April 3, 1862.

*Chas. Treadwell,* nativity unknown. Enlisted November 1 1861, at Flint. Aged 28 years. Discharged February —, 1862, at Flint.

*Vinson Teeler,* born in Tompkins N. Y. Enlisted October 28, 1861, at Spring Arbor. Aged 34 years. Farmer.

*Benj. F. Vreeland,* born in Bergen, N. J. Enlisted November 20, 1861, at Adams. Aged 23 years. Blacksmith. Appointed Corporal June 23, 1862.

*John VanDuzer,* born in Hillsdale county, Mich. Enlisted January 1, 1862, at Hillsdale. Aged 25 years. Laborer. Appointed Corporal April 3, 1863.

*Wayne Vosberg,* born in N. Y. Enlisted December 7, 1861, at Woodbridge. Aged 18 years. Laborer.

*Alonzo Wood,* born in Steuben county, N. Y. Enlisted January 18, 1862, at Hillsdale. Aged 30 years. Laborer. Died July 12, 1862, at Mound City, Ill., of fever.

*Alexander Williams, Jr.,* born in Madison, O. Enlisted December 7, 1861, at Woodbridge, Mich. Aged 18 years. Laborer. Died September 21, 1862, at Jackson, Miss., of chronic diarrhœa.

*C. B. Winget,* born in Ontario county, N. Y. Enlisted December 9, 1861, at Fentonville. Aged 40 years. Carpenter. Discharged September —, 1862, at Camp Dennison, O.

*Peter West,* born in Tuscaroras county, O. Enlisted December 1, 1861, at Cambria. Aged 36 years. Laborer.

*Joseph Wolfe,* born in Hungary. Enlisted February 17, 1862, at Hillsdale. Aged 36 years. Laborer.

*Geo. Young,* born in Wayne county, N. Y. Enlisted November 22, 1861, at Woodbridge. Aged 20 years. Laborer.

*Ezra C. Yost,* born in Erie county, N. Y. Enlisted January 8, 1862, at Ransom. Aged 19 years. Laborer. Died August 16, 1862, at Mound City, Ill., of billious fever.

*Emery Yost,* born in Erie county, N. Y. Enlisted January 8, 1862, at Ransom. Aged 18 years. Laborer.

## VETERAN ORGANIZATION.

### FIELD OFFICERS.

CHARLES M. LUM,    -    -    *Colonel.*
CHRISTOPHER J. DICKERSON, *Lieutenant Colonel.*
HENRY S. BURNETT,    -    - *Major.*

### STAFF OFFICERS.

FRED. W. SPARLING,  -  -   *Surgeon.*
DANIEL A. SPICER,    -    - *1st Assistant Surgeon.*
DAVID W. VANDERBURGH,    *2d Assistant Surgeon.*
EDWIN A. SKINNER,  -  -   *Quartermaster.*
FRED. S. STEWART,    -    - *Adjutant.*
——— ———,   -   -   -   - *Chaplain.*

### NON-COMMISSIONED STAFF.

ERASTUS B. PAXSON,  -  - *Sergeant Major.*
AMI M. ROBERTS -    -    - *Quartermaster Sergeant.*
JAMES. W. ARMSTRONG.    - *Commissary Sergeant.*
WM. H. HANNA,  -  -   - *Hospital Steward.*
——— ———,   -   -   - *Prixcipal Musician.*

### COMPANY A.

#### COMMISSIONED OFFICERS.

——— ———, *Captain.*      ——— ———, *2d Lieut.*
DeWitt C. Welling, *1st Lieut.*

#### NON-COMMISSIONED OFFICERS.

*Sergeants.*

——— ———, *First.*      Wm. B. Pratt, *Fourth.*
Samuel S. Tower, *Second.*      M. P. Andrews, *Fifth.*
Charles P. Rice, *Third.*

*Corporals.*

James Atherton, *First.*      ——— ———, *Fifth.*
George E. Mills, *Second.*      ——— ———, *Sixth.*

14

Chas. Robinger,* *Third.*      —— ——, *Seventh.*
H. S. Calkings *Fourth.*      —— ——, *Eighth.*

### Privates.

Abel, Godfrey.
Botsford, Jonas W.
Beard, Henry.
Brown, William.
Campbell, Albert.
Cook, Lyman V. D.
Conden, Lampson.
Cowles, Edward D.
Colburn, Benjamin,
Crawford, Silas.*
Darby, Charles.
Ervey, Judson.†
Gove, Wm.

Miller, Henry.
Mills Orlando.
Marsh, Henry. †
Minor, R. Blake.
O'Rourke, Alexander.
Parker, George A.
Putnam Monroe.
Palmer, Christopher H.
Riegle, Abram.
Tower, William J.
Welch, Edgar D.
Wooliver, Peter.

## COMPANY B.

### COMMISSIONED OFFICERS.

Charles H. Richman, *Capt.*      Wm. A. Copeland, 2d *Lieut.*
George Turner,   1st *Lieut.*

### NON-COMMISSIONED OFFICERS.

#### Sergeants.

Wm. B. Walker, *First.*      Wm. A. Stewart, *Fourth.*
Theo. V, Kelsey, *Second.*      Isaac Hanson, *Fifth.*
Thomas Horner, *Third.*

#### Corporals.

Alexander H. Allen, *First.*      Hiram Braley, *Fifth.*
Wm. Dennis, *Second.*      Samuel B. Andrews, *Sixth.*
John B. Herriman, *Third.*      Henry Taylor, *Seventh.*
Lewis D. Kelsey, *Fourth.*      Wm. Chatfield, *Eighth.*

#### Privates.

Brown, Wm. N.
Brown, George.
Byron, Robert.

Pierce, Phinneas.
Pierce, Henry F.
Patterson, William.

Bradgro, Francis,

Cole, Eugene.

Crydeman, Jefferson W.

Cronkwright, Abraham.

Gruet, James.

Hull, Cyrus E.

Hough, Robert B.

Hough, Elijah.

McMellin, Neil.

McGrowry, John.

Miner, Geoge H.

Munger, Stephen B.

Rodell, George.

Rozell, Laperose.

Spencer, James.

Saxton, Washington.

Soule, John D.

Truax, Charles,

Turner, Junius O.

Vosburgh Ralph.

Westbrook, William.

Wisner, Allen E.

Woodard, Myron O.

## COMPANY C.

### COMMISSIONED OFFICERS.

Sylvan TerBush, *Captain.*    Geo. A. Allen, *2d Lieut.*

Alva A. Collins, *1st Lieut.*

### NON-COMMISSIONED OFFICERS.

#### *Sergeants.*

Esli R. Redfield, *First.*    James R. Kipp, *Fourth.*

Fletcher W. Hewes,§ *Second.*    Milo Swears, *Fifth.*

Mark H. Ridley, *Third.*

#### *Corporals.*

Edmond O'Neil, *First.*    Geo. R. Collins, *Fifth.*

S. J. W. Gibbs, *Second.*    G. W. Richmond, *Sixth.*

F. B. Casamar, *Third.*    H. S. Bidwell, *Seventh.*

J. C. Inglehart, *Fourth.*    M. C. Barney, *Eighth.*

#### *Privates.*

Arman, Elihue.

Bush, George.

Bush, John,

Becket, George W.

Clark, John.

Crittenden, Frank.

Cheney, Lewis C.

Cornish, James H.

Chapman, Freeman.

Confer, Nelson.

§ Detailed as Ordnance Sergeant for the Regiment,

Corwin, Erastus.
Casamer, Theodore F.
Cummings, Oscar.
Colvin, Joel P.
Hedglen, Edmond E.
Husted, Stephen J.
Hewes, Edgar I.
Hibbard, Harker.
Ingleheart, George.
Landon, James C.
Merritt, Thomas J.
Marvin, George C.
Payne, Martin B.

Carter, Richard.
Ford, Ira C.
Grilley, Edgar E.
Hedglen, Seely S.
Potter, John.
Richmond, George S.
Rogers, Ira.
Ramlow, Charles H.
Rutherford, George M.
Stowe, George.
Saunders, John W.
Sprague, William E.
Volentine, Asa.

## COMPANY D.

### COMMISSIONED OFFICERS.

Israel Huckins, *Captain.*        Richard Teal, *2d Lieut.*
Watson Beach, *1st Lieut.*

### NON-COMMISSIONED OFFICERS.

#### *Sergeants.*

Henry Wideman, *First.*        S. R. Moore, *Fourth.*
Hugh McCaffrey, *Second.*      James D. Close, *Fifth.*
Thomas Oldfield, *Third.*

#### *Corporals.*

James W. Eaton, *First.*       *Phillip Knapp, *Fifth.*
William. J. Hoey, *Second.*    *Charles Cissman, *Sixth.*
George Henry, *Third.*         William Hale, *Seventh.*
Amos L. Ellsworth, *Fourth.*   Lemuel House, *Eighth.*

#### *Privates.*

Amon, Jacob.                   Miles, Ira M.
Belknap, Stephen.              Moore, Freeman Q.
†Briggs, Charles N.            McKenzie, John D.
Brimley, George.               Patterson, John.
Byam, Frederick C.             Randall, Charles.

Campbell, James.

†Clukey Joseph.

Cross, Charles M.

Edwards, George.

Foster, W. S..

Gardner, George.

Gordon, John W.

Henderson, William.

Henry, John.

Heeler, Heman.

Lakin, Daniel A.

Louks, Alonzo.

Maskell, James.

Merrick, Robert.

Rockwood, Annanias.

Ross, Nelson F.

Seymore, Walter.

Shaver, Horace.

Sherman, Augustus,

Smith, Levi.

Stacy, Alexander.

Vancamp, Samuel.

Wahley, Charles.

Ward, Lyman.

Wilson, George.

Dixson, Daniel.

Wright, Austin.

## COMPANY E.

### COMMISSIONED OFFICERS.

Bradford Cook, *Captain.*    Rudolph Papst, *2d Lieut.*

Harrison H. Wheeler, *1st Lieut.*

### NON-COMMISSIONED OFFICERS.

#### Sergeants.

—— ——, *First.*    Robert P. Settell, *Fourth.*

Orange F. Linsday, *Second.*    —— ——, *Fifth,*

Joseph T. Moore, *Third.*

#### Corporals.

Wm. H. Parsons, *First.*    Wm. H. Robinson, *Fifth.*

John Henries, *Second.*    Henry Smith,, *Sixth.*

Geo. Watkins, *Third.*    —— ——, *Seventh.*

Frank Thomas, *Fourth.*    —— ——, *Eighth.*

#### Privates.

Allen, Luther.

Ayers, William.

Banfill, George.

Carl, John G.

Lamphier, Henry H.

Lowe, James.

Linen, James.

Leverre, Theopholis.

Chase, Eugene K.
Duchene, Benjamin.
Dewar, James.
Fry, Edward.
Flynn, Michael.
Farrell, James,
Flanagan, S. A.
Johnson, John.
Jones, Johnathan.

Pomeroy, John T.
Rewhle, Valentine.
Smith, Peter.
Strickland, Thomas.
Sheldon, Henry.
Stephens, Robert.
Westbrook, Chas. H.
Wasey, Mathew.
Williams, Michael.

## COMPANY F.

### COMMISSIONED OFFICERS.

Noah H. Hart, *Captain.*
Wm. McDonald, 1*st Lieut.*

—— ——, 2*d Lieut.*

### NON-COMMISSIONED OFFICERS.

#### *Sergeants.*

—— ——, *First.*
Samuel Starmer, *Second.*
Mathew M. Hedges, *Third.*

Andrew W. Bradley, *Fourth.*
Lewis B. Wells. *Fifth.*

#### *Coporals.*

Wm. A. France, *First.*
James H. Robinson, *Second.*
Calvin H. Bentl,y *Third.*
Cornelius McMonagal, *Fourth.*

Lafayette M. Reed, *Fifth.*
† Jas. O. Hodgson, *Sixth.*
* Alexander Officer, *Seventh.*
—— ——, *Eighth:*

#### *Privates.*

Alport, James G.
Alger, George W.
Burton, Norman.
Bradshaw, Ruben.
Currey, Andrew.
Crankshaw, Jacob.
Clark, George.
* Douglas, Dexter.
Evans, Edward.

Horton, Horace F.
Haskill, Albert.
Lucas, Wm.
Morrison, George.
Mercer, Morgan D.
† Mattison, Ezra B.
Nolin, Owen.
Owen, Thomas C.
Reid, Darwin.

Fisher, Warren.
Ferguson, James A.
Glover, Wm. M.
Gummerson, Aaron.

*Stone, Wheeler H.
Sutphon, Horace W.
Watson, Myron C.
Wealsh, Michael.

## COMPANY G.

### COMMISSIONED OFFICERS.

Wm. H. Dunphy, *Captain.* ——— ———, *2d Lieutenant.*
John Algoe, 1*st Lieutenant.*

### NON-COMMISSIONED OFEICERS.

*Sergeants.*

Joseph A. Gleason, *First.*
Henry W. Shipman, *Second.*
Wm. Keene, *Third.*

Chas. Bennett, *Fourth.*
Chas. Cook, *Fifth.*

*Corporals.*

Thomas Weaver, *First.*
Standish Waxfield, *Second.*
Gordon Rudd, *Third.*
Joseph Barber, *Fourth.*

Jacob E. Johnson, *Fifth.*
Jason Clark, *Sixth.*
Bradley Mattoon, *Seventh.*
Putnam Welling, *Eighth.*

*Privates.*

Ashby, Charles L.
Appley, William.
Bunker, William.
Bailey, Wm. H.
Cudworth, Joseph T.
Derby, Wm. H.
Delong, Enos.
Edwards, John.
Ellsworth, Charles.
Gordinier, Asa.
Gordinier, Martin.
Gordinier, Jay.
Glover, Joel.
Haynes, George A.
Huntly, Mortimer.

Hands, Benjamin F.
Lenox, Marvin.
Lawrence, Rasselous E.
Mattoon, Christopher.
McCoy, Peter.
McGary, John.
Mitchell, Ira.
Osgood. H. C.
Proctor, Thomas.
Phillips, Chas. J.
Parrish, Eli.
St. John, James.
Spencer, Henry C.
Trew, Samuel.
Volker, Frederick.

Howard, Myron.
Hooper, Samuel A.
Huntly, Wallace.
Hedgers, Justus.

Walters, Jeffries.
Webster, Wm. W.
Wildy, Albert S.

## COMPANY H.

### COMMISSIONED OFFICERS.

John Pierson, *Captain.* —— ——, *2d Lieutenant.*
H. Walter Nichols, *1st Lieut.*

### NON-COMMISSIONED OFFICERS.
### Sergeants.

—— ——, *First.*
William Clark, *Second.*
John Chamberlain, *Third.*

Ruben Wright, *Fourth.*
§ Hiram E. Belcher, *Fifth.*

### Corporals.

Albert W. Simmons, *First.*
Hiram R. Beach, *Second.*
Edwin F. Holmes, *Third.*
Constantine Miller, *Fourth.*

John Butler, *Fifth..*
Cornelius L. Smith, *Sixth.*
Abram J. Sloat, *Seventh.*
—— ——, *Eighth.*

### Privates.

Butler, Lawrence.
Basler, Jacob.
Credit, George W.
Carman, Francis.
Crothers, John.
Derrick, John.
Evans, Samuel.
Hungerford, Myron M.
Harris, Wm. G.
*Harris, Abram.
*Hope, John H.
*Kipp, Frederick.
McCarthy, James.
Mosey, Frank.

Madison, Archie.
Meeker, Lewis.
*Ovaitt, Levi.
Porter, Wm.
Post, Ransell L.
Palmer, Porter.
Reynolds, Robert.
Rogers, Samuel.
Shaw, Alfred J.
Starks, Danford.
Sloat, Silas J.
*Thomas, Simmons.
Vancamp, Jessie.
Wheeler, Nathan.

§ Detailed as Color Sergeant for the Regiment.

## COMPANY I.

### COMMISSIONED OFFICERS.

Platt S. Titus, *Captain.*     Thomas Branch,     *2d Lieut.*
—— ——,     1st *Lieut.*

### NON-COMMISIONED OFFICERS.

*Sergeants.*

Charles P. Stewart, *First.*     Wm. H. Davie, *Fourth.*
Newton D. Hodge, *Second.*     Gleason F. Perry, *Fifth.*
George Alpin, *Third.*

*Corporals.*

Worthy E. Millard, *First.*     —— ——, *Fifth.*
Hiram E. Howell, *Second.*     —— ——, *Sixth.*
William O. Morse, *Third.*     —— ——, *Seventh.*
George Marshall, *Fourth.*     —— ——, *Eighth.*

*Privates.*

Bard, John.                 Messerall, Isaac.
Brabson, Thomas E.          Perrigo, Simeon.
Crittenden, Edwin.          Raisin, Lewis.
Currier, John W.            Rice, Langdon B.
Gordon, Oliver.             Sherman, James E.
Hathley, Rufus.             Taylor, Nathaniel.
Houghton, Abraham G.        Vantassell, Henry.
Klock, Prismus.             Vite, Michael.
Lake, William H.            Walters, Aaron.
Lamphierd, Wilbur.          Whitney, Henry.
Livermore, Edward.          Winters, John.

## COMPANY K.

### COMMISSIONED OFFICERS.

Hannibal H. Nims, *Captain.*   John Knox, *2d Lieutenant.*
Avery A. Smith, 1st *Lieut.*

### NON-COMMISSIONED OFFICERS.

*Sergeants.*

Gideon H. Sherman, *First.*     Jasper Bryan, *Fourth.*

Frederick J. Baker, *Second.* —— ——, *Fifth.*
Volentine Riggs, *Third.*

## Corporals.

Benjiah C. Baker, *First.*      John Vandusen, *Fifth.*
Christian Howald, *Second.*     Oscar Tuttle, *Sixth.*
Benj. F. Vreeland, *Third.*     —— ——, *Seventh.*
John C. Olin, *Fourth.*         —— ——, *Eighth.*

## Privates.

Bostwick, William.            Merrill, Daniel S.
Curtis, Shelden W.            Otto, William.
Fishell, Geo. G.             Russell, Thomas.
Freedon, George.             *Robins, Sanford.
Faulkner, Thomas.            Rose, George.
Goodrich, Charles.           †Reeder, Franklin.
Giles, Mesick.               Spencer, Phillip.
Holion, Thomas.              †Spencer, George G.
Harpster, James R.           Thornton, Charles H.
Hardin, Jeremiah.            Vosburgh, Wayne.
Houk, Chase F.               Wolf, Joseph.
Jay, George D.               Yost, Emery.
Lewis, Eben M.               Youngs, George.

† The names marked with dagger, are of men who were not eligible to muster when the regiment mustered, but did so before we obtained a furlough.

* The names marked with a star, are of those who had served over 21 months, and not two years, and who signed pledges to re-enlist when they became eligible.

In Company G, the names are not marked on account of the list having been lost. All other companies containing no marked names had no pledged men.

## EXPLANATORY.

It was the intention of the author to carry the date of this work only to February 16, 1864, (the date when the regiment was mustered as veterans,) but owing to circumstances which were developed shortly afterward, it was thought best to continue it a little later.

It is for this reason that the account of the reconnoisance and fight at Buzzard's Roost is detached from the main history.

F.

---

## RECONNOISANCE IN FORCE.—FIGHT AT BUZ-ZARD'S ROOST, GA.

February 23. At daylight this morning an order came for the regiment to move immediately, with sixty rounds of ammunition, and three days rations.

Although we were partially prepared for this, by having received an order the evening previous to prepare, and keep constantly on hand three days rations and sixty rounds of ammunition per man. Yet we could hardly believe that we should have to leave our camp and go to the front before going home, for we were daily and hourly expecting that our furlough would come.

The day before, the first and third Divisions of our army corps (the 14th) passed by our camp en route for " the front." And we well understood that a reconnoisance in force was to be made. But our division was so scattered, being on duty at several different points, we thought it would not be called upon.

At eight o'clock, A. M. the regiment moved out of camp, or a part of it did. A portion was on picket, and not being yet relieved did not move until about 10 o'clock, A. M., when it followed the advance.

One half of Companies D and G, and a detail of enough men from the balance of the companies to complete the number of the said companies to their full size, had been sent out the night before several miles, on guard duty, and were consequently left back. Although they followed on, the second day after the regiment, they did not arrive in time for the fight. Several of the men were almost or entirely without shoes, and of course could not accompany the regiment. And it is but justly due that we say that several of these men felt disappointed that they could not accompany the regiment. Thus it will be seen that the regiment was very small. But small as it was, the men who composed it were as "plucky" as ever, and found no word of fault at their having their expectations thus unhappily disappointed. But little did we dream of what was in store for the 10th.

The day was sunny, warm and pleasant, and we marched to within a mile of Ringgold, where we halted at about two o'clock, P. M., having marched 14 miles. Here we leisurly prepared our meals, and the pickets having come up we went to rest for the night.

February 24.—We were astir early, and just after daybreak on the move. We marched through Ringgold, and immediately reached "Hooker's Gap" in the white oak ridge, through which we passed, and soon after came up with the main force which had left Chattanooga on the 22d.

We moved on with the army until within one and a half miles of Tunnel hill, when our forces were drawn up in several lines of battle on either side of the road. Our line being next to first on the right of the road, and on a ridge. As we supposed we were to advance in the position or order in which we were disposed, we were a little surprised when our Brigade was ordered to move by the left flank, after we had been halted for about an hour. And leaving the force still lying there we moved directly to the left, passing directly in front of a line on the left of the road. We continued this direction across roads and fields, striking to the left of the rebel camps, which stretched away to the front and right, occupying a space nearly a mile in length, and which we had been comfortably watching while lying in line of battle.

After moving a mile by the left flank, and getting nearly opposite the rebel camps, the direction of march was changed by moving by the right flank, which of course brought us into line of battle. In this way we moved forward and soon crossed over the tunnel through which the railroad runs, and came to the rebel earthworks, which we mounted immediately, our batteries at the same time throwing shell and shot into their camps. The rebels beat a hasty retreat when they found themselves so completely flanked. ·We made a momentary halt after crossing their fortifications, and as our batteries were still shelling the camps and vicinity, Gen. Morgan called for our colors, and had them planted in the highest part of the camps, and as they floated out triumphantly on the breeze our batteries ceased firing, and we had peaceable possession of the viper's nest, with our stars and stripes proclaiming victory where but a few moments before our enemy had thought to defy us. But although we had the nest, the vipers themselves true to their subtle instinct, had fled for safer lodgings. We swept past and through this extensive camp for nearly a mile, the rebels flying before us at every step.

After passing their camps we formed in column in the road, and moved toward Dalton. At half-past four o'clock, P. M., we arrived at Buzzard's Roost, a very rocky, rough, stronghold, in a pass known as Kenyon's Gap, three miles from Dalton, Georgia. Here the rebels had taken a strong position on and in rear of Rocky Faced Ridge, commanding the gap through which both the railroad and wagon road pass to Dalton.

After crossing the railroad we formed in line of battle facing the gap, and on the right of the wagon road, and threw out skirmishers, for the enemy had skirmishers on the ridge to the right of the gap; which ridge sloped upward gradually from near the road, for some distance, and then grew steeper until it formed a heavy ridge, and a difficult one to dislodge the enemy from. A battery partially in rear of and protected by this . ridge, at the same time began dropping shells all around and among us. Our skirmishers forced the enemy to retire from the ridge and held it. Here we remained exposed to fire until dark without serious damage being done.

Just at dark Gen. Morgan ordered us to recross the railroad, and passing by a spur on the left of the railroad, (where we were exposed fully to the fire from the battery,) on double-quick, we took our position for the night between two spurs of "Rocky Faced" where we were partially protected from the fire of the enemy. Orders were given that no fires be built, as that would discover our position to the rebels.

Companies C and F were detailed as pickets. Our picket line was advanced to within a few rods of the enemy, and all night we could hear them engaged at pounding, chopping, etc., as though planting batteries. Our pickets were even so far advanced as to be able, when daylight came, to look right down upon the rebel camps, and force, or at least a part of it, just beyond the gap.

February 25.—When morning came and we could see how the "land lay," we could partially understand our position.

From the ridge on the left (north) of the railroad, a number of spurs put out, running nearly parallel to each other, toward the railroad. The sides of these spurs were steep and rocky, and covered with brushwood and logs. On the first, running a little obliquely to the direction of the others, they had built some earth works, but had vacated them on our approach.

These spurs were from 30 to 50 feet high, and very rugged, and at the top had no breadth, descending immediately from the crest, on either side. Altogether they bore the resemblance of the sea, were it lashed into fury by the power of the tempest, and suddenly congealed so as to retain all its roughness.

Close to the railroad, also on the left, rose a "round top," a sort of rough, scraggy knoll, but entirely separated from the spurs.

The main ridge on the left, rose up from the spurs quite steep, and so high as even to command the narrow ravines between the spurs at its foot. On this bold front there was a large force of sharpshooters annoying our pickets, and they were so well entrenched, and the ridge was so steep, that it was vain to think of dislodging them with the small force in our command, under the circumstances.

On the right of the railroad, the main ridge rose up without spurs, from close to the track. A battery—the one which annoyed us the evening previous,—planted on that ridge, was also in position to throw its death dealing missiles into every ravine on the opposite side of the gap. Hence, if we were to advance over these ridges, we should be exposed to a raking fire from the right, by the battery, and on the left by the sharpshooters, with their deadly rifles. What was in front was yet to be developed.

Company A relieved a portion of the pickets in the morning, and companys B and I were thrown out as skirmishers, covering the remainder of the picket line of the right, and extending some distance farther, to drive the enemy back as far as possible, and ascertain their position and strength in front.

Steadily, step after step the enemy's skirmishers were driven back, and as steadily our line advanced, pressing forward anxiously, yet cautiously. The regiment in the mean time being drawn up in line of battle on the first spur, on the west opening of the gap, exposed to the fire of the sharpshooters, and the battery too, had it chosen to open.

At times the rebels contested stubbornly, as if determined to yield not a foot of ground, but by the sternest necessity. Again they would fall back hurriedly, as if entirely routed, and then rally and oppose stubbornly again. At 3 o'clock, P. M., our skirmishers had advanced well up the side of the ridge, but as the enemy had a very heavy line of skirmishers, supposed to be strongly supported, it was thought best not to advance farther without strengthening our lines. For that purpose a portion of the 60th Illinois Infantry,—the only one present with us of our brigade, comprising all of that regiment who were not already out, moved forward in accordance with orders of Gen. Morgan, and our regiment accompanied them. We could not move forward in the valley or gap through which the railroad ran, for we would be entirely exposed to the fire of the battery on the right, and the sharpshooters on the left, and also to whatever might be in front. The only alternative left for us was to advance over the spurs directly in our front, as these would protect us from a front fire.

Up to this time our efforts had failed to draw fire from the enemy, and hence we did not know their exact position or force. As soon as the movement had well begun, and the two regiments commenced advancing, the sharpshooters poured a most galling fire into the ranks from the left, and the battery on the right opened, throwing shot and shell with deadly accuracy, raking the ravines, and sweeping the tops of the spurs. But on, coolly, calmly and steadily our lines advanced over two of these rugged spurs, and through two of the ravines, coming each moment more and more into certain range of the sharpshooters, now directly opposite the left flank; nor did they halt here, but pressed on hurriedly yet steadily to the top of the third, our colors flying defiantly in the very faces of the enemy. As soon as we reached that point, a battery directly in front, and one a little to the left, and heavy lines of Infantry opened a most galling and murderous fire, beneath which it is impossibe to understand how a single life could stand preserved a single moment. It was as though heaven's loudest thunders were all about us, and breaking up the foundations of the mountains under feet. The regiment was ordered to lie down, and obeying, we returned as best we could, the fire of the triple number in our front. And all the time the shells from right, left and front, came howling and shrieking like hellish fiends, seeking our lives; with unearthly yells and demon thunder bursting at every point, tearing and furrowing the earth like thunderbolts, while a hail of lead, terrible and devastating, pored in from front and left. The sharpshooters did fearful execution, as they were so elevated that our lying down afforded no protection whatever. Turn which way we might, and the earth seemed constantly lifted and thrown into the air by striking shot and bursting shells. Each moment some one cries "I'm hit! what shall I do?"

and his officer orders him to retire from the field. Men never deported themselves better in such circumstances. Every one seemed cool, and determined to do the best they could. Men, comrades were being killed on every hand, and yet, just as determined fought those who still survived. It was a desperate courage; a terrible energy; a dreadful necessity which nerves the hero to deeds of undying valor. And well did it tell on these brave men. Never for a moment were the officers without coutroll over the men.

It is true there were a few, very few, who had played the coward's part. Some who were recklessly daring, loaded their pieces, and standing boldly erect, bade defianco to their foes, and dealt death for death. We shall not say that it is foolish to thus expose life in such instances. Who can say but it was the terribly brave example of these men which saved the rest from panic and demoralization.

Here tho regiment remained under that deadly enfilading fire for some forty minutes, and all the time Lieut. Col. Dickerson paced back and forth along the lines, bidding his men to be cool and take sure aim. "Fire low" said he. And it was not until he saw that the last man would soon be lost that he gave the order to retreat. Hastily the men moved to the bottom of the first ravine on the retreat, and although by this time apparently confused and scattered, only a word from their commander and they formed in line of battle, and waited until Col. Anderson, commanding the 60th Illinois Infantry, came and consulted with Lieut. Col. Dickerson, and the retreat was ordered to be completed, which was done in good order, the men being constantly under control of their officers. It was not until the retreat was completed that we missed our Lieut. Col. Commanding. The last that had been seen of him was in the first ravine we entered on our retreat, and as the enemy pressed forward when we left the field, and the battery on the right and tho sharpshooters on the left raked the ravines constantly with a heavy fire, he was supposed to have been wounded and taken prisoner. Some of the men talked with

15

him after he had fallen behind, and he said he was wounded. How badly, was not ascertained. He seemed to be unwilling that any one should help him, as they would have to expose themselves more to danger, but told them to press on and save themselves. We feel his loss very deeply. He proved himself courageous, bold and fearless, amid the greatest dangers of a soldier's life.

Many of our wounded, and all of the dead had to be left behind. But as the enemy did not advance their pickets, and the force fell back, some of the wounded dragged themselves from the field by the greatest efforts, which seemed like taking life. Some who were not wounded were so entirely exhausted as to be unable to leave the field, and they lay until late at night, and one or two even until daylight, concealed, yet close to the rebel pickets, so that they could hear them talk.

The retreat was ended where the advance began. And we rested on the ridge from which the desperate charge was made, in just one hour and five minutes from the first advance.

The whole proceeding was watched by Gen's Thomas, Palmer, Davis, Morgan and others. All of them spoke very highly of the conduct of our regiment. They did not hesitate to make the most praiseworthy remarks in regard to the controll of the officers over the men; and the daring coolness and veteran bearing of the men all through the whole action. And we feel proud that we have thus far kept the honor of our state, as regards our conduct on the field of battle.

It was very sad that we should loose so many when home seemed just in our grasp. Indeed it seemed worse that we had to fight at all at that time than it would at any other. Our commanders wished that it might not have been. Still we felt ready to "do and dare," ill as it seemed.

When night came we were very tired, and rest seemed refreshing, but the thoughts of dead, dying and wounded comrades so close by, troubled our slumbers.

February 26.—We laid here all day to-day, but were not engaged, having been relieved by another brigade the night before. At dark we fell in and marched to Ringgold, and passing through, halted on the same ground we did on our way out, to stay until morning, having come ten miles from Buzzards' Roost.

February 27.—Lay near Ringgold until about 2 o'clock, P. M., when we fell in and marched to camp, a distance of fourteen miles, where we arrived at dusk.

Our wounded were carried in ambulances to Chattanooga, as fast as possible. A hospital was established at Tunnell Hill as soon as our forces had possession of it; and here most of the wounded received very good care until they could be sent away.

This demonstration at Buzzards' Roost, was undoubtedly the hottest, and by far the most desperate of any part of the reconnoisance. Indeed men who have seen hard service, and long service, say they never saw hotter or more destructive fire. And we cannot imagine how a fire could well be arranged to be more destructive and terrible.

It would be very interesting to record personal examples of noble and daring deeds, and to condemn cowardly ones; but we have neither the time nor space. We are glad that of the cowardly, there were but one or two; while of the opposite there were many. But we purpose to give general features of our particular regiment, having no personal heroes.

We give below an accurate list of killed, wounded and missing.

————

HEADQUARTERS 10TH REG'T MICH. V. V. INFANTRY,
NEAR ROSSVILLE, GA., FEB. 29, 1864.

The following is a list of killed, wounded and missing of the Tenth Regiment of Michigan Veteran Volunteers, Infantry, during a reconnoisance upon Dalton, Georgia, on the 25th day of February, 1864.

| Comp'y, | Rank. | Killed. | |
|---------|-------|---------|---|
| B. | Private. | Ezekiel Bourbina, - - - - | |
| C. | Corporal. | Samuel J. W. Gibbs, - - | Veteran. |
| C. | Private. | James H. Cornish, - - - | " |
| C. | " | Erastus Corwin, - - - - | " |
| C. | " | Stephen Husted, - - - - | |
| E. | " | James Farrell, - - - - | Veteran. |
| E. | " | Mathew Wasey, - - - - | " |
| F. | Sergeant. | Samuel Starmers, - - - | " |
| F. | Corporal. | William H. Watson, - - - | |
| F. | Private. | Michael Welch, - - - - | Veteran. |
| K. | Corporal. | Oscar Tuttle, - - - - - | " |
| K. | " | John Vanduser, - - - - | " |
| K. | Private. | Ira E. Payson, - - - - - | |

Total killed 13.

| Co. | Rank. | Wounded. | Nature of wound. |
|-----|-------|----------|------------------|
| B. | Sergt. | Thomas Horner, | Slight; left side. |
| B. | Private. | Robert Byron, | Middle of thigh. |
| B. | " | George Brown, | Severe; left shoulder. |
| C. | " | George Rutherford, | Slight; contused. |
| C. | " | George Inglehart, | Slight; left leg. |
| C. | " | Ira C. Ford, | Slight; left hand. |
| C. | " | Sylvester Haynes, | Severe; right leg and right shoulder. |
| C. | " | Edgar I. Hewes, | Serious; right side. |
| D. | " | Daniel Lakin, | Slight. |
| D. | " | Berry B. Miller, | Severe; right shoulder. |
| D. | " | Levi Smith, | Slight. |
| E. | 1st Lieut. | Harrison H. Wheeler, | Slight; hip. |
| E. | Sergt. | Robert P. Settell, | Severe; thigh and left hand. |
| E. | Private, | Peter Smith, | Slight; right shoulder. |
| E. | " | John T. Pomeroy, | Slight; left leg. |
| E. | " | Jerry Tracy, | Slight. |
| E. | " | Peter O'Neill, | Slight. |
| E. | " | Michael Flynn, | Severe. |
| F. | Corp. | William A. France, | Slight. |
| F. | Private. | James A. Ferguson, | Severe; left arm. |
| F. | " | George Clark, | Slight. |

| F. | " | Miron C. Watson, | Slight. |
|---|---|---|---|
| G. | " | James St. John, | Slight. |
| H. | Sergt. | Ruben Wright, | Slight. |
| H. | Corp. | Hiram R. Beach, | Severe. |
| H | " | John Butler, | Slight. |
| H. | Private. | Francis Carman, | Severe. |
| H. | " | Archibald Madison, | Slight. |
| H. | " | John Marshall, | Severe. |
| H. | " | Lewis Meaker, | Slight. |
| H. | " | Robert Reynolds, | Serious; leg. |
| I. | " | Nathaniel Taylor, | Slight. |
| K. | " | Emory Yost, | Severe. |
| K. | " | William Otto, | Severe. |
| K. | " | Charles Goodrich, | Severe. |

Total wounded 35.

| Comp'y. | Rank. | Missing. |
|---|---|---|
| | Lieut. Col. | C. G. Dickerson. |
| C. | Private. | George Stowe. |
| D. | " | Ignatus Horn. |
| E. | " | James Lowe. |
| E. | " | Thomas Strickland. |
| F. | " | Wheeler H. Stone. |
| F. | " | George Alger. |
| F. | " | Horace F. Horton. |
| F. | " | Horace W. Sutphen. |
| F. | " | John A. Miller. |
| G. | " | Kenneth McKay. |
| H. | " | John H. Hope. |
| H. | " | Porter Palmer. |
| H. | " | Ransell L. Post. |
| I. | 1st Sergt. | Charles P. Stewart. |
| K. | Private. | John Gibson. |
| K. | " | Joseph Wolfe. |

Total missing 17.

Total loss 65.

# OUTLINE

# VETERAN SERVICE

# Tenth Regiment of Michigan Veteran Volunteer Infantry.

February 6, 1864—July 19, 1865.

# BRIEF VETERAN RECORD.

———⊷>◆<⊷———

Feb. 16. In camp near Rossville, Ga. Mustered as *Veterans*, to date from Feb. 6, 1864 (two years from date of volunteer muster). The number mustered, including those who pledged to muster as soon as eligible was four hundred sixteen.

Feb. 17 to 22. In camp near Rossville, Ga.

Feb. 23. Ordered to the front. Marched 14 miles. Camped 1 mile from Ringgold at 2 p.m.

Feb. 24. Took Tunnel Hill. Reached "Buzzard's Roost" (Kenyon's Gap) at 4.30 p.m. Skirmished till night, and at dark stole close up to the rebel lines and lay without fires until morning.

Feb. 25. Battle of "Buzzard's Roost." Killed, 13; wounded, 35; missing, 17. Total 65.

Feb. 26. At "Buzzard's Roost" until dark; then marched to near Ringgold, 10 miles, and camped in the same place as on February 23.

Feb. 27. Lay in camp until 2 p.m., then marched to camp near Rossville.

Feb. 28 to March 5. In camp near Rossville, waiting for transportation to take us home on our veteran furlough.

March 5 to 11. On the way home. Left camp at 2.30 p.m. and marched to Chattanooga, 8 miles, in one hour and thirty minutes. Train left for the *north* at 12, midnight.

March 11. Arrived in Detroit (as I was not with the regiment I have not the points and dates of the route. F. W. H.)

March 12. Furloughed for 30 days to report at Flint, April 12.

March 12 to April 12. Every man detailed on "Special Duty." Obeying his own orders.

April 12.   Reported at Flint.

April 12 to 20.   At Flint, waiting U. S. Orders, to return to the field.

April 20 to 24.   From Flint, Mich., to Nashville, Tenn.

April 24.   Arrived at Nashville and took up quarters at Barracks No. 1, at 8 a.m.

April 25.   At Nashville.   Ordered to move to-morrow.   Order countermanded.

April 26.   Drew ordnance stores for the entire command.

April 27.   Marched at 9 a.m. on the Murfreesboro "Pike."   Made only 8 miles.   Camped early.

April 28.   Marched 13 miles.

April 29.   Reached Murfreesboro, 9 miles.   Camped nearly south of Murfreesboro, near a large spring. Drew clothing.   Heavy rain in the night.

April 30.   Marched 14 miles on the Shelbyville "Pike."

May 1.   Marched 11 miles to Shelbyville. Quartered in buildings.

May 2.   Left Shelbyville at 3 p.m.   Marched 6 miles.   About 600 cavalary near our camp to-night.

May 3.   Marched to Tullahoma.   (12 miles.)

May 4.   Marched to Decherd.   (15 miles.)

May 5.   Marched to Tantallon.   (15 miles.)

May 6.   Marched 13 miles.   Camped in the woods.

May 7.   Marched into Stevenson (very hot.)

May 8.   Marched to Bridgeport, 10 miles.   Camped on the island.

May 9.   Marched 11 miles.   Camped near White-side's Mountain.

May 10.   Marched 12 miles.   Camped at the foot of Lookout Mountain.   During the night a heavy rain. The water from the mountain side deluged the camp, and a high wind threw down the tents.

May 11.   Marched to Chattanooga, 6 miles. Camped south of the town.

May 12.   Marched at 3.45 p.m., 6 miles, to the old camp where we re-enlisted as Veterans, near Ross-ville, Ga.

May 13.   Marched at 5.30 a.m., 16½ miles, to 1 mile S. E. of Ringgold.   3 p.m.

May 14.   Marched at 6 a.m., 14 miles; reached "Buzzard's Roost" at 10 a.m.   Looked over the battle-ground until 11.30 a.m.   Found the following inscrip-tion on a board raised over some graves: "8 *Yankees*

*gone to Heaven, I hope ; where there is no fighting,
and where God judges who is right or wrong.*"
Passed through Tunnel Hill and Dalton. Camped at
3 p.m., 1 mile south of Dalton.

May 15. Marched at 11 a.m. Rebels made a
charge on our corps at midnight, last night, and
"skedaddled." Inscription found on a guide board
to-day: "*Masonic Hall, 1½ miles beyond Hell.
Hell, 4½ miles.*" (No record of the day or number of
miles marched.)

. May 16. In pursuit of rebels. Regiment joined
the brigade this a.m. near Resaca. Left Resaca at
7.30 am. (20 miles.) Camped at 9 p.m. (Where?)

May 17. Left camp at 6.30 a.m. Marched
rapidly. Halted at 1.30 p.m. near Ogee Creek.
Moved forward at 3 p.m. Met Rebels at 5 p.m. 3d
Brigade threw out skirmishers and drove rebel skirmishers to their line of battle. The rebels in turn
drove our skirmishers back to our line of battle. An
action followed and the rebels were driven. Heavy
fighting for awhile. Barnett's 5th Wisconsin Battery
shelled the "Johnnies." At 8.30 p.m. our brigade
moved to the right flank two miles and took position
for the night. Some girls came into our lines during
the fight and reported very few rebels in Rome, but
we were afraid to trust their story. We are about
1 mile from Rome, Ga. Marched 18 miles.

May 18. At 6.30 a.m. formed line of battle and
advanced through a dense fog, towards the rebel
works on a hill overlooking our position. Skirmishers (A and part of D) soon found that the works had
been abandoned during the night. We took possession just after day-break. Rebels threw a few shells
at us from the town across the river (Rome.) Our
forces occupy the town to-night.

May 19. On picket near Rome, Ga.

May 20. On picket until 2.30 p.m. In camp
near Rome, Ga.

May 21. In camp near Rome.

May 22. Left camp at 2 p.m. Crossed the
Oostanaula river, into Rome; then crossed the Etowah
to the south bank of the Coosa. Marched 2½ miles.

May 23. At 9 a.m., moved camp one mile farther
from town, into a clump of young pine. Corn meal
for rations during the last three days. Hard-tack
again to-night.

May 24. Left camp at 5 a.m. Made 18 miles on

the Atlanta road and camped at Peak's Spring. Water very scarce on the march.

May 25. Marched at 7.30 a.m., 15 miles, camped at 8 p.m., 5 miles from Dallas, Ga., in a rye field. Heard fighting from 5.30 p.m. until dark. Country very hilly. Rained hard in the evening.

May 26. Marched at 7 a.m.; advanced 2½ miles, toward Dallas (as we supposed) over a very hilly road, and then halted until 10 a.m., when we retraced our march to last night's camp, took another road and reached Dallas at 2 p.m. Found the town nearly deserted. Passed 1½ miles beyond the village and formed line of battle. Heavy fighting east and south of us. (11½ miles).

May 27. Lay all last night in line of battle, fronting north. Reveille at 4 a.m. At 6.30 moved line 80 rods to front and right, facing N. E. At 9 a.m. formed new line ¼ mile to right, fronting E. Lay in this position all day. Brisk skirmishing all day in our front. Cannonading on both flanks.

May 28. In line of battle, in yesterday's position. Co. G on skirmish line. Brisk firing. Heavy attack on our right in p.m. Rebels repulsed with severe loss.

May 29. Still in line of battle as yesterday. Very quiet all day. At 9.30 p.m. we moved silently to the right rear flank and took position to support a battery. At 10.30 p.m. the rebels charged our lines, coming down the mountain. Masked batteries opened fire and raked the side of the mountain down which they came, and our infantry met them with a hot fire. They were repulsed. At 12 midnight they charged again, and were again repulsed.

May 30. Twice between midnight and 3.30 a.m. the rebels charged our lines with a decided repulse each time. Rumor said that they were made drunk and told that they had only a lot of 100 day men in their front, and that they should each have a negro as personal property if they would break our lines. The sight, at the time of each charge, was a splendid affair; the stillness between the charges, like the silence of death. At day-break, resumed position in line of battle.

May 31. In line of battle, of the last three days. Rebels shelling from the mountain.

June 1. Left the line at 6.30 a.m. 14th, 15th, and 16th Army Corps are taking a new position. March very tiresome and day hot. At 4.30 p.m. took position in rear of 23d Army Corps, on a hill, and supposed we should remain until morning. At 9 p.m. fell in, moved 1½ miles and took position in the front lines, facing Lost Mountain. (10 miles.)

June 2. Threw up works and held our position. Rebels close in front. Sharpshooters throw an occasional "minnie" in our lines. They think us surrounded and ask our skirmishers if we are going to surrender or cut our way through. Rebel earthworks about 600 yards from ours. Skirmishers in rifle-pits.

June 3. In works. Line of yesterday. An effort was made to draw the rebel forces out by withdrawing our skirmishers and marching our troops out in plain sight of the enemy, and returning them to their works by a masked passage, but it failed. They would not take the bait. We had a very large number of cannon masked to rake the field if they had come.

June 4. Left our works at day-light. Moved slowly. Roads muddy. Camped at 12.20 p.m. on Stoneman's Hill. 14th Michigan Infantry rejoined our Brigade to-day.

June 5. In camp on Stoneman's Hill. Rebels skedaddled from Lost Mountain last night and this morning. Orders to march at sunrise.

June 6. Ready at sunrise. Moved at 8 a.m. Marched slowly (8 miles). Formed line of battle at 5 p.m. and threw up breast-works in a field, near a piece of woods. Near Acworth, Ga.

June 7. Lay in works, near Acworth, Ga. Received large mail.

June 8. Lay in works, near Acworth, Ga. Orders to march at 6 a.m. to-morrow.

June 9. Ready to march at 6 a.m. Order countermanded at 8 a.m. Lay in works.

June 10. Orders at midnight to move at 5 a.m. Delayed until 6.20 a.m. Heavy thunder-shower at 12.30 p.m. We were in the rear and so marched heavily and slowly on account of train delays. Camped at 3.30 p.m., having made only about 4½ miles.

June 11. Ready to move at 5 a.m. Moved at 9.30 a.m. Rain all the morning. Marched only about two miles (east) by a series of short moves, and at 11.45 a.m. made camp. At 3.30 p.m. comes the " fall in." Struck tents and were until after dark moving one mile—in double column at half distance. (3 miles.)

June 12.  In camp.  Rained all day.

June 13.  In camp.  Rained until noon.

June 14.  Left camp at 9.10 a.m. without striking tents or taking blankets.  Moved ¾ mile nearly south and massed by division.  Whole force moved forward 1½ miles and massed in a piece of woods.  Cos. E, K, G and B skirmishers.  Co. E lost Michael Williams (shot in the head).  Wounded—Corporal Thomas, ankle, and Corporal Vreeland, slightly.  (Did we put up works?)

June 15.  In camp, a little in rear of our earthworks, near Big Shanty.

June 16 and 17.  In position of the 15th.  Steady firing in our front.

June 18.  In position of the 15th until 4 p.m. Moved half mile to the front and threw up earthworks. We built fires and tried to dry our clothing.

June 19.  Left our lines at 7.50 a.m.  Moved slowly, often halting.  Approaching Kenesaw Mountain.  Artillery passed us and took position in rebel works, and begun shelling the mountain.  At 9.40 a.m. we had advanced two miles.  At 11 a.m., a heavy rain.  We advanced half mile beyond the works and halted in close column by division.  Artillery moved up.  We approached the mountain, slowly supporting our skirmishers as they cleared the way, until we formed our lines close to the foot of the mountain.  (4 miles.)

June 20.  Skirmishing on the side of Kenesaw. Carrier and Van Tassel, Co. I, wounded.

June 21.  In camp near Kenesaw Mountain. Lieut. Wheeler, Co. E, and Private Butler, Co. H, wounded this morning.

June 22.  In camp near Kenesaw Mountain.  Most of us lay in the works a good share of the day as the Rebels were shelling our lines.  H. Bidwell, Co. C, wounded.

June 23.  In camp near Kenesaw Mountain.  Several artillery duels occurred to-day, and several skirmish spirts that called us into the trenches.

June 24.  In camp near Kenesaw Mountain.  Artillery quiet.  Sharpshooters annoyed us some.  Asa Gardinier (G) wounded.  Went on skirmish on the side of Kenesaw.

June 25.  On skirmish on Kenesaw.  Several artillery duels, but our guns soon silenced the rebels.

June 26.  Relieved from skirmish line at midnight.  Marched to the rear at 12.40 a.m. but had made only 1¾ miles at day-break, then moved to the right 3 miles. Although we made only 5 miles, yet it was a hard march on account of the previous skirmish of 30 hours.

June 27. At 2 a.m. received orders to be ready to march at sunrise without knapsacks. Moved at 6 a.m. Took position in breastworks half mile out. Captain Cook mortally wounded. Our entire line charged the rebel works, but did not carry them. Union loss, 3,000. Confederate loss, 450.

June 28. In works, south of Kenesaw Mountain. Sharpshooters on both sides kept up a constant fire.

June 29. In works, south of Kenesaw Mountain. At 11 a.m. a truce of four hours to bury the dead, lying between the lines (killed the 27th.) Our soldiers mingled with the rebels during the interval. Time up and the dead not all buried. 1½ hours more allowed. Captain Cook died.

June 30. In works, south of Kenesaw Mountain. No decided move on either side. Sharpshooting brisk.

July 1. In works, south of Kenesaw Mountain. Sergeant Baker (K) wounded last night. Briggs (K) severely wounded in hip to-day.

July 2. Rebels abandoned their works last night. We started in pursuit at 7 a.m. Overtook their rear guard two miles out. Threw up breastworks at dark, 7 miles out.

July 3. Completed earthworks. At 5 p.m. moved half mile to the front and threw up a new line of works. Pioneer detail of 50 men built 5 bridges.

July 4. Rebels ran again last night. We pursued them, skirmishing and worrying their rear guard. Took 50 prisoners. (6 miles).

July 5. Threw up works. At 4 p.m. relieved by 20th Army Corps and moved quarter mile to the left and rear, and bivouacked for the night.

July 6. Moved quarter mile to left and rear again, and pitched camp in a fine grove of young pines. Our camp 1½ miles south of the Chattahoochee River.

July 7 to 17. In camp of July 6. July 10—our regiment on skirmish discovered that the rebels had run, and we reached their works before any other skirmishers, either right or left. Picked up 33 deserters from the rebels. Found railroad bridge burning.

July 17. Crossed the Chattahoochee, and halted about 1½ miles from the pontoon bridge for the night.

July 18. Lay in the position of last night until

3 p.m., then moved two or three miles, and formed line of battle, and threw up breastworks.

July 19. Lay in works until 2.45 p.m., and then began the Peach-tree Creek movement. Some of our sharpshooters wounded. Lay in a small ravine expecting to charge the enemy.

July 20. Lay in the position of last night. Threw up works in a.m. Sustained more losses to-day—some 20 in all. Just at sundown the rebels retreated and we possessed their works, advanced some distance beyond, and bivouacked.

July 21. Marched at daylight toward Atlanta. Crossed Peach-tree Creek. Made reconnaissance of two miles toward Atlanta, worrying the rear of the enemy. In the middle of the afternoon they stood, and by flank movement forced our skirmishers to retire. All the regiments except A, F, and D, on skirmishing line. Corporal Herriman (B) killed; Sergeant Shipman (G) wounded, and left on the field. Hedges (G) slight. Returned to our works of the night of the 18th inst.

July 22. At 12 noon ordered to march. Report that Atlanta is ours. Halted 3½ miles from Atlanta at 6 p.m. Found report false. Bivouacked for the night. Recovered Sergeant Shipman this a.m.

July 23. Moved into front line at 9 a.m. Threw up breastworks and made abattis. Our position is the right rear flank of the army, 3½ miles west of Atlanta.

July 24 to 26. In works, 3½ miles west of Atlanta.

July 27. At 1.10 p.m. moved out in light order and assisted in driving back the rebels, and advancing our lines. Returned just before dark· A hard day's work.

July 28. Moved at 9 a.m. in heavy order, carrying everything. Made a circuit of some 8 miles or more in our rear and right, and after a hard day's marching passed the line of works which we left in the morning, and bearing to the right continued the march until midnight. Men so exhausted that many of them dropped down to sleep without any supper. (12 miles.)

July 29. Lay in line until 12 noon. Companies A, F, D, H and E, skirmishers pressed the enemy back about a mile. Regiment on picket to-night.

July 30. Relieved by the 60th Illinois. Took position in their works, but at 12 noon moved ¾ mile to the right and threw up works. Our men are becoming worn by these constant moves. To-morrow is Sunday and of course a move.

July 31. Made a reconnaissance in front, occupying the entire day, from 9 a.m. until just before dark. We are very close to a R.R.

Aug. 1, 2 and 3. In works of July 30 (Aug. 2). Strengthened our works as we expected an attack.

Aug. 4. Moved at 2 p.m. Advanced a little beyond the position reached Sunday and lay until dark; then went on picket duty and advanced as skirmishers; nearly a mile. Pushed steadily forward until 11 p.m. passing through an open field, across a creek, and up a very steep hill in woods to an open field. Very dark, and *hard* work. Held position until morning.

Aug. 5. Advanced as skirmishers. Crossed the Sandtown road and passed through a field, driving rebel skirmishers about half a mile. Relieved at night and bivouacked about where our line rested this morning.

Aug. 6. At 8 a.m. ordered out to occupy the works of the 60th Illinois, while they went out as skirmishers. Lay until nearly dark and then put up works in position occupied this morning. Made camp at dusk in a heavy rain.

Aug. 7. At 3.15 p.m. advanced and took possession of the rebel works, vacated by them because of a flank movement against their left. After passing their first line we threw up works. The rebels shelled us during the whole move. O. Mills (A) wounded. Brought up knapsacks and put up tents.

Aug. 8. At 1 p.m. marched in light order to the right and rear, making a circuit of some four miles, and halting 1¾ miles from the position of this morning. Threw up works expecting a cavalry attack, but it failed.

Aug. 9. In position of yesterday. Our boys drove some rebel cavalry out of an orchard for the sake of the apples.

Aug. 10. Position unchanged.

Aug. 11. At 3 p.m. returned to camp of the 7th inst.

Aug. 12. Moved at 5.10 a.m. half a mile to the right, and relieved the 104th Ohio Infantry.

Aug. 13. In position of yesterday (S. W. of Atlanta.) Half of the regiment on picket. Geo. Jay, musician (K) killed. Dawson (K) wounded.

Aug. 14 to 18.   Still in the position taken on the 12th.   We are here, as in many other places on this campaign, exposed to continual fire from rebel batteries and musketry.

Aug. 19.   Made a sortie to the right and front, leaving camp at 3.45 a.m., then assisted to support the 23d Army Corps while they continued the movement.   Returned to works at 7.30 p.m.

Aug. 20.   Moved out at 4 a.m. and made a more extended sortie.   Did some foraging.   Returned to the works at 6 p.m.   (15 miles.)   Nearly reached the Montgomery R.R.

Aug. 21.   17th New York Infantry joined our Brigade.

Aug. 22 to 25.   Position unchanged.   Our camp is about six miles from Atlanta and nearly opposite East Point.

Aug. 26.   Still in the same position.   Comparatively quiet for a few days past.   Under orders tonight to move at a minute's warning.   A little before midnight rebels began shelling our camp.

Aug. 27.   Moved out at 2.30 a.m.   Rained just at daybreak.   Marched very slowly all day, halting frequently, working to the right.   At 1.30 p.m. threw up temporary works, facing the rear.   (3 miles.)

Aug. 28.   At 5.20 a.m. moved *rapidly* 4 miles south, then S.S.E., then S.E., and crossed the Montgomery R.R. at about 3 p.m., and halted in a cornfield.   *We* harvest this crop and stay to-night.

Aug. 29.   Moved out at daybreak, and advanced through fields and woods 1½ miles, and threw up works. Then we moved out in light order and captured one rebel and 15 horses and equipments.   The rebels ran at the first volley.   Skirmished toward Atlanta 1½ miles, then returned to within ¾ mile of our works, cutting a road (that ¾ mile) to get back by the best route.   Got back about sundown.   (7 miles.)

Aug. 30.   Left at 5.30 a.m. on the route of yesterday.   Cut a road through the woods 1½ miles. Had 6 Companies out as skirmishers.   Met no opposition except a vidette post.   They ran after the first volley.   Reached the road where we went yesterday at 9 a.m.   Were relieved at 10.40 a.m., and marched east past a rude church and across a small creek. Pursued that direction some 4 miles.   Bivouac in a grove.   (Distance marched ?)

Aug. 31.   At 12 noon moved into breastworks of

the 1st Division. In the middle of the afternoon moved to the left ¼ mile, then to the right 1¾ miles, and formed line of battle.

Sept. 1. At 7 a.m. moved toward Jonesboro, until within two miles of it, when our Army Corps struck the Johnnies. After crossing a bridge we were posted on the right of the Jonesboro road, and rested in an open field. Rebels shelled some. A charge on our right. Rebels driven. Moved to the left of the Jonesborough road, and our Brigade formed lines -of battle in a piece of woods. Moved out of the woods and into an open ravine in front of the enemy's line of works, which were on the crest of the opposite side of the ravine. Our movement was partially concealed by the smoke from our skirmish line, but the enemy threw grape and canister along our lines from a battery in our right front. In the ravine we rested to support a charge against Clayborne's Division of the rebel army. Clayborne's Division had never been driven, and repulsed the charging force, which broke into confusion before the murderous fire. Our lines now advanced and in a few minutes rested against Clayborne's works. Major Barnett, commanding the regiment, was, at this point, killed. Only a moment's halt and our boys scaled the works, and fought the enemy in their trenches, finally causing them to yield, and the victory of the Jonesboro battle was won. We took two lines of works, and one rebel regiment, and stand of colors. The fight was severe but we maintained our record, for like the rebel division under Clayborne, ours had never, during the whole service, been driven. Our loss in officers and men was very heavy. Reported to-night at seventy-one (71.) (At this writing I have not at hand the names of the killed and wounded.)

Sept. 2. At daylight began burying our dead. Picked up and turned over ordnance stores. We were busy all night, after the close of the battle, taking care of the wounded. At 8.30 a.m. moved 1½ miles to near Jonesboro, then went on picket on the R.R. Our troops tearing up the R.R. this p.m. Captain Dunphy placed in command of the regiment.

Sept. 3. Relieved from picket at 4 p.m. Marched to Jonesborough and pitched camp. Congratulatory orders read and Official Orders of the fall of Atlanta.

Sept. 4 and 5. In camp at Jonesborough.

Sept. 6. Left camp at 8 a.m. Formed line of

battle a few rods in rear of camp.  At noon moved out
1½ miles and formed a new line.  Stay to-night.

Sept. 7.  Moved six miles across lots toward
Atlanta.

Sept. 8.  A move of 5½ miles toward Atlanta.  At
one point our Brigade was massed and Brigadier Gen.
J. D. Morgan read congratulatory orders from Presi-
dent Lincoln, General U. S. Grant, and General
Sherman.  Camped at White Hall, two miles from
Atlanta.

Sept. 9 to 27.  In camp at White Hall, Ga.  Ordinary camp and picket duties.

Sept. 28.  Moved to Atlanta at 8 a.m.  Took cars
and lay on board all night

Sept. 29.  Left Atlanta at 7 a.m.  Arrived at
Marietta at 10 a.m.  Passed through Big Shanty,
Altoona, Kingston, Adirsville, and Calhoun, and
reached Resaca at 6 p.m.  Soon moved on and passed
through Dalton, Ringgold, and Graysville, and at
midnight stopped near Chickamauga.

Sept. 30.  Moved at 2.40 a.m.  Reached Chickamauga Bridge at 3 a.m.  At 11 a.m. moved forward.
Chattanooga at 12 noon.  Stevenson at 3 p.m.  In the
evening moved out one mile and stayed over night.

Oct. 1.  Left Stevenson by the Huntsville road,
at 9.20 a.m.  Made Huntsville at 8 p.m.  Stay on the
cars for the night.

Oct. 2.  Left cars at 8 a.m.  Made camp at once,
quarter mile west of town.  At 3.30 p.m. broke camp
and took cars for Athens.  Found the road torn up
4 miles out, and lay by to repair it, and stay over night.

Oct. 3.  Road repaired at 6 a.m. and we moved on
cautiously to a point two miles from Athens, when we
left the cars, and at 1 p.m. moved forward, reaching
Athens at 2 p.m.  Camped on the Florence road.

Oct. 4.  At 6 a.m. marched out on the Florence
road.  Waded Elk River at 4 p.m.  Rained most of
the afternoon.  Camped at Rogersville a little after
dusk, while it rained in torrents.  (20 miles.)

Oct. 5.  Left camp at daylight  Marched to within 6 miles of Florence.  Rained most of the day.
Received a large mail, which had to be distributed on
the march, while it was raining heavily.  (18 miles.)

Oct. 6.  Moved at 9 a.m. in light order.  Advanced 1½ miles toward Florence.  Our cavalry were, at
that point, trying to drive a force of rebels.  They
failed, and we were ordered forward and drove them

beyond Florence. We then returned to camp. (12 miles.)

Oct. 7. Moved at 1 p.m. to within a mile of Florence. Camped at sunset. Rosencrans in possession of Florence, having arrived from Nashville with a large force. (5 miles.)

Oct. 8. At 10 a.m. fell in and marched to Florence, and after passing through most of the principal streets, stacked arms and rested awhile; then returned to camp at 1 p.m.

Oct. 9. In camp at Florence, Ala.

. Oct. 10. Moved at 6 a.m. Marched 18 miles toward Athens. Waded Blue Water Creek and camped on the east bank.

Oct. 11. Marched 19 miles toward Athens. Forded Elk River at 12 noon. It was deeper than the last time we forded it and had a strong current. Camped at sunset 7 miles from Athens, Ala.

Oct. 12. Left camp at 7 a.m. Marched to Athens, Made a short stop and moved out on the Huntsville road one mile, and camped at 1 p.m.

Oct. 13. At 7 a.m. marched back to town and took cars for Chattanooga, Tenn., where we arrived at midnight.

Oct. 14. Left the cars in the morning and stacked arms near the depot, and got breakfast. At 10 a.m. took position S. W. of the town and repaired fortifications.

Oct. 15. In works at Chattanooga. Exciting rumors that the enemy were advancing. Reinforcements coming in.

Oct. 16. In works at Chattanooga. Rumors that the rebels are moving toward Bridgeport.

Oct. 17. In works at Chattanooga. Under orders to move.

Oct. 18. Left works at 7 a.m. Marched rapidly 13 miles up the Chattanooga Valley, and camped at 2 p.m. at Gordon's Mills.

Oct. 19. Left camp at 8 a.m. Had a drove of 2,000 cattle to move. Marched 13 miles to Lafayette, and camped at 4 p.m.

Oct. 20. Marched 16 miles toward Summerville, and camped at a creek at 4 p.m.

Oct. 21. Left camp near Summerville and marched 18 miles toward the Alabama line. Camped at dark,.

Oct. 22. Marched 12 miles to Galesville, Ala. Rejoined the 14th Army Corps to-day.

Oct. 23 to 28.   In camp at Galesville, Ala.

Oct. 28.   At 2 p.m. marched 8 miles toward Rome.

Oct. 29.   Marched at 6 a.m.   Arrived at Rome, Ga., at 3 p.m.   (18 miles.)

Oct. 30 and 31.   In camp at Rome, Ga.

Nov. 1.   Marched to Kingston. (18 miles.) Camped at 2 p.m.

Nov. 2 to 7.   In camp at Kingston, Ga.   Nov. 3. John Potter, Co. C, accidentally killed at the slaughter yard.   Nov. 4. Received pay.   Nov. 5. A great deal of gambling.

Nov. 8.   Marched to Centreville, Ga.   Voted for President.   Made camp at 2 p.m.

Nov. 9 to 12.   In camp at Centreville, Ga.

Nov. 13.   Marched at 6.30 a.m. to R.R.   Tore it up and burned the ties at several points.   Made 14 miles.   Camped ¾ mile from (Ackworth?) at 8.30 p.m.

Nov. 14.   Heavy frost last night.   Marched at 6 a.m. (20 miles.)   Camped at sunset.

Nov. 15.   Left camp at 6 a.m.   Crossed the Chattahoochee River and reached Atlanta at 2 p.m.   Camped outside of the fortifications south of the city at 4 p.m. (distance ?)

Nov. 16.   Left camp at 1 p.m.   Marched through Decatur.   Saw very few men.   We marched slowly across stony fields, driving cattle.   Camped after dark in a grove of young pine.   (10 miles.)

Nov. 17.   Passed through Lithonia.   Found the R.R. destroyed and the depot and several dwellings burned.   Tore up R.R. in two places.   Camped after dark.   Made awkward work getting into camp.   Rations short.   Some forage, potatoes and meat. (19 miles.)

Nov. 18.   Train guard.   Hard march.   Passed Covington about 3 p.m.   Crossed Yellow River on a pontoon bridge.   (Two bridges—one for troops and one for teams.)   Camped just beyond the Ulcofanhatochee River a little before dark.   One day's rations issued to last 3 days.   (14 miles.)

Nov. 19.   Passed through Sandtown a little before noon.   Found plenty of forage in the shape of sweet potatoes, meat, honey, etc., also forage for animals.   No traces of frost.   Roses and other flowers in bloom. (18 miles.)

Nov. 20.   In advance of the Corps to-day.   Foraged considerable.   Captured several mules and a few horses.   Passed through Shady Dale.   (12 miles.)

Nov. 21. In rear of the Division. Repairing road. Moved very slowly. Roads muddy. Rained most of the day. Crossed Muddy Creek in a.m. and Cedar Creek in p.m. Left the Milledgeville road this p.m. and took the Macon 'road. Camped at 4 p.m. ½ mile beyond Cedar Creek. 12 miles.

Nov. 22. In camp near Cedar Creek, Ga. 2d and 3d Divisions passed us to-day. Camp very smoky and disagreeable.

Nov. 23. Froze hard last night. Ice lasted all day in ditches and sheltered places. Kilpatrick's train was in our way in the forenoon so that we had to move slowly. Marched faster in p.m. Camped at night 2 miles from Milledgeville. (14 miles.)

Nov. 24. Left camp at 10 a.m. Passed through Milledgeville, and then marched rapidly some 8 miles and caped at 4 p.m. (10 miles.)

Nov. 25. Moved slowly at first. Crossed Gum Creek and reached Buffalo Creek about noon. Waited for a bridge to be built—as the guerillas had destroyed one. Had a hard, slow time crossing the swamp through which the Creek runs, as the teams were often stalled. Made camp at midnight. (12 miles.)

Nov. 26. Marched at daylight. Moved rapidly. And just before reaching Sandersville, as we came near Keg Creek, the 3d Brigade, in advance, had a skirmish with some cavalry, fighting them all the way into Sandersville. The town was nearly deserted and our men sacked it and burned some buildings. Halted ¾ hour just after passing the village, then advanced ¾ mile and halted for the night. Found an abundance of persimmons in this region. (8½ miles.)

Nov. 27. Marched at 6 a.m. Moved rapidly. Crossed two small streams. Crossed the Ogeechee River a little after noon, then took the (Louisville ?) road and marched 3 miles on it. (16 miles.)

Nov. 28. Rear guard. Marched rapidly to Rocky Comfort Creek. Here a bridge had been destroyed. Pontooned the Creek and corduroyed the swamp. This took several hours and being rear guard we did not move forward until dark. Passed through Louisville, and camped a mile beyond at 8.30 p.m. Most of the town was burned by our advance. (10 milesi)

Nov. 29. In camp near Louisville, Ga. A skirmish between some rebel cavalry and a force of our foragers, took place in our rear. Foragers driven in.

Nov. 30. In camp, near Louisville, Ga. A part

of our regiment on picket. Rebels drove a force of foragers in, but our pickets stopped the rebels. Capt. Dunphy in command of picket forces, took about 20 prisoners, drove the rebels back, and rescued six companies of foragers and their wagons.

Dec. 1. Marched at 12 m., nearly in the direction of Wanesborough. Camped at 7 p.m. (11 miles.)

Dec. 2. Repairing roads on the march. Also delayed by waiting for the 1st Division to pass. Made camp at dusk. (10 miles.)

Dec. 3. Flankers for 3d Division train. Moved slowly, only about 2 miles in a.m. In the p.m. crossed two small streams. Left the Wanesboro road and took the Millen road. Camped at 12 midnight. Rained while we were camping. (8 miles.)

Dec. 4. Moved toward the Savannah river to the Jacksonboro road. Crossed the Augusta R.R. at station No. 1, and soon after reached Haversen. Camped at 7 p.m. (13 miles.)

Dec. 5. Train guard. Marched rapidly toward Savannah. Struck the river road at a point opposite Sylvania. Road slashed but our pioneers soon cleared it. Warm marching. Halted at Buck Creek P. O. just at dusk. Our regiment on picket. A swamp slashed just ahead of us. (15½ miles.)

Dec. 6. Marched at 11.15 a.m. Moved rapidly until dark, when a swamp road had to be repaired, then moved rapidly on a very sandy road. Hard marching. Camped at 8.30 p.m. near a large swamp, through which the road was slashed full of trees. (18 miles.)

Dec. 7. Pioneers having cleared the road, we marched at 8.30 a.m. Moved steadily. Had to wait once for some 40 rods of slashing to be cleared out. Camped one mile from Ebenezer Creek. Crossed two small streams, with high steep banks to-day. Soil better, plantations richer, and forage more plenty than for a few days past. (16 miles.)

Dec. 8. Fell in at 7 a.m. Order to march countermanded. Moved out at 10.45 a.m. Crossed Ebenezer Creek on a bridge made by pontooniers, on the timbers of the old bridge. Marched nearly to Lockner's Creek. Waited for the creek to be pontooned, and for the pioneers to clear out a slashing. Camped at dusk, 3 miles beyond the creek. Supper nearly ready when "Fall in," and marched back nearly to the creek, and camped at 11.45 p.m. in a corn field. (10 miles.)

Dec. 9. Moved at 8 a.m. directly back to the point we halted at last evening, and lay until 1 p.m. while the road was cleared and Kogler's Creek bridged. At 3.30 p.m. halted in a piece of pine timber on the right of the road. At dark, when camp was nearly made, ordered to move. Marched ¾ mile ahead, and ¼ mile to the right, and camped in a cotton-field. A rebel battery just ahead annoys our column. One of our battery lieutenants killed by a shell from the rebels. (8 miles.)

Dec. 10. Marched at 8 a.m. and soon reached the works of the rebel battery that fired at us yesterday p.m. They evacuated last night, (14 miles from Savannah.) Shortly after crossing Black Creek we overtook the 20th Army Corps, who were burning the Savannah and Charleston R.R. Brigade camped at this point. Regiment on picket, 1 mile to the right. (6 miles.)

Dec. 11. Withdrew pickets at 9 a.m. Marched to the right, crossed the Charleston R.R. and the Georgia Central R.R. Heard heavy firing this a.m. The rebels threw shells both on our right and left flanks. They have batteries ranging on each flank of our brigade. Rained considerable and was muddy. Camped at 2 p.m. (9 miles.)

Dec. 12. Frost last night. In camp near Savannah, Ga. No fires after dusk.

Dec. 13 to 21. In camp near Savannah, Ga. Our position, in front of a large swamp, and between us and it is a *heavy* belt of pine. Dec. 14. Put up breast-works. We hear that our forces have taken Fort McAllister with 17 guns and 300 men. This opens our communication with the ocean, and "hardtack." We have had but one-third rations of bread for several days. This with fresh meat and a little rice has been our diet. Dec. 17. Our first mail from home since leaving Atlanta. Dec. 20. Making fascines for works in the swamp. Dec. 21. Under orders to march all day. Put up tents again just at night. Heard that the enemy had evacuated Savannah.

Dec. 22. Moved out slowly toward the city, on the main road. Took the R.R. to cross over a district flowed by cutting the canal embankment. After reaching the rebel works by this means, we turned to the right, left the R.R., crossed the canal, followed its course ¾ of a mile and camped in a grand piece of Georgia pine, 2¼ miles from the "Forest City." 2 miles.

Dec. 23 to Jan. 1. In camp 2½ miles from Savannah, Ga. Built a comfortable log camp, "chinking" our cabins and making our beds of the Spanish moss, which we found in great abundance hanging from the branches of the trees in this latitude. Rations *short.*

Dec. 27. Our Corps reviewed in the streets of the city by General Sherman. 10th Michigan specially complimented.

Jan. 2. Moved camp to the left ¼ mile to get better ground, as a part of the regiment were on low ground.

Jan. 3 to 13. In camp 2¾ miles from Savannah, Ga. Jan. 3 and 4. Regiment on picket—on the "Butterfield plan". Jan. 8 and 9. On outlying picket at Cherokee Hill—7 miles from camp. Drill and parade while out. (14 miles.) Jan. 13. Clothing issued—we needed it badly. A horse presented to Adjutant Jewell on Dress Parade.

Jan. 14. At 10 a.m. marched to the city and encamped S. W. of it on a sand plain. Plenty of *grit* now (in our rations.) (2½ miles.)

Jan. 15. Reported to Q. M. General in the city, and took quarters in a brick building on the corner of Abercorn and Bryan Streets.

Jan. 16 to 18. In the quarters occupied the 15th, doing heavy guard and fatigue duty, unloading boats, etc.

Jan. 19. Moved into quarters previously occupied by a regiment of the 16th Army Corps, on Bay Street. Found a camp of 8 streets, which made it inconvenient for our regiment of 10 Companies.

Jan. 20. Moved out hurriedly at 7 a.m., taking the Louisville road. Passed our old camps, the ones made on our first arrival at Savannah. Overtook the Brigade 8 miles out. Camped about noon in a yellow pine forest. (10 miles.)

Jan. 21. Moved our line a little by "refusing" the right (so as to avoid a piece of low ground), and put the camp in order.

Jan. 21 to 24. In camp 10 miles from Savannah, Ga. Picket duty. Very bad weather. Rain and clouds.

Jan. 25. Reported on the Louisville road at 8 a.m. to wait for headquarters train. Lay all day in a muddy field, 80 rods from a good camp. At dark the train came and we marched forward. Camped at 8.30 in an open field, then changed camp. Three Companies did not get in until 3 a.m., as they were helpthe train over a bad piece of road. (4½ miles.)

Jan. 26. Train guard for the Corps headquarters train. Left the Louisville road and struck toward the Savannah River. Roads very muddy. Moved slowly. Camped in a swamp at 7 p.m. on account of the pontoon train, ahead of ours, getting stuck in a quicksand swamp, and we could not advance until after midnight. (12 miles.)

Jan. 27. Found better roads. Passed through Springfield, where we left the Headquarters train, and guarded a part of the Division supply train. Soon after leaving Springfield we reached Ebenezer Creek, and waited until nearly midnight to "corduroy" the crossing. The logs used being green, the bark soon wore off, and the water which run over the logs froze on, making the "corduroy" very slippery and dangerous. It took a long time to get the train across. Camped at 3 a.m. (10 miles.)

Jan. 28. After moving out three miles, we struck the river road on which we approached Savannah. Marched a couple of miles on it, and camped at 11.30 a.m. near "Sister's Ferry," in an old corn-field. (5 miles.)

Jan. 29 to Feb. 4. In camp at "Sister's Ferry," Ga. Feb. 1. R. Hathaway, Co. I.; Ira Mitchell, Co. G.; S. Robbins and M. Maskell, Co. K., captured while foraging.

Feb. 5. At 1.20 p.m moved toward the ferry. Delayed until 8.30, then crossed the Savannah River on a pontoon bridge; then over "corduroy" to Upper Landing, and struck out into pine openings, and camped at 10 p.m. (5 miles).

Feb. 6. In camp at "Sister's Ferry," S. C. Officers and clerks busy all day and all night making out rolls to muster out non-veterans. Dug up furniture.

Feb. 7. In camp at "Sister's Ferry," S. C. Capt. Richman, Capt. Hart, 1st Lieut. Beach, 2d Lieuts. Allen and Branch, and the non-veterans, started for home to-day.

Feb. 8. Marched to Brighton Cross Roads. Roads miry. A large detail repairing them. Camped at 2.15 p.m. in pine woods. (8 miles.)

Feb. 9.   Marched to King Creek P. O.   Rear guard.   Camped at 7.30 p.m.   (20 miles.)

Feb. 10.   After passing through Irvington and crossing Briar Creek we left the Augusta Road and took the Barnwell Road.   Camped a little after sunset within six miles of Barnwell.   Passed over a pleasant region to-day.   Neat country churches.   (21 miles.)

Feb. 11.   Left camp at 5.25 a.m.   Four miles out ran against Gen. Catlin's train (1st Division 14th Army Corps) and halted until 12.20 p.m.   Fish pond on a plantation near our halt.   We tapped the pond, and had fresh fish for a change of diet.   Passed through Barnwell with bayonets fixed, colors flying, and bands playing.   Ruins smoking on either hand.   Crossed the Salkehatchie River twice to-day.   Camped at 3 p.m., two miles beyond Barnwell, on the Williston Road.   (8 miles.)

Feb. 12.   Passed through Williston at 11.45 a.m.   Town burned and R.R. destroyed.   Eight miles further on, reached the South Edisto River, and camped at 5.30 p.m.   (17½ miles.)

Feb. 13.   Moved at 8.30 a.m.   Immediately crossed the river and passed over a long "corduroy" through a swamp.   Camped 1 mile beyond the river at 9.30 a.m.   At 1 p.m. struck tents and took the Columbia road and camped again at 3.15 p.m.   (6½ miles.)

Feb. 14.   On the Columbia road.   At 10 a.m. reached the North Edisto River and built a bridge. Moved forward at 12.30 p.m.   Made a rapid march while a drizzling rain froze to our clothes.   Camped just before dark.   Plenty of pitch-pine, so we readily built hot fires and "thawed out."   Water to drink *scarce* this p.m.   (20 miles.)

Feb. 15.   Retraced our line of march 1 mile and took the Lexington road.   A poor country, being the watershed, between the Saluda and North Edisto rivers.   Camped at 6 p.m. 2¼ miles from Lexington. Water scarce.   (17 miles.)

Feb. 16.   (1st anniversary of our Veteran Muster-in.)   Passed through Lexington at 9 a.m.   The town was nearly destroyed by fire.   At 3 miles from Columbia, halted for dinner.   20th Army Corps came in on our right.   At 4 p.m. retraced our march 3 miles and turned to the north, and camped 6¼ miles from

Columbia at sunset. At Lexington found the first stony ground since leaving Savannah. (16 miles.)

Feb. 17. Crossed the Saluda River ¾ mile from camp, and struck a road running nearly with Broad River. Followed it some 13 miles and then turned toward the river and camped on its bank at sunset. Fine residences burning. Plenty of red clay. (16 miles.)

Feb. 18. In camp on Broad River, S. C. Orders to march. Countermanded after dark.

Feb. 19. Crossed Broad River on pontoon bridge. Moved up the river 3 miles over a rich undulating country. Fine residences burning. A great abundance of forage. After dinner, left arms and knapsacks, and went up the Spartanburg R.R. a couple of miles destroying and burning as we went, then returned to our dining-ground and camped. Captured several horses and mules. (8 miles.)

Feb. 20. Followed the Broad River road to Long Run, then took the Winsboro road and camped at 11 a.m. on Little River. (8 miles.)

Feb. 21. Crossed Little River. Took the Winnsboro road 8 miles, then retraced our steps a short distance and crossed to another road leading to Winnsboro and struck Kilpatrick's train moving in upon our road. Camped at 4.30 p.m. near a fine spring. Country still *very* good. Forage plenty. (12 miles.)

Feb. 22. Took the Adger's Turnout road, and at Adger's Turnout, waited an hour for a train to pass, then followed the Columbia and Charlotte R.R. to White Oak Turnout, then the Camden road for 5 miles, and camped at 2.30 p.m. (11 miles.)

Feb. 23. Left the Camden road early in the morning and took Rocky Mount road. Crossed Gladden's Creek, Big Wateree Creek, Little Wateree Creek and Hog Fork. Bothered by a part of the 20th Army Corps being in our way. Camped soon after dark, raining. (10 miles.)

Feb. 24. *Raining, muddy, large hills.* Crossed Fishing Creek and Catawba River. Kilpatrick's train delayed us. Helping trains. Hills and mud badly mixed up. Character of country changed. No more long-leaved pine. Oak, hickory and short-leaved pine. Camped at 3.10 p.m. near Rocky Mount, at which point were, in the time of the Revolution, barracks for quartering troops. Huge boulders. (4 miles.)

Feb. 25. In camp at Rocky Mount, S. C. Corduroying roads.

Feb. 26. In Camp at Rocky Mount. Fatigue and scouting. Inspection at 4 p.m. by Col. Lum.

Feb. 27. In Camp at Rocky Mount. Delayed by breaking of pontoon bridge yesterday.

Feb. 28. Marched at 11 a.m. Corduroyed some road before the train could pass. (4 miles.)

Mar. 1. Train guard. Most of the fences had been used for corduroy. Moved slowly. Tops of the hills covered with huge boulders. Crossed Hanging Rock Creek at Hanging Rock, S. C. (famous in Revolutionary History.) Camped at midnight, but the rear Companies did not get in until 1 a.m. (20 miles.)

Mar. 2. Reveille at 4 a.m. giving us but 3 hours to rest. Marched at 6. Crossed Little Lynch Creek and Flat Creek. Character of the country variable. (12 miles.)

Mar. 3. Crossed Thompson's Creek at noon. A mill on fire above the road threatened to burn out the gates, and inundate our road. Gen. Morgan helped to put out the fire, and put in the upper gates of the floom, which saved us. Left the Chesterfield Court House road which we had been on for two days, and took Hailey's Ferry road at Mount Craughin. Camped at 4 p.m. one mile from the state line. Corduroyed road after camping. (21 miles.)

Mar. 4. Left camp at reveille, (before day break) and corduroyed a long piece of road, and repaired a bridge on Thompson's Creek, then returned and got breakfast, after which we started out, stacked arms in the mud and went at it again. Rear guard. marched at 11.45 a.m. Crossed the State line into North Carolina at Maysville, moved eastward, south, and re-crossed the State line into South Carolina. Camped at 7 p.m. on the Great Peedee River in South Carolina. (14 miles.) *Mud, mud, mud. Rain, rain, rain.* Have scarcely seen the sun for 10 days.

Mar. 5 and 6. In camp on the Great Pedee River, waiting for a pontoon bridge to be built.

Mar. 7. At 3 p.m. left camp, and after long delays crossed the river at the mouth of Mark's Creek. Marched 1 mile and camped at sundown. (1½ miles.)

Mar. 8. Marched at 6 a.m. Crossed the State line into North Carolina, about 2 miles out. Crossed several small streams, moved rapidly on the watershed between Peedee and Lumber rivers. Barren. Scarcely any houses. Camped at dusk. (23 miles.)

Mar. 9. Struck the Charlotte and Fayetteville plank road 10 miles from camp. Crossed Lumber River soon after. Camped on Rock Fish Creek, while it was raining like 77½. (22 miles.)

Mar. 10. Stragglers from Kilpatrick, coming in, from early day light. (Wade Hampton attacked and threw Kilpatrick into confusion, just at day light.) We are train guard. Passed 5 vats of turpentine in flames, at Gruppy's Creek. Found one distillery of spirits of turpentine standing. Two had burned. (11 miles.)

Mar. 11. Rear guard. Camped 2½ miles from Fayetteville, N. C. (13 miles.)

Mar. 12. Lay until 5.45 p.m. when an order to march immediately, set us all in commotion. On the road in 15 minutes. Marched through Fayetteville, N. C. Crossed the Cape Fear River, and camped at Terryl's Creek. Could not cross as the rebels had destroyed the bridge. Camped at 9.30 p.m. (4 miles.)

Mar. 13. Crossed Terryl's Creek, took a by road to the left and struck another main road at 9.45 a.m. Camped at 12 m. Went out light in p.m., and skirmished, pressing the enemy steadily back some two miles. Ordered back just after pushing the rebels across a swamp. Reached Camp at 4.30 p.m. James Patterson, Co. B, wounded in the head. (6 miles.)

Mar. 14. In camp 3¼ miles from Fayetteville, N. C.

Mar. 15. Struck the Raleigh road 4 miles from camp. Soon after, overtook the rear of the 2d Division, 20th Army Corps and moved slowly. Camped at 6 p.m. (11 miles.)

Mar. 16. *Heavy skirmishing.* Battle of Averysboro, N. C.

Mar. 17. Occupied the rebel works early. Left camp at 11 a.m. Passed through the rebel works. Took the Goldsboro road. Crossed Black River. Bridge covered with rosin, ready to burn. Camped 1 mile beyond Mingo River soon after dark. (18 miles.)

Mar. 18. Six miles out reached a slough and had just begun bridging it, when we were ordered forward. Moved rapidly and soon encountered the enemy's pickets. Deployed six Companies as skirmishers, and pressed them back to their main line of barricades, and dislodged and routed them. (Godfrey Abel, Co. A, killed.) Took dinner on the skirmish line. Lay until 5 p.m. Moved to Smithfield road and followed it 1 mile to Mill Creek, expecting to bridge it. Countermanded. Moved back to the Goldsboro road. Camped and threw out pickets on both roads. Those on the Goldsboro road were attacked, but they repulsed the attack. (10 miles.)

Mar. 19. Battle of Bentonsville. "Gen. Johnson who had been concentrating the Confederate forces from Georgia, South Carolina and Tennessee at Smithfield, N. C. (said to amount to 40,000) slipped out at night in light marching order, expecting to fall upon the left wing of Sherman's army under Gen. Slocum, and crush it before support could reach him. Slocum was at first driven back, but hastily throwing up rifle-pits, assumed the defensive; Kilpatrick's cavalry supporting his left. Six, assaults were made by Johnston, which failed to dislodge Slocum's veterans from their position, while the artillery fire upon the Confederates was very damaging. Night caused a cessation. Gen. Slocum still holding his ground." "Federal loss 1,600 killed and wounded. Rebel loss not known. They left 267 dead on the field, and lost 1,600 taken prisoners."

Mar. 20. Right wing of Sherman's army on hand and we take the *offensive*. Companies H, E, G and B, skirmishing. Pressed the rebels back one mile.

Mar. 21. Still on the field of the Bentonsville fight. Put up heavy timber works. Our forces succeeded to-day in clearing the Goldsboro road.

Mar. 22. Johnston retreated last night. We left the swamp in which the battle occured (known in the neighborhood as the "Scott Place") moved out on the Goldsboro road. Camped at 4.30 p.m. (10 miles.)

Mar. 23. Crossed Neuse River at 10 a.m. R. & N. R. R.R. at 2.15 p.m. Little River at 3.45 p.m. Passed through Goldsboro in column by Companies with bayonets fixed, colors flying and bands playing. Camped 2 miles north of Goldsboro at 6.30 p.m. Wood and water scarce. (14 miles.)

Mar. 24. Moved camp a few rods and put up tents in order.

Mar. 25 to Apr. 9. In camp 2 miles north of Goldsboro. Mar. 25. Foraging. Mar. 26. Received a large mail. Mar. 27. Another large mail. Dress Parade. Mar. 28. Promotions in line officers read on parade. Mar. 31. Captain Dunphy takes command of the regiment. Meeting of the Regimental

Commanders of the Brigade at Col. Lum's quarters
this evening. Resolutions attesting esteem and respect for Col. Lum, and expressing regret at losing
him, were passed. Apr. 6. News of the fall of Richmond read to the Brigade by Capt. Wiseman, Asst.
Adjt.-Gen. of the 2d Division 14th Army Corps.
Apr. 8. Col. Lum made his farewell address to the
regiment after dress parade. Apr. 9. Col. Lum
started for home.

Apr. 10. En route for Raleigh, N. C. Train
guard. Rebels opposed our progress, so we moved
slowly. Camped on the bank of Buffalo Creek. Rebels
here last night. Several " Yankee Johnnies " came
in this p.m. One who once belonged to our regiment.
(12 miles.)

Apr. 11. Swampy ground. Reached Smithfield
at 3.40 p.m., and camped east of it at 7 p.m. When
we were just turning in were ordered to move immediately. Climbed out, marched through town, crossed
Neuse River, moved out one mile and camped at 10
p.m. (13 miles.)

Apr. 12. In camp in a.m. Noon ordered to get
dinner. Countermanded. Emptied our dishes of
water. Fell in, marched half mile. Stacked arms in
camp order. Moved out into an open field. Order
issued to the Brigade by Gen. Vandevere, announcing
the surrender of Lee's army to Grant on the 9th.
P.M. moved steadily forward on the Raleigh road.
Camped at sunset at Claydon. (11 miles.)

Apr. 13. Rear guard of Corps train. Crossed
R.R. seven times to-day. Entered Raleigh at dusk.
Marched through to music. Camped soon after dark
one mile from town. (15 miles.)

Apr. 14. Followed Charlotteville R.R. several
miles, crossing it nine times. After leaving the R.R.
bore southward, then westward, moving rapidly.
Camped at 5.30 p.m. (18 miles.)

Apr. 15. A continuous rain during the entire
march to Aven's Ferry, Cape Fear River, some two
or three miles below the junction of Haw and Deep
Rivers. Had to wade several small stueams. Camped
near Aven's Ferry at 11 a.m. (14 miles.)

Apr. 16 to 20. In camp at Aven's Ferry, N. C.
Apr. 16. Rumors, " Johnston surrendered to Sheridan.
We are to go back to Raleigh," etc., etc. Apr. 17.
More rumors, nothing official. Apr. 18. Official notice
of President Lincoln's assassination. We were at first

greatly shocked and pained. This gradually gave place to a deep rooted feeling of determination to avenge his death. Official notice that negotiations were in progress between Johnston and Sherman. Apr. 19. Negotiations still in progress. Foraging to cease. Apr. 20. Official negotiations concluded, which need ratification only to make peace from the Potomac to the Rio Grande. Sherman believes he will soon lead his army home.

Apr. 21. Train guard. Camped at Holly Springs a little past noon. Good water and a pleasant camp. (14 miles.)

Apr. 22 to 28. In camp at Holly Springs, N. C. Apr. 24. Rumor that Johnston has played traitor. Apr. 25. Rumor of a forward movement. Two days rations to last four. Orders to be ready to march to-morrow. Apr. 26. Order countermanded. Rumor that Johnston has "Skallahooted" and that his Adjt.-Gen. has surrendered the army. Another, that Johnston was killed by his own men because he tried to run away. Apr. 27. Rumors, rumors, rumors. Apr 28. Orders to march to Richmond, also that we should soon return to our homes.

Apr. 29. Marched to Morrisville, on the Goldsboro and Charlotte R.R. Camped 12.30 p.m. (14 miles.)

Apr. 30. In camp at Morrisville, N. C.

May 1. Crossed Neuse River at Fish Dam at 1.30 p.m. Camped 7 miles beyond at 4.15 p.m. (21½ miles.)

May 2. Crossed Ledge of Rocks Creek, a mile below Dutchville, and Tar River at Upper-Ferry. Passed through Oxford at 4 p.m. Camped two miles north in a pine grove, 5 p.m. (22 miles.)

May 3. Left camp at day-break. Gave way twice for 20th Army Corps. Passed them twice. Crossed the State line into Virginia. Camped 2 miles south of Roanoke River at sunset. Orders for reveille at 2 a.m. and to march at 4 a.m. to-morrow. (21 miles.)

May 4. Marched at 4 a.m. Crossed Roanoke River just at the first light of morning, and passed the camp of the 20th Army Corps soon after. Passed Rudolph, Macon College at 7.45 a.m. Camped at 5 p.m ½ mile from Mehevrin River. (23½ miles.)

May 5. Rear of the Brigade Crossed South and North Mehevrin Rivers and Reedy Creek, and passed through Lewiston (Lunenburgh C. H.). P.M. crossed the Nottaway River at the "Falls." Camped 4 miles south of Nottaway C. H. at 6 p.m. (25 miles.)

May 6. Passed through Nottaway C. H. and Furgesonville, also Dannsville. Crossed the Appomattox River on a pontoon bridge at 7.30 p.m. Camped at 8 p.m. It became evident to-day that we are racing with the 20th Army Corps. (32 miles.)

May 7. Marched steadily and camped at 3.30 p.m. 5 miles from Richmond, Va., in a pine grove, in which we could plainly trace the rows made when the last crop of corn or cotton was raised. Trees 12 to 14 inches in diameter. (25 miles.)

May 8 to 10. In camp 5 miles south of Richmond, Va. May 8. Rumors of our having to stay here several days. May 9. Orders to march to-morrow. Are to be reviewed by Gen. Halleck in the streets of Richmond. May 10. Countermanded. Rumors of a fuss between Gen. Howard and Gen. Halleck, about Halleck's calling our army thieves, and asking Howard, who is temporarily in command, to keep them out of the city. Rumor that Sherman has returned from Alexandria and decides that Halleck cannot review our army.

May 11. Marched at 7 a.m. In Manchester a Division of the 24th Army Corps " turned out " and we gave them the " fisic and the rag." Crossed James River just above " Libby " and " Castle Thunder," at 9 am. Were *not* reviewed in Richmond. Passed the Capitol, Washington Monument, and other notable places. Crossed the Chickahominy at 5 p.m. (22 miles.)

May 12. In camp until noon. Passed Hanover C. H. (built in 1735.) Crossed Pamunkey River on a pontoon bridge. Camped at dusk at Mill Swamp Creek. (9 miles.)

May 13. Passed through Chesterfield. Water scarce. Camped at 4.15 at Rehoab Church. (20 miles.)

May 14. Sunday. In a.m. passed a neat brick church, at which services closed on account of our passing. Saw Blue Ridge occasionally. (20 miles.)

May 15. Blue Ridge in sight most of the day, some 50 miles on our left. Crossed Rapidan River, at Raccoon Ford, water knee deep, and camped one mile beyond at 5 p.m. (18 miles.)

May 16. Waded Rappahannock River, leg deep, at noon. Camped at 5.15 p.m. (21 miles.)

May 17. Struck O. & A. R.R., east of Catlett's Station, and followed its course (crossing several times) to Manassas Junction. Took the road toward

Fairfax C. H.  Waded Bull Run and camped at 6 p.m. (23 miles.)

May 18.  Left camp at Bull Run at 5 a.m.  Passed through Fairfax with music and colors.  (14 miles.)

May 19.  Marched to near Fort Wade, on Arlington Heights, and camped a little past noon.  (Distance?)

May 20 to 25.  In camp 4 miles from Alexandria, Va., near Fort Wade, on Arlington Heights.  May 24. Reviewed in the City of Washington by Gens. Grant and Sherman, and President Johnson.  (18 miles.)

May 25.  Moved camp to north of Washington.  While passing through Washington the citizens visited the column, at its several halts, in large numbers, and distributed crackers, pickles, water, handkerchiefs, boquets, wreaths, etc., and begged caps and cartridges, and expressed their surprise and admiration because Sherman's army was so different from what they thought us, and gave us many compliments as being the best appearing and best drilled troops in the whole review of yesterday.  (10 miles.)

May 26 to June 13.  In camp 3 miles north of Washington, D. C. near Fort Totten.  May 30. Ex-Lieut. Col. Dickerson came to camp to-day.  Eight month's pay rolls signed.  May 31.  Gov. Crapo and Adjt.-Gen. Robertson visited us, and Gov. Crapo and Lieut. Col. Dickerson addressed the 10th and 14th Regiments.  June 12.  Received an unexpected order to make out muster-out rolls, for all whose terms expire before Oct. 11, 1865.  Said rolls made out, and men mustered out.

June 13 to 18.  En route from Washington, D. C. to Louisville, Ky.  June 13.  Left Washington on baggage and flat cars, at 8.30 a.m. at the viaduct across the Potapsco River, took the Grafton R.R. and reached Harper's Ferry just after dusk.  Soon after leaving Harper's Ferry, A. Houghton (musician of Co. I) jumped from the cars while asleep.  June 14. Paw Paw Ridge at day-break and Grafton after dark. Run out from Grafton 26 miles and lay over until 4 a.m.  Passed through Kingswood Tunnel at 6 p.m. This Tunnel is ⅔ mile long.  9½ minutes.  June 15. Reached Parkersburg in p.m.  Bivouac in a grove ¾ mile out.  June 16. At day-break shipped aboard the "Revenue."  Left Parkersburgh at 10 a.m.  28 miles below, re-shipped on the "Blue Wing" No. 3. People *patriotic* on the Ohio side.  June 18.  Arrived at Louisville, Ky. at 8.30 a.m. and landed immediately and marched nearly east 4 miles and camped at 1.30 p.m. in an open field.

June 19 to July 20. In camp near Louisville, Ky. June 20. Moved camp 1 mile nearer town. June 22. Col. Lum visited us. Promotions read. June 24. More promotions. July 1. Saturday. A sermon by Mrs. Stoner of Ohio. July 2. Sunday. Preaching. Dress parade. Col. Lum made a brief and cheering speech to us. July 4. Reviewed by Gen. Sherman. He made a speech. The day was hot, *hot*, ʜᴏᴛ. July 5. Received orders to make out muster-out rolls, and were busy from to-day in the long, slow work of perfecting the rolls, until July 19, when we were mustered out by Rudolph Papst, Capt. and A. C. M. 2d Division 14th Army Corps.

July 20 to 23. En route for *Michigan*. July 20. Took train for Indianapolis, Ind. July 21. Indianapolis at daybreak. At Soldier's Home until 11 a.m., then took train for Sidney. Arrived at 8 p.m. July 22. At 3 a.m. took train from Sidney for Toledo, O. From Toledo to Jackson, where we arrived a little after noon. *Reception* and *dinner* by the ladies of Jackson, at Union Hall. Speeches by Mr. Bristol, Capt. Tower, of Jackson, and Ex-Gov. Blair. Marched to barracks and found comfortable quarters.

July 23 to Aug. 1. In camp, Blair Barracks, at Jackson, Mich. July 24. Signing Pay-Rolls and getting ready to turn over Camp and Garrison Equipage, and Ordnance Stores. July 29. Some excitement about pay, for we expected it to-day sure. July 31. Monday. A large number of our men visited the paymaster, demanding pay. Aug. 1. *Men* paid off and most of them started for home. Aug. 2. *Officers* paid off.

The future—HOME.

To the Survivors of the Tenth Regt.
of Michigan Veteran Volunteers—
Infantry.

*My Esteemed Comrades:*

Since, by your pleasure, I have been appointed historian; and as I received no instruction as to the particular field in which I was to work; and as I have often heard earnest expressions of a wish that we had in tangible form, at least an outline of our *Veteran Service*, I think it best to begin with that. The plan formed in my own mind is this:

1. To prepare a mere brief outline of our Veteran Service (sent you herewith.)

2. To prepare a plain map, showing all our movements after leaving Camp Thompson, Flint, Mich.

3. To make copies of our Muster-out Rolls. These rolls account for every man ever belonging.

4. To make a list of survivors on July 19, 1865, showing date, place, and cause of death, of those who have died since that date.

5. To make a record of each Reunion, showing place, exercises, and "Roll Call" of each separately.

These several records to be a nucleus for the final complete history of our service, both Volunteer and Veteran, in one volume.

Allow me to make the following suggestions as to the carrying out of this plan:

1. Make yourselves a committee of the whole to help write a full history.

2. Each one begin at once, and write out and send to Col. Chas. M. Lum, at Detroit, Mich., any narrative suggested by the outline. Let these narratives be of skirmish, or battle, or scout, or foraging, or capture, or escape, or camp-story, or joke, or anything else of our four years of service. There are scores of such things belonging to our history, which no *one* man can tell. Be sure to give *dates* and *places*, if possible, and at the same time correct any errors you find in this outline, and also add the date, place, and cause of death of any of our comrades, since the muster-out of 1865.

3. When the several parts are in approved shape, take the proper steps to raise a fund among ourselves, and have them printed in a single large volume.

I see no other as effectual and satisfactory way to accomplish this work; and it seems to me, that by this means, we can have ready for distribution, at an early date, the best Regimental Record ever prepared.

Allow me to express my sincere regret that I could not grasp your friendly hands at Detroit. I sincerely trust that the future may give me the proud privilege of greeting you again.

Hoping that this outline may meet your approval, and trusting that you will each lose no time in writing out your part, so that the work may be done quickly and thoroughly, I subscribe myself,

Your comrade and obedient servant,

F. W. LEWES.

DEAR COMRADES:

*Feeling that all of you who have not a copy of "Sherman's Memoirs" would be glad to have a copy, now that it can be had for so little money, I have made an arrangement with the publishers to give me special terms, for your benefit.*

*I can, therefore, send you post-paid a copy of the $2.00 volume (advertised on the back cover) at $1.50, and shall take pleasure in doing so, for all who send the $1.50 before next January.*

*All good war volumes are of value to old soldiers, and Sherman's own book, "Sherman's Memoirs," of special value to each of us, because it contains his own account of the "March to the Sea."*

ADDRESS,

F. W. HEWES,

BLOOMFIELD, N. J.